Doyle's Practical Guide to Business Law in Emerging Countries in Asia

Other Books by Michael Doyle

Doyle's Practical Guide to Thailand Business Law

Doyle's Practical Guide to Thailand Intellectual Property Law

More Praise for Doyle's Guide

"This is a book that every transnational business lawyer, whether in private practice or in-house, will want. Its lucid exposition also makes it a valuable tool for non-lawyer international investors and traders."

Charles E. McCallum, Former Chair
American Bar Association, Business Law Section

"A useful resource for entrepreneurs and managers planning business start-ups or expansion in Asia."

Dr. Philip Hallinger, Professor of Management
Hong Kong Institute of Education

"Michael Doyle's book provides a much-needed guide to navigating through the sometimes bewildering maze of government rules and bureaucracies for doing business in Asian countries."

Bill Hannay, Former Chair
American Bar Association, Section of International Law

"This book is the ultimate reference for doing successful business in Asia!"

William E. Heinecke, Chairman & Chief Executive Officer
Minor Group

"Michael Doyle provides crucial reading for doing business in emerging Asia, including India and China. In this book, the authors share insight and practical advice into the different legal and business systems in some of the world's most critical markets."

Ashish Sudhakar, Senior Asia Pacific Manager
DISYS Singapore Pte Ltd

"Michael Doyle manages to communicate—in plain English—the key legal issues facing foreign investors in developing Asia today."

Michael S. Murray, Regional Chief Executive Officer
East Asia Coats Plc

Doyle's Practical Guide to Business Law in Emerging Countries in Asia

Michael Doyle

Edited by Millie Lindsay

Carolina Academic Press
Durham, North Carolina

Library of Congress Cataloging-in-Publication Data

Doyle, Michael.
  Doyle's practical guide to business law in emerging countries in Asia /
Michael Doyle.
    p. cm.
  ISBN 978-1-59460-777-6 (alk. paper)
  1. Business law--Asia. 2. Commercial law--Asia. I. Title. II. Title: Practical
guide to business law in emerging countries in Asia.

  KMC84.B87D69 2010
  346.507--dc22

                                    2009053510
CAROLINA ACADEMIC PRESS
700 Kent Street
Durham, North Carolina 27701
Telephone (919) 489-7486
Fax (919) 493-5668
www.cap-press.com

Printed in the United States of America

For my mother,
Kathryn Doyle

From left to right: Benjamin Yap representing Kelvin Chia Partnership (Vietnam); Ravi Singhania representing Singhania & Partners (India); Jiang JIANG representing Hylands Law Firm (China); Renato Leuterio representing Grant Thornton Hendrawinata (Indonesia); Michael Doyle representing Seri Manop & Doyle (Thailand); Michael Lee representing Pamir Law Group (China); and Azmi Mohd Ali representing Azmi & Associates Advocates & Solicitors (Malaysia).

Angara Abello Concepcion Regala & Cruz (the Philippines) not pictured.

Picture taken in front of The Opera House in downtown Ho Chi Minh City, Vietnam.

Contents

India

Indonesia

Malaysia

Philippines

Thailand

Vietnam

China

Capital City	Beijing
Major Financial Center	Shanghai
Population (projected 2010)	1354 million
Location	Eastern Asia, between North Korea and Vietnam
Major Languages	Standard Mandarin (spoken), Simplified Chinese (written)
Legal System	Civil law
Square Miles	3,704,427 sq mi
Gross Domestic Product (projected 2010)	USD 5303 billion
Major Exports	Manufactured goods, including textiles, garments, electronics, arms
Currency	Renminbi (RMB or CNY)
U.S. Dollar Exchange Rate (as of November 2009)	USD 1 = RMB 6.8279
Euro Exchange Rate (as of November 2009)	EUR 1 = RMB 10.1052

Section Authors

Jiang Jiang	Michael Lee
Partner	Partner
Hylands Law Firm	Pamir Law Group
Email: jiangjiang@hylandslaw.com	Email: mlee@pamirlaw.com
Website: http://www.hylandslaw.com	Website: http://www.pamirlaw.com
(Chapters 1, 4 and 6)	(Chapters 2, 3 and 5)

Chapter 1

Should Our Business Establish as a Limited Company, Representative Office, or Branch?

One of the first issues faced by prospective investors in China is choosing the appropriate type of legal structure through which to operate their business. The most commonly used of the structures available are limited company, representative office, and branch.

When choosing the structure that is appropriate for your business you should consider a number of factors, including

i.   the intended activities to be pursued, i.e. operational activities or non-operational activities

ii. familiarity with the Chinese market and business culture

iii. industry entry policies and restrictions

iv. capital requirements

v.   liability issues

vi. tax treatment

1. Limited Company

The limited company (company) in China is similar to a Limited Liability Company (LLC) structure in the US and is the most utilized type of legal entity in China.

A company is owned by shareholders (minimum one) and managed by directors (minimum one). The liability of each of the shareholders is generally limited to the total par value of their shares. The shareholders' participation in company affairs (unless there is only a single shareholder) is achieved through voting at the shareholders' meeting or making decisions in case there is only one shareholder. Generally, it is the directors who are responsible for managing company affairs and who owe various fiduciary duties to the shareholders and the company (duty of care, duty of loyalty, etc.).

Unlike a branch and representative office, a limited company is treated under Chinese law as a stand-alone legal entity.

EXAMPLE: If a multinational wishes to establish a subsidiary in China, it will likely do so as a privately held company. If individual investors wish to establish a stand-alone business to generate income in China, they will most likely do so as a company.

EXAMPLE: Suppose a multinational establishes a wholly owned subsidiary in China as a limited company. That new limited company then executes a contract with another Chinese company to supply electronic components, but then fails to supply those components. In this situation, the Chinese purchaser would generally be limited to suing the Chinese subsidiary for the breach of contract, not its headquarters overseas.

The most common types of limited companies utilized by foreign investors are Joint Ventures and Wholly Foreign Owned Enterprises, which are discussed in detail in Chapters 2 and 3.

2. Branch and Representative Office

Many times, however, foreign investors will not want to operate as a limited company. This is most likely to be true when a multinational company seeks to establish a presence in China, but does not wish to establish a separate legal entity. For accounting, tax, and other reasons, the multinational company may instead want the China office to function as a part of the head office overseas. If that is the case, the multinational will normally choose to establish a representative office or branch office, not a company limited.

Chinese law treats each of these two entities as extensions of the head office overseas, not as separate legal entities. Their activities are the activities of the head office.

3. Representative Office

A representative office can act as a local liaison for the head office overseas and engage in product promotion, market research, exchange of technology, and other non-operational activities permitted in China. For a detailed list of activities a representative office can and cannot do in China go to www.doylesguideasia.com/china/chapter1/appendixa. For a foreign investor, the main advantage of establishing as a representative office is that it is simpler and cheaper to establish than either a JV (Joint Venture) or a WFOE (Wholly Foreign Owned Enterprise) since no registered capital is required and the startup costs are considerably low.

Since a representative office is not considered an independent legal entity, but rather an extension of its parent company, it cannot enter into contracts in its own name, issue tax invoices, or hire employees directly. Therefore, all business contracts must be entered into in the name of the parent company, and all local employees must be hired through local staffing companies.

Consulting companies and trading companies may find the representative office particularly useful, as their business usually only needs some office space and a few employees and usually does not need to purchase manufacturing equipment and raw materials.

EXAMPLE: A Swiss sourcing company establishes a representative office in China. The representative office performs the following activities:

i.   Acts as a liaison between the head office in Switzerland and suppliers and clients in China

ii. Carries out import and export trading through an import and export agent and markets products

iii. Selects source suppliers

iv. Engages in quality control of functions

v.   Performs market research and general facilitation, etc.

EXAMPLE: A Korean consulting company establishes a representative office in China and engages in market research and establishing contacts with prospective customers and partners; provides data and promotional materials to clients; conducts research and marketing surveys; liaisons with local contacts in China on behalf of the head office overseas; and acts as a coordinator for the parent company's activities in China and other non-revenue generating business activities.

A representative office is not allowed to directly engage in revenue generating activities, unless otherwise permitted by certain bilateral treaties between China and other countries, or by regulations applicable to special industries.

EXAMPLE: According to the Sino-US Civil Aviation Transportation Agreement, representative offices established by American civil airlines may sell civil air transportation services provided by American civil airlines, as well as engage in administration, inquiry, and other business activities.

EXAMPLE: Representative offices of foreign accounting firms are allowed to provide accounting, tax, and other services to foreign clients who come to invest or do businesses in China, and provide information, international tax, and other consulting services to Chinese clients.

Establishment of a representative office is easier than the establishment of other business presences. Normally, the investor can directly register its representative office with the Administration for Industry and Commerce office in the province where the representative office is located. However, if the representative office is to participate in such sectors as banking, insurance, securities, law, and accounting, it must first obtain approval from competent government agencies (which agency depending upon the sector the investor seeks to engage in). For the usual steps to set up a representative office go to www.doylesguideasia.com/china/chapter1/appendixb.

Generally speaking, the entire process to establish a representative office takes about three to six weeks, depending on the specific circumstances of preparation work and the governmental authority.

4. Branch

In general, Chinese law allows foreign companies to set up branches in China. In practice, however, the government seldom grants approval for setting up a branch of a foreign company, due to the lack of implementing regulations regarding its establishment. As a result, it is possible for foreign companies to get approval to establish a branch in China only in specific industries, such as banking and insurance.

5. Capital Required

The rules governing the amount of investment required for a limited company are presented in Chapters 2 and 3. To see a list of the minimum registered capital required per total investment, go to www.doylesguideasia.com/china/chapter1/appendixc.

There are no minimum capital requirements for a representative office.

For a branch, however, the amount of capital required varies in different industries. Branches of foreign banks and foreign insurance companies must have adequate working capital of not less than RMB 200 million.

6. Official Fees

The official fees payable to the Administration for Industry and Commerce (AIC) for registration of a limited company, representative office, and branch are calculated as follows:

The registration fee for a representative office is RMB 600.

If the registered capital of a limited company is RMB 10 million or less, the registration fee is 0.8% of the registered capital of the limited company, with a minimum registration fee of RMB 50.

If the registered capital of a limited company is more than RMB 10 million, the registration fee for the part of the registered capital exceeding RMB 10 million is 0.4%.

Chapter 2

What Legal Issues Are Associated with the Start-Up of a Foreign-Held Company?

There are several legal and practical issues associated with the legal start-up of a private company limited (company) by foreign investors in China.

There are three stages associated with the start-up:

i.   Obtaining approval for the proposed company name

ii. Obtaining approval for the foreign investment, based on the submission of a detailed feasibility study and/or project proposal

iii. Obtaining a business license and related approvals and registrations

There are no shelf companies in China, so this process must be followed each time a company is formed.

A company with foreign investors may take the form of a wholly foreign-owned enterprise (WFOE) or a joint venture (JV). The definitions and requirements applicable to WFOEs and JVs are further discussed in Chapter 3.

To see a detailed explanation of the process to establish a new company go to www.doylesguideasia.com/china/chapter2/appendixa.

1. Formation Agents

Investors may arrange for one or more individuals or hire an agent in China to represent them during the various stages of the registration process. Investors usually do not need to be physically present in China to complete the company's formation.

Note that the concept of "company promoter" does not exist in China.

2. Shareholders

There are certain rules as to who may act as company shareholders, depending on whether the company is to be established as a WFOE or JV and whether the shareholder is an individual or business entity.

If a foreign individual is the sole shareholder of a WFOE, then Chinese law prohibits this individual from being the sole shareholder of any other WFOE.

EXAMPLE: A German businessman comes to China and establishes a WFOE in which he is the sole shareholder. This is permissible under Chinese law. However, he will not be legally allowed to be the sole shareholder of any other WFOE.

In addition, any WFOE with a foreign individual as its sole shareholder may not be the sole shareholder of another Chinese company.

EXAMPLE: Using the same facts as above, the company would not be legally allowed to act as the sole shareholder of any other Chinese company.

Also note that only Chinese corporate entities (not Chinese individuals) are allowed to act as shareholders in a JV.

EXAMPLE: Suppose a Korean company and a Chinese individual wish to establish a JV. Using these facts, the Chinese individual would not be allowed to act as a shareholder of the JV.

3. Filings

There are two Chinese government agencies primarily involved in the start-up process:

i.   The local branch of the State Administration of Industry and Commerce (usually referred to as AIC), which is responsible for registering company names and issuing business licenses

ii. The local branch of the Ministry of Commerce (MOFCOM), which is responsible for processing applications for foreign investment approval

Other government formalities related to the start-up process include registering at the local taxation bureau office, statistical bureau, and customs office, and with the environmental protection authorities having jurisdiction over the location of the new business (as applicable). (See Chapter 1.)

4. Timing

The amount of time required to register a new company varies widely depending on a number of factors, including

i.   the business activities it is to engage in

ii. which government agency applications are required to be submitted (central, provincial, or local)

iii. the speed with which the required information and documents can be prepared and submitted (in particular the Feasibility Study Report and Project Proposal discussed below)

iv. the availability of the parties required to sign various documents

The average processing times for approval of various applications are presented below:

Average Processing Times

Application Type	Where Submitted	Average Time Required For Approval
Proposed Company Name Registration	Local Office of AIC	Approved (or Rejected) Immediately
Foreign Investment Approval	Local Office of MOFCOM	30 Working Days (WFOEs) 45 Working Days (JVs)
Business License	Local Office of AIC	7 Working Days
Tax Registration Certificate	Local Office of Taxation Bureau	5 to 10 Working Days (Depending on Locality)

* Note that the above table applies to companies that do not have business activities requiring special approvals. Also note that processing times may vary according to local rules and practices.

5. Company Name

The first step in the company registration process is reserving the company name.

Under Chinese law, company names must be presented entirely in Chinese characters (with no foreign language words or letters).

There are no general restrictions on what company names may be used. A common practice with regard to company names is to use the following word order:

Company Name + Type of Industry + Province or City Name + Type of Proposed Company

The proposed company name and at least one alternative name are required to be included in an application submitted to the local AIC office for approval. Once approved, the name will be reserved for three to six months, depending upon the policies of that particular local AIC office.

An English or foreign language counterpart name may also be submitted but is not required. When used, there is no requirement for the non-Chinese language counterpart names to be consistent with their Chinese versions. However, many foreign investors use names which are consistent with the Chinese versions in terms of either pronunciation or meaning.

EXAMPLE: The Chinese name used by Wal-Mart is *woerma baihuo youxian gongsi* (written in Chinese characters) with the name Wal-Mart transliterated into Chinese characters as *woerma*.

EXAMPLE: The Chinese name used by Microsoft is *weiruan (zhongguo) youxian gongsi* (written in Chinese characters), which is a literal translation of micro (*wei*) and soft (*ruan*).

EXAMPLE: The Chinese name used by Citibank is *huaqi yinhang zhongguo youxian gongsi* (written in Chinese characters). The Chinese characters *huaqi* have no connection to either the meaning or sound of Citibank's English name, but instead is a seldom used way of referring to the United States.

Shareholders should not invest in marketing materials containing the company's proposed name until after AIC's approval of that name. This sounds like common sense, but many people make this mistake.

6. Feasibility Study Reports and Project Proposals

In China, the foreign investment approval process for both WFOEs and JVs requires the submission and approval of a Feasibility Study Report (the Report) to MOFCOM. The contents of the Report normally include

i.   a general market study description

ii. source of investment

iii. schedule of investment

iv. description of the company's proposed work force

v.   technology to be used or developed

vi. raw materials needed

vii. site of the company

as well as other relevant information.

All applications for foreign investment approval for a JV also require submission and approval of a Project Proposal.

Project Proposals are also submitted to MOFCOM and normally contain a description of the company's intended objectives and operations, total investment and registered capital, capital contributions of the foreign and Chinese partners, supplies of raw materials, and estimates of foreign exchange income and economic benefits.

Some local branches of MOFCOM also require WFOE applicants to submit a separate Project Proposal as well.

The amount of time needed to receive foreign investment approval from MOFCOM depends on each individual application. However, MOFCOM usually issues approvals between one and three months after applications are filed.

To see further details on this go to www.doylesguideasia.com/china/chapter2/appendixa.

7. Business License

Prior to beginning operations, the company is also required to obtain a business license from the local AIC office. The business license application is submitted after receiving foreign investment approval from MOFCOM as described above, so the process is normally only a formality. Business licenses are usually issued by AIC within seven working days of submitting the application.

Once the business license is received, the company may begin operations.

8. Company Address

Companies are required to have a physical address at an appropriate location zoned for industrial or commercial use. Companies may not be registered at a residential address or a post office box.

Note that an executed office lease or production facilities lease is required to be submitted as a supporting document when registering the company's address with MOFCOM and AIC.

When entering into the lease agreement for the new company's premises, in order to save time it is important to have a sufficient number of original leases executed by the parties. This is because MOFCOM, AIC, and other government agencies may require originals of the executed lease to be submitted.

9. Registered Capital and Total Investment

The capital contributions made to the company by the shareholders are referred to as the total investment (representing the shareholder's total investment in the company) and registered capital (representing the shareholder's maximum liability associated with the company).

EXAMPLE: A US company establishes a WFOE in China and designates $20 million US as its total investment in the company, with $12 million of the $20 million as the company's registered capital. In this situation, $20 million represents the US company's total investment in the WFOE, and $12 million represents the US company's total legal liability associated with the WFOE.

The total investment is generally required to reflect the scale of the business as stated in the company's official documents, including the Feasibility Study Report (see above), and the Articles of Association (see below). The amount of registered capital should be sufficient for the preparation and initial operation of the new company.

The balance of total investment (above the registered capital amount) may be paid in at any time or not at all.

EXAMPLE: Using the same facts as above, after the shareholders pay in the registered capital amount of $12 million, there is no further legal requirement to pay in the additional $8 million representing the balance of the total investment.

The minimum amount of registered capital for both a WFOE and JV depends in large part upon the investors' total investment in the company.

Total Investment Amount	Required "Minimum Registered Capital Amount"
Above US $30,000,000	1/3 of Total Investment or US $12,000,000 whichever is higher
US $10,000,001 to US $30,000,000	2/5 of Total Investment or US $5,000,000 whichever is higher
US $3,000,001 to US $10,000,000	1/2 of Total Investment or US $2,100,000 whichever is higher
US $3,000,000 or below	7/10 of Total Investment

EXAMPLE: A UK company and a Chinese company seek to establish a JV and set the total investment in the JV at $5 million US. In this situation, the minimum registered capital amount would be $2.5 million US.

Note that there are also minimum requirements for registered capital for insurance and other specified industries.

Capital contributions may be made using both cash and non-cash assets, but the total non-cash investment (if any) may not exceed 70% of the total registered capital. Note that when non-cash assets are used they must be properly appraised.

EXAMPLE: A Canadian investor seeks to register a WFOE in China, sets the company's registered capital at $10 million US, and wishes to use non-cash assets to the greatest extent possible to fund the registered capital. In this situation, the investor would only be allowed to use non-cash assets to fund $7 million US of the registered capital. The remaining $3 million US must be paid in cash.

The total initial contribution of registered capital by the shareholders must not be less than 20% of the total stated registered capital amount and may not be lower than the "minimum *statutory* registered capital amount" required. The minimum *statutory* registered capital amount for both JVs and WFOEs is RMB 30,000 unless a WFOE has only a sole shareholder, in which case the minimum statutory registered capital amount is RMB 100,000 and must be fully paid in.

EXAMPLE: A Spanish company and a Chinese company establish a JV in China and set the registered capital at $10 million US. In this situation, the shareholders' total initial capital contribution may not be less than $2 million US.

After the initial contribution, the balance of registered capital must be completely paid into the company within two years of the company's registration.

10. Articles of Association

The Articles of Association (Articles) is the company's charter on file with AIC, which sets forth the company's objectives and the basic rules by which it is to operate. The Articles detail information such as the number of directors required on the board, frequency of shareholders and directors meetings, what constitutes a quorum, etc.

In the case of a JV, it is very important to make sure that the Articles and the joint venture agreement between the parties are consistent and do not contradict one another.

EXAMPLE: A Chinese company and a Belgian company enter into a joint venture agreement to form a JV in China to produce beer. The joint venture agreement sets forth information such as the composition of the JV board of directors, voting rights, meeting notice requirements, and various JV decision making mechanisms. In order to avoid confusion, the parties should ensure that the provisions of the JV Articles are consistent with the provisions of the joint venture agreement.

11. Legal Representative

Chinese law requires that companies designate one individual to be the company's legal representative. The legal representative is the official representative of the company and may be personally liable if the company is found by a court to have violated the law. The legal representative is also responsible for receiving service of process for all court proceedings in which the company is a party.

EXAMPLE: A Swiss company registers a WFOE in China and designates a Swiss national managing director as the WFOE's legal representative. Later the WFOE is charged with smuggling goods into China. In this situation, if the company is found guilty, the Swiss national may also be found criminally liable for the illegal action.

The legal representative is the most powerful position in the company because this person can legally bind the company with his or her signature (even without approval from the company board of directors).

Foreign investors commonly appoint their top Chinese executive or Chinese business partner to serve as legal representative, but if there is a disagreement between the foreign investor and the legal representative (such as on employment matters), tensions may adversely impact the operations of the company.

It may also be administratively difficult to replace a legal representative when the parties are not cooperating, which may further impact the business. The person appointed as the legal representative should ideally be someone the foreign investor trusts and who can be relied on to act in the best interest of the company, even when this would be against his or her own personal interest.

For the above reasons, the selection of the person to be the company's legal representative is a very important decision and should be carefully considered.

EXAMPLE: In a JV between a UK party (holding a 55% interest) and a Chinese party (holding a 45% interest), the JV agreement allows the Chinese party to designate the Legal Representative. Later, a dispute between the two parties arises over a particular business project, and the Legal Representative stops reporting for work. It is discovered that the JV chop (a Chinese seal required to authorize the payment of employee salaries and many other documents, as discussed below) has been removed by the Legal Representative without permission. As a result, employees cannot be paid on time, and the company's reputation and operations are adversely affected.

12. Directors

Different rules apply concerning the minimum number of directors allowed for a WFOE and JV. WFOEs must name at least one director, who may be a Chinese or foreign national. JVs must have at least three directors, who may be Chinese or foreign nationals. Only individuals may act as company directors, not companies.

13. Official Fees

The application fees payable to AIC at the time of registration for the business license are calculated based on the stated registered capital as shown below:

Amount of Registered Capital	Official Fees
Less than 10 million RMB	0.0008% x Registered Capital
Greater than 10 million RMB	[0.0008% x 10 million RMB] + [0.0004% x (Portion of Registered Capital over 10 million RMB)]
Greater than 100 million RMB	44,000 RMB

EXAMPLE: A company's Registered Capital is RMB 14,000,000. The application fee payable to AIC would be [0.000008 x 10,000,000] + [0.000004 x 4,000,000] = RMB 9,600.

14. Bank Accounts

After receiving its Business License and Tax Certificate, a company is required to open a RMB bank account and a foreign exchange bank account at a Chinese bank.

Requirements to open a corporate bank account vary from bank to bank, but a Foreign Exchange Certificate from the State Administration of Foreign Exchange (SAFE) is required to open an account in a foreign currency. Such accounts may only be opened at banks designated by the government to conduct foreign exchange.

15. Chops and Chop Controls

A "chop" is a traditional Chinese seal having the same legal effect as a signature outside of China. Chops are routinely used instead of signatures on a company's agreements, bank paperwork, regulatory filings, and other documents. The person holding the company chop has apparent authority to act and make decisions on behalf of the company.

To see a list of the types of chops typically used by a Chinese company, go to www.doylesguideasia.com/china/chapter2/appendixa.

Foreign investors must take special care to implement control mechanisms to prevent misuse of the company chops and avoid the inadvertent creation of unknown and unwanted liabilities. Internal controls, such as chop use logs and a system of approvals, should also be established as standard operating practices in the company.

EXAMPLE: A Chinese company and a Swiss company establish a JV in China with the JV company chop to reside with the JV financial controller. The JV does not implement controls as to who has access to the chop, and it is later stolen and fraudulently used to authorize bank transfers.

16. Public Access to Company Details

The general public cannot access company information on China registered companies on the internet or on public databases. Chinese attorneys, however, have the right to request and receive such information, such as the names of a company's legal representative, directors, shareholders, annual financial reports, government approvals, and other documents from relevant government officials.

Chapter 3

What Legal Issues Are Associated with Operating as a Foreign-Held Company?

The Chinese government regulates the activities of foreign-held companies (commonly referred to in China as Foreign Invested Enterprises or FIEs) operating in China at both at the national and provincial levels. An FIE is a Chinese registered company with any foreign investors.

This chapter discusses the applicable legal rules associated with establishing and operating a business as an FIE.

1. Regulated Activities

FIE regulated activities are divided into those which are Prohibited, Restricted, Encouraged, and Permitted.

Prohibited activities generally include those activities which affect state security or public interests, are highly polluting, occupy a huge amount of farmland, or are detrimental to human health and natural resources. Foreign investment in Prohibited sectors is completely banned.

To see a complete list of Prohibited Activities go to www.doylesguideasia.com/china/chapter3/appendixa.

Restricted activities are subject to heightened regulatory scrutiny and, depending on the type of investment, may be required to use a joint venture (JV) ownership structure (see Chapters 1 and 2), with certain limits on the percentage of equity ownership held by foreign investors.

EXAMPLE: Foreign investors seeking to engage in passenger transport activities by rail are required to do so through a JV in which a Chinese party has a controlling interest.

Restricted activities include those that are deemed technologically backward, are bad for the environment, involve exploration or mining, or sectors that the Chinese government has not yet fully opened to foreign participation.

To see a complete list of Restricted Activities go to www.doylesguideasia.com/china/chapter3/appendixb.

Encouraged activities include engaging in new agricultural technology, information technology support and management, banking industry support centers, and sports and fitness centers, as well as clean energy, anti-pollution equipment, urban waste processing, and recycling industries.

Encouraged activities are regarded as benefiting China's economic objectives of abandoning outdated, energy-intensive and low-technology production, while encouraging development of renewable energy resources, clean and efficient production, service and support industries, and sectors seen as promoting public health.

To see a complete list of Encouraged Activities go to www.doylesguideasia.com/china/chapter3/appendixc.

Permitted activities are those that are not included in the Encouraged, Prohibited, or Restricted lists. Typical examples of Permitted industries include restaurants, toy manufacturing, and management consulting services.

2. WOFE and JV Activities

The two most common types of FIEs are Wholly Owned Foreign Enterprises (WOFEs) and JVs between Chinese and foreign investors.

WOFEs and JVs may engage in a restricted activity(ies) upon receiving approval from the local branch of the State Administration of Industry and Commerce and Ministry of Commerce (MOFCOM) to engage in that activity(ies). In this situation, MOFCOM will review whether the FIE meets the particular criteria governing the proposed activity when the FIE applies for foreign investment approval. To see a description of the process go to www.doylesguideasia.com/china/chapter2/appendixa.

Some criteria for restricted and encouraged activities require a certain percentage of ownership or even majority control by the Chinese parties, so those activities may only be engaged in by JVs. All FIEs may engage in permitted activities.

3. Nominee Shareholders

Generally, nominee shareholders are individuals or companies that agree to hold shares on behalf of the true owner(s) of the shares. Under this arrangement, typically the nominee shareholder and the true owner execute an agreement stating that the nominee shareholder agrees to hold the shares in name only and that the nominee shareholder will exercise all shareholder rights (voting rights, rights to transfer, rights to receive dividends, etc.) in accordance with the true owner's instructions.

Chinese law neither expressly permits nor expressly prohibits nominee shareholder arrangements. In practice, the actual investors and nominee shareholders may use contractual arrangements, such as voting agreements, to govern the relationship. The risk for the true owner, however, is that since the nominee shareholder's name appears on all the shareholder documentation, the shareholder rights all legally reside with the nominee shareholder, not the true owner.

Therefore, in the case of a dispute between the local nominee and the foreign investor involving the nominee relationship, the court may choose to rule that such agreement is unenforceable on the basis that the agreement is attempting to avoid the legal rules which would otherwise be applicable or seen as harmful to government or social interests.

EXAMPLE: A French company wants to hold an interest in a book distribution company, a business that is categorized as Prohibited for foreign investment. The French company enters into an agreement with a Chinese company, where the French company pays the Chinese company an amount of money equal to the total registered capital of a book distribution company, which the Chinese company uses to form a 100% domestically-owned book distribution company using its own name. The book distribution company makes a profit and declares dividends, but the Chinese company does not pass on the profits to the French company as agreed. The French company sues the Chinese company for breach of their agreement. In this situation, the Chinese court may rule that the nominee arrangement was meant to circumvent the rules prohibiting foreign investment in book distribution companies, so it is unenforceable.

4. Common Offshore Structures

The foreign investor and Chinese investor interested in establishing a new business in China may establish a JV in China. It is also common for parties to establish a company in Hong Kong or a tax haven jurisdiction (such as the Cayman Islands or the British Virgin Islands) and use that offshore company to establish a WOFE in China. Some of the typical reasons for using this type of corporate structure include

i.   Foreign investment incentives: Some foreign investment incentives are only available to WOFEs.

ii.   Lower withholding rates: Advantageous withholding tax rates for dividends, royalties, and interest for companies in Hong Kong and other countries pursuant to tax treaties with China.

iii. Streamlined corporate governance in China: Since a WOFE only has one shareholder, fewer corporate approvals are needed and obtaining regulatory approvals may be easier.

iv.   Familiar corporate rules: Corporate rules governing a Hong Kong or Cayman Islands company tend to be more familiar to foreign investors, so they may be more comfortable resolving shareholder disputes in a Western-style legal system.

v.   Exit strategy: Offshore entities can be publicly listed outside of China, or the entire Chinese operation can be sold to a buyer without obtaining Chinese government approval.

This was a popular investment structure for some time; however, in 2005, the Chinese government began to require Chinese individuals and companies to obtain prior approval from the State Administration of Foreign Exchange (SAFE) before purchasing shares of companies registered outside of China. As a result, this has become an obstacle for foreign investors seeking to partner with Chinese investors using the above described structure. Therefore, in order to avoid associated complications, foreign investors should carefully consider these issues and receive legal advice before proceeding to use such structures.

EXAMPLE: A German company and a Chinese company form a company in the British Virgin Islands (BVI) in which the German company holds 40% of the shares and the Chinese company 60%, for the purpose of the BVI company establishing a WFOE in China. The Chinese partner wires funds abroad to capitalize the BVI company (before first obtaining permission to do so with SAFE), which then applies for permission to establish a WFOE in China. By doing so, the Chinese company has violated foreign exchange controls by failing to register the offshore investment with SAFE. Although the WFOE might be successfully formed, the Chinese government is likely to later deny the offshore parent company's applications to repatriate dividends, withdraw investment, decrease the amount of registered capital, or transfer equity from the WFOE.

5. Stock Options and Employee Incentives

Many foreign investors in China who typically grant stock options to select employees globally often seek to do the same for their Chinese employees. Note, however, that the above described rule also applies in this situation.

EXAMPLE: A Canadian company listed on the New York Stock Exchange establishes a WFOE in China and offers certain employees in the office the opportunity to participate in a stock options plan whereby the employee would have the opportunity to purchase shares of the Canadian company at a special discounted rate. Before the employees would be legally allowed to participate in this plan, they must obtain approval from SAFE.

There are ways to avoid the requirement of SAFE approval in some situations, (such as stock options granted that can be exercised only if the employer's stock becomes listed or if the employer is acquired by a listed company, and "phantom stock" plans that give Chinese employees cash rewards based upon stock appreciation). However, it is recommended that foreign investors seek the advice of legal counsel before implementing such plans.

Chapter 4

What Is the Process to Obtain a Work Permit?

Foreigners are required to obtain a work permit and residence permit in order to legally work and live in mainland China (China).

The application process consists of two applications:

i.   An application to receive a work permit from the designated Labor and Social Security Bureau office

ii. An application for a residence permit from the designated Exit-Entry Administration Division of the Public Security Bureau office

The work permit is the permission to work in China. The residence permit is the permission to reside in China. The applicant must obtain both in order to work and live in China.

Some foreigners with special status are exempted from obtaining a work permit. To see the list of categories of foreigners who are exempted from the requirement to obtain an employment license or/and work permit go to www.doylesguideasia.com/china/chapter4/appendixa.

The work permit and residence permit are normally valid for a period of one year. After one year, both the work permit and residence permit must be renewed (see below).

Keep in mind that the application and procedure to obtain a work permit and residence permit may vary depending upon the province in China where the applications are submitted. The information set forth in this chapter is mainly based on the practice in Shanghai.

Furthermore, note that different rules apply to persons from Taiwan, the Hong Kong Special Administrative Region, and the Macao Special Administrative Region seeking work and residence in China, which are not covered in this chapter.

1. Qualifications of Foreign Employees

The following are the general requirements applicable to foreign individuals seeking to work and reside in China:

i.   Must be at least 18 years of age and in good health
ii.   Possess the requisite professional skills and work experience needed for the position
iii. Have no criminal record
iv.   Have an employer in China
v.   Possess a valid passport or equivalent international travel document

EXAMPLE: Suppose a foreigner is to be employed as a company's financial controller in China. In this situation, the applicant would likely be required to produce the following documents (in addition to the other documents described in this chapter) when applying for a work permit:

i.   Health certificate issued by a hospital designated by the Chinese government and a certificate of an educational degree
ii.   Certificates of professional qualifications, such as a certificate regarding accounting or finance or a reference letter issued by the previous employer
iii. Passport

2. Restricted Professions

Employers in China may only employ foreigners for those positions in which special skills are required and the position cannot be filled by domestic Chinese employees, and the employment does not violate any relevant regulation.

3. Application Process

The following authorizations are required when applying to obtain a work permit and residence permit:

Authorization Required	Estimated Processing Time
Applying for and obtaining Employment License	15 working days
Applying for and obtaining Visa Notification Letter	2–3 working days
Applying for and obtaining Employment Visa (Z Visa)	(varies widely)
Applying for and obtaining Temporary Residence Certificate	1 working day

Applying for and obtaining Health Certificate	4 working days
Applying for and obtaining Work Permit	5 working days
Applying for and obtaining Residence Permit	5 working days

Also, note that the above estimated time frames are applicable to Shanghai only.

a. Employment License

In order for the foreign employee to receive an employment license, his employer must submit relevant supporting documents before he enters China. To see a list of the supporting documents go to www.doylesguideasia.com/china/chapter4/appendixb. For employers in Shanghai the validity period of the employment license is normally six months.

The applicant will then be required to enter China and submit his application for a work permit (see below) within the period stated in the employment license.

EXAMPLE: An employer in Shanghai seeks to employ a Dutch national. In this situation, the employer would be required to apply for and obtain an employment license on the Dutch national's behalf before the Dutch national would be allowed to enter China and continue the process. After the employee enters the country, the Dutch national would be required to submit a work permit application within the period stated in the employment license (which for Shanghai employers is normally six months).

Foreigners, however, who qualify under either of the following categories may be exempt from the employment license requirement and, therefore, be allowed to apply for a work permit without the requirement of first obtaining the employment license prior to entering the country:

i. Chief representatives and representatives of the representative offices of foreign enterprises in China

ii. Foreigners who are employed to work in China according to agreements and protocols signed between China and foreign governments or international organizations, or who are employed to implement Sino-foreign cooperative projects or employee exchange programs

b. Visa Notification Letter

After obtaining the employment license, the employer applies to the authorized government agency (which is usually the local branch of the Ministry of Commerce) to request a visa notification letter (the Letter).

Upon receiving the Letter, the employer sends it and the original employment license to the foreign employee. Keep in mind, the Letter has a stated validity period. In Shanghai the validity period is set at one month.

If the dependents (parents, spouse and/or children under 18 years of age) of the foreign employee intend to accompany the employee to China, information regarding the dependents is included in the application for the Letter.

The Letter will be a necessary supporting document when the foreign employee applies for the Z visa with the authorized Chinese Embassy or consulate in his home country (see Section 3 below).

To see the list of supporting documents required to be submitted to obtain the Letter go to www.doylesguideasia.com/china/chapter4/appendixc.

c. Applying for and Obtaining the Employment Visa (Z Visa)

The foreign employee is required to send the employment license, the Letter, the application for the Z Visa, and other relevant documents to the appropriate Chinese embassy or consulate in the foreigner's home country before the expiration of the Letter.

EXAMPLE: A US national accepts a position to work for a company located in Shanghai and seeks to obtain the necessary government authorizations to do so. The employer applies for and obtains an employment license and the Letter on the foreigner's behalf and sends those documents to the US employee. The US employee then sends the employment license, the Letter, a completed Z visa application form, and required supporting documents to the Chinese embassy in the US within the period stated in the Letter.

If the foreign employee's dependents' information is included in the Letter, those dependents may also apply for the Z Visa at the same time as the foreign employee.

EXAMPLE: Using the same facts as above, the US employee would be required to send the following documents to the Chinese Embassy in the US in order to receive the Z Visa:

   i. Passport

   ii. Application form

   iii. Photo

   iv. A visa notification letter (the Letter) issued by the authorized Chinese government agency (see above)

v.   An original and a photocopy of the employment license issued by the Labor and Social Security Bureau or the original of other documents applicable to foreigners who are exempted from the employment license or work permit requirements

vi. Proof of kinship, e.g. marriage certificate, birth certificate, etc. for the foreign employee's spouse and any other dependents

d. Temporary Residence Certificate

After the foreign employee and dependents (if any) arrive in China (holding a Z Visa), they are required to obtain a temporary residence certificate within twenty-four hours of their arrival.

The temporary residence certificate may be issued by the hotel (if the foreign employee and dependents stay in a hotel) or the competent local police station (if the foreign employee and dependents are accommodated in a rented flat or house).

This temporary resident certificate will be a necessary supporting document for the work permit application.

e. Health Certificate

The foreign employee and dependents (if any) are required to have a medical examination at the designated hospital and obtain the health certificate after their arrival in China. Children who are under 18 years of age do not need to undergo the medical examination. This document will be a necessary supporting document when applying for the work permit.

f. Work Permit

Within fifteen days after the entry of the foreign employee with a Z Visa, the foreign employee is required to apply for the work permit with the Labor and Social Security Bureau. To see a complete list of the documents required go to www.doylesguideasia.com/china/chapter4/appendixd.

g. Residence Permit

After the foreign employee obtains a work permit, he is required to apply for a residence permit for himself and his dependents (if any) with the Exit-Entry Administration Division of the Public Security Bureau. To see a complete list of supporting documents required go to www.doylesguideasia.com/china/chapter4/appendixe.

If this is the first time the foreign employee and dependents (if any) have applied for a residence permit they are required to go to the Exit-Entry Administration Division of the Public Security Bureau in person to make the application. Their passports will be kept in the Public Security Department for five working days. During this period, they will be required to remain in China.

h. Applicable Fees

Applicable government fees payable during the process to obtain a work permit and other authorizations required may vary among areas in China. The following is the list of fees for Shanghai:

i.   Fee for employment license: RMB 10

ii.   Fee for visa notification letter: RMB 20

iii. Fee for employment visa: depends on the stipulation by the Chinese embassy

iv.   Fee for medical examination: RMB 702 per person

v.   Fee for work permit: RMB 10

vi.   Fee for residence permit: RMB 800/person/year (might be different depending on the nationality of the foreign employee)

EXAMPLE: Using the same facts as above, a summary of the complete procedure for applying for a work permit and residence permit for the US employee and his dependent spouse would be as follows:

Step 1   The US employee provides his Chinese employer with the copies of documents and information which are required to apply for an employment license and visa notification letter.

Step 2   The US employee's Chinese employer applies for the employment license before he and his spouse enter China.

Step 3   The US employee's Chinese employer applies for the visa notification letter for him and his spouse.

Step 4   The US employee's Chinese employer delivers the employment license and the visa notification letter to him.

Step 5   The US employee and his spouse apply to the Chinese embassy in the US for Z visas.

Step 6   The US employee and his spouse enter China by holding Z visas.

Step 7 The US employee and his spouse obtain a temporary residence certificate within twenty-four hours of their arrival in China.

Step 8 The US employee and his spouse undergo a medical examination at the designated hospital and obtain the health certificate.

Step 9 The US employee's Chinese employer applies for his work permit within fifteen days of his arrival in China.

Step 10 The US employee and his spouse apply for a residence permit within thirty days of their arrival in China.

i. Renewal of Work Permit and Residence Permit

The employer must apply for an extension of the work permit thirty days prior to the expiration date indicated in the employee's work permit. To see a complete list of the supporting documents required for the work permit renewal application go to www.doylesguideasia.com/china/chapter4/appendixf.

After the renewal of the work permit is approved, the foreign employee then applies for the extension of his residence permit. To see a complete list of supporting documents required for the residence permit renewal go to www.doylesguideasia.com/china/chapter4/appendixg.

Chapter 5

What Investment Incentives Are Available to Foreign Investors?

1. General Tax Incentives

The Chinese government encourages certain types of business activities by granting tax exemptions and tax reductions (the standard corporate income tax rate in China is 25%).

Foreign investors seeking to benefit from these tax incentives are required to either apply for prior approval, or submit supporting documentation when filing their tax returns, depending on the type of business and the incentives sought.

Also, note that tax exemptions and reductions described below only apply to income derived from the promoted activity, not to the company's income in general.

EXAMPLE: A joint venture between Chinese and UK investors engages in research and breeding of new crop varieties (see below) and earns income from this activity. The joint venture also earns income from other unrelated activities not promoted by Chinese tax law. In this situation, the joint venture's income derived from research and breeding of the new crops would be fully exempt from income tax; however, income derived from its other activities would be subject to normal tax rates.

a. Agricultural Activities

Corporate income derived from one or more of the following activities is permanently exempt from corporate income tax:

33

i.   Cultivation of vegetables, grains, tubers, oil-bearing crops, beans, cotton, certain fiber crops, sugar crops, fruits or nuts

ii.   Breeding of new varieties of crops

iii. Cultivation of traditional Chinese medicinal materials

iv.   Fostering and cultivation of forests

v.   Raising of livestock and poultry

vi.   Gathering of forest products

vii. Agricultural, forestry, animal husbandry and fisheries service projects, such as irrigation, primary processing of agricultural products, veterinary medicine, agricultural technology promotion, agricultural machinery operation and repair, etc.

viii. Offshore fishing

These activities enjoy a permanent 50% reduction on corporate income tax:

i.   The cultivation of flowers, tea and other beverage crops, and spice crops

ii.   Marine aquaculture and inland aquaculture

EXAMPLE: A Korean investor engages in marine aquaculture in China and derives RMB 10,000 in income from the activity in Year One. In this situation, the investor's corporate income tax would total RMB 1,250 (income RMB 10,000 x tax rate 25% = RMB 2,500 / 2 = RMB 1,250).

b. Participation in Infrastructure Projects

Income derived from participation in major government infrastructure projects, such as the construction and/or development of ports, airports, railways, highways, urban public transport, electricity, water conservation, etc., is exempt from corporate income tax for years one through three and is given a 50% tax reduction in years four through six.

EXAMPLE: The Chinese government awards a project to a French company to construct a port in China, and the project takes four years for the French company to complete. In years one through three, the French company's income derived from this project is completely exempt from corporate income tax. In Year Four, in which the French company earned RMB 10,000 from working on the project, the company only pays RMB 1,250 in corporate income tax ([10,000 x 25%]/2 = 1,250).

Further details are available at www.doylesguideasia.com/china/chapter5/appendixa.

Note, however, that the above-mentioned tax incentives do not apply to parties who build infrastructure or take part in other construction projects for their own benefit.

EXAMPLE: Same facts as above, except that the Chinese government also grants the same French company the right to operate the port for ten years after the port is completed. In this situation, the French company would not enjoy exemption or reduction of taxes on any income earned from the project in both the construction and operational phases.

c. Environmental Protection

Companies engaging in environmental protection, energy conservation, and water conservation projects are exempt from tax for years one through three and need only pay 50% tax in years four through six.

Examples of eligible activities include projects involving public sewage treatment, public waste disposal, comprehensive development and utilization of methane, improvement of energy conservation and emissions-reducing technologies, and desalination of sea water.

EXAMPLE: The local government in Shenzhen hires a Canadian company to develop and implement a new system to operate the public sewage treatment facility. The Canadian company earns a total of RMB 12 million during the first three years, and another RMB 7 million in its fourth year of operation. In this situation, the RMB 12 million earned during the first three years is completely tax exempt. For the fourth year, the total corporate income tax due is RMB 875,000 ([7,000,000 x 25%]/2 = 875,000).

d. Transfers of Technology

Annual income derived from activities related to transfers of technology up to RMB 5 million is exempt from corporate income tax, and for income exceeding this amount the normal corporate income tax is reduced by half.

EXAMPLE: A Chinese company seeks to manufacture computer chips, but lacks the technological know-how for a critical part of the manufacturing process. A German company possessing the critical technology agrees to license it to the Chinese company for a one-time payment of RMB 10 million. In this situation, the German company would be exempt from paying tax on the first RMB 5 million of this income, while it would only pay RMB 625,000 in corporate income tax on the remaining RMB 5 million ([5,000,000 x 25%]/2 = 625,000).

2. Western Development Tax Incentives Investment

The Chinese government has also enacted special incentives to encourage economic growth in its less-developed central and western regions. These investment incentives apply to six provinces (Gansu, Guizhou, Qinghai, Shaanxi, Sichuan, and Yunnan), as well as five autonomous regions (Guangxi, Inner Mongolia, Ningxia, Tibet, and Xinjiang), and one municipality (Chongqing). Collectively, these provinces are called the Western Region.

a. Tax Incentives

Foreign-invested companies operating in the Western Region in the fields of transportation, power generation, water conservation, and other related fields for at least ten years are granted full tax exemption for years one and two of operation and 50% reduction of tax for years three through five. Normal tax rates apply from year six onwards.

EXAMPLE: A Korean company is constructing an electric power plant in the Western Region and plans to operate the plant for fifteen years. The project would receive the following tax incentives:

Years One and Two	Tax exempt
Years Three to Five	50% tax reduction
Year Six and onwards	Normal tax rate (25%) applies

b. Access to Restricted Activities

In China, certain business activities are generally restricted to domestic held companies only.

Foreign investors in certain sectors, such as commercial retail enterprises and trading companies, are only permitted to operate their businesses for a maximum of thirty years. However, if foreign investors make these same investments in the Western Region, they may operate for a maximum of forty years with government permission.

EXAMPLE: A French retail chain establishes a retail outlet in southwestern China's Sichuan province. Normally, a foreign-owned retail outlet could only operate for a maximum of thirty years. However, since the outlet is in the Western Region, the French company may apply to operate for as long as forty years.

To see a list of sectors eligible to operate for forty years in the Western Region, go to www.doylesguideasia.com/china/chapter5/appendixb.

3. Special Economic Zones and the Shanghai Pudong Zone

China grants special tax incentives to foreign investors establishing high-technology businesses in the country's Special Economic Zones (SEZs): Shenzhen, Zhuhai, Shantou, Xiamen, and Hainan Island, as well as the Shanghai Pudong New Area. These businesses are exempt from tax in years one and two of operation (starting from the date of the first sales transaction) and will enjoy a 50% tax reduction in years three through five.

EXAMPLE: German investors establish a new factory in Shenzhen to produce semiconductors. In this situation, the project would likely qualify for the following tax incentives, starting from the year in which the first sales transaction is reported:

Years One and Two	Tax exempt
Years Three through Five	50% corporate income tax reduction
Year Six and onwards	Normal tax rate (25%) applies

Note that if the foreign-invested company has production or operational facilities both within and outside of an SEZ, only the income generated from within the SEZ qualifies for this tax incentive.

Chapter 6

What Legal Issues Are Associated with Foreign Ownership of Land?

The private ownership of land is generally not allowed in mainland China by either foreigners or Chinese nationals. This is because urban land is owned by the central government and rural land is owned by farm collectives.

Chinese law does, however, allow qualifying foreign individuals and foreign companies to acquire a right to use (not own) land for a period of time specified in the law and even transfer that right of use to third parties in some situations. This right is comparable in many respects to a leasehold.

Also, qualifying foreign individuals and foreign companies are legally allowed to purchase and own buildings, houses, condominiums, and other immovable property during the period of land use, subject to certain conditions described below.

1. Land Use Right

China has a system under which land ownership is separated from land use rights (with both Chinese nationals and foreigners only afforded land use right). Under this system, urban land is generally owned by the government (State Land) and rural land is generally owned by farm collectives (Collective Land).

Normally, foreigners (individuals and foreign registered entities) can only buy the right to use State Land, not Collective Land.

The maximum period of use of State Land is prescribed by law, depending upon the legal classification of the purchaser's intended use.

Intended Use	Use Period
Residential use (including condominiums)	70 years
Industrial use	50 years
Health, educational, or athletic use	50 years

Cultural, scientific, or technological use	50 years
Business, tourist, and recreational use	40 years
Offices, mixed purpose use, or other uses	50 years

Chinese law states that land used for residential purpose is automatically renewable at the end of the term, and since the law does not specifically state that additional fees will be payable, it is widely held that no additional fees would be applicable to renew the use period. On the other hand, land use for a business related purpose would be renewable upon the owner paying an additional amount to the government, called a land grant fee, upon the expiration of the term.

Note, however, that whether or not the above use periods are actually renewable by the purchaser at the end of the use term is currently not well settled under Chinese law. This is because these rules were only introduced by the government in the early 1990's, so the initial land use periods have not yet expired.

EXAMPLE: A Korean businessman purchases a seventy-year land use right to land and a house in 2005. Under the current status of the law, since the use of this land is for residential purposes, upon its expiration in the year 2075 that land use right should be automatically renewable.

EXAMPLE: An Australian company purchases office space in 2003. Under the current status of the law, in the year 2053 that land use right can be renewed by the Australian company; however, there may be a question concerning the amount of the land grant fee payable to the government.

2. Purchase for Self Use

Chinese law allows certain types of foreign parties to purchase land use and/or immovable property for self use.

Foreign companies with branch offices or representative offices, WFOEs, and JVs in China are allowed to purchase a right to use land and own immovable property (during the period of use) for self use according to their actual needs, without requesting additional permission from the government to do so.

EXAMPLE: A Finnish company with a branch office already registered in China seeks to purchase office space for self use in Beijing. This should be permissible under the law.

EXAMPLE: Same facts as above, except the Finnish company wishes to purchase the office for the purpose of leasing the property out to third parties. This purchase would not be permissible under this rule.

EXAMPLE: A US company in the process of establishing a representative office in Shanghai seeks to purchase office space for self use. This would not be allowed until the representative office is properly established in China according to the law.

Foreign individuals who have worked or studied in China for more than one year are also permitted to purchase immovable property for self use.

EXAMPLE: A German engineer who has worked for a Chinese company for only three months seeks to purchase a condominium in Guangzhou. This would not be permissible under this rule as the German has not yet worked or studied in China for the requisite one year.

3. Purchase for Business or Other (Non-Self Use) Purpose

Chinese law requires that foreign companies and foreign individuals that wish to acquire a land use right for land and/or immovable property for a purpose *other than* self use must establish a special purpose legal entity called a Foreign Invested Real Estate Enterprise (FIREE) (see applicable financing rules below).

A FIREE is a foreign owned enterprise registered in China to engage in real estate investment, development, or business operations.

The normal time necessary to register a FIREE is about three to six months, at which time the foreign investor should have already entered into a contract to purchase the land use right for land and/or immovable property.

This is referred to in China as the rule of business presence, which means that any foreign investment in real estate for a purpose other than self use must be approved by the Chinese government in advance.

EXAMPLE: A US real estate company seeks to purchase a condominium building in Xiamen for the purpose of converting the building into a hotel. After execution of the sale and purchase agreement by the US real estate company with the seller, Chinese law would require the US company to first apply to establish a FIREE with the Chinese government and then, if successful, to operate the building under the FIREE.

4. Financing and Foreign Exchange Controls

Chinese law regulates how the purchase price for land use and/or immovable property are paid for by the foreigner, both in terms of the source of funds and where the funds are paid.

Qualifying foreign individuals and foreign companies, as described above, purchasing land use and/or immovable property in China may pay the purchase price either from an offshore source or from a foreign currency account in China.

If the purchase is by a foreign registered company the following documents are required to be presented to the Chinese bank responsible for converting the foreign currency payment to RMB:

i.   Sale or pre-sale contract for the property

ii. Approval and registration certificate of the foreign company's onshore branch or representative office

iii. Registration of the purchase with a competent property administration authority

iv. Written declaration that the purchased property will be for self use

Upon its receipt of the above documents, the bank should allow the foreign purchaser to convert the foreign currency into RMB so that he can pay the seller.

EXAMPLE: A Danish company with a representative office in China seeks to purchase office space in Beijing for self use and wishes to wire in Euros from a source outside China to make the payment. Before the Danish company would be allowed to convert the Euros into RMB, the Danish company would be required to present the above four listed documents to the Chinese bank, including a declaration that the property is for self use only.

If the purchase is by a foreign individual, the following documents are required to be presented to the Chinese bank responsible for converting the foreign currency into RMB:

i.   Sale or pre-sale contract for the property

ii. Written proof of personal identity such as passport or identity card

iii. Registration of the purchase with a competent property administration authority

iv. Written proof of one-year stay in China for employment or study, such as an employment contract or certification of recruitment

EXAMPLE: A Canadian student studying the Chinese language seeks to purchase a land use right and a house in Shanghai and successfully negotiates the terms of the deal with the owners. Before the Canadian would be allowed to convert the purchase price from foreign currency to RMB, he would be required to present the above documentation, including evidence that he has lived in China for employment or study for the past year, to the converting bank.

Note that the above one-year proof of stay requirement is waived for individuals with Hong Kong, Macao, and Taiwanese citizenship.

EXAMPLE: Same facts as above, but the purchaser is from Taiwan instead of Canada. In this situation, the purchaser would be required to provide the bank with the same documentation as stated above with the exception that the written proof of one-year stay would not be required.

The law requires the sale proceeds be paid by the foreign purchaser into the seller's RMB bank account.

EXAMPLE: A German company with a representative office in China seeks to buy office space in Shanghai for self use. The seller requests that the German company pay 50% of the purchase price in RMB into a Chinese bank account and the other 50% into an account offshore in foreign currency. This would not be permissible as the payment does not comply with the above requirement.

5. Primary and Secondary Markets

There are basically two sources of land in China: land in the primary market (which is held by the government) and land in the secondary market (which was formerly owned by the government, but has subsequently been sold to a third party).

In order for foreigners to obtain a land use right for land in the primary market a very strict (and many times very time consuming) bidding or auction procedure must be followed; therefore, many times, foreigners interested in acquiring rights to land prefer to do so from the secondary market, where the requirements are more easily met (as generally set forth in this chapter.)

6. Title Search

It is very important that any prospective purchaser of land use and/or immovable property in China conduct a thorough title search prior to closing. By conducting a title search, a prospective purchaser can obtain basic information concerning the property's precise location, borders, and usage, and whether any liens, mortgages, or leases are registered on the title.

The prospective purchaser should also review documents such as the property ownership certificate (the landowner's primary evidence of ownership), and if the landowner does not have the property ownership certificate, the prospective purchaser should review the following documents:

i. Construction land planning permit

ii. Construction planning permit

iii. Construction permit

iv. Certificate for land use right (for state owned land)

v. Property pre-sale permit (commonly referred to as the "five permits")

vi. Other relevant documents

Note that in some provinces the local land offices have data bases to assist interested persons in obtaining information concerning properties located in those provinces.

Note too, that the original registration documents may also be available for search by the owners, persons authorized by the owners, land registration agencies, judicial authorities (such as the courts and procurators), and other government agencies.

India

Capital City	New Delhi
Major Financial Center	Mumbai
Population (projected 2010)	1224 million
Location	Southern Asia, bordering the Arabian Sea and the Bay of Bengal, between Burma and Pakistan
Major Languages	Hindi, English
Legal System	Common law
Square Miles	1,269,210 sq mi
Gross Domestic Product (projected 2010)	USD 1234 billion
Major Exports	Agricultural products, textile goods, gems and jewelry, software services and technology, engineering goods, chemicals, leather products
Currency	Indian rupee (INR)
U.S. Dollar Exchange Rate (as of November 2009)	USD 1 = INR 46.569
Euro Exchange Rate (as of November 2009)	EUR 1 = INR 69.5225

Section Authors

Ravi Singhania
Managing Partner
Singhania & Partners
Email: rs@singhania.in
Website: http://www.singhania.in

Dipak Rao
Partner
Singhania & Partners
Email: dr@singhania.in
Website: http://www.singhania.in

Chapter 7

Should Our Business Establish as a Company, Branch Office, Liaison Office, or Project Office?

One of the first issues faced by prospective investors in India is choosing the appropriate type of legal structure through which to operate their business.

The most commonly used structures available are private company, liaison office, project office, and branch office.

When choosing the structure that is appropriate for the business, the foreign investor should consider a number of factors, including

i.   the intended business activities

ii. liability issues

iii. tax treatment

iv. capital requirements

v.   accounting issues

1. Private Limited Company

The private limited company structure (company) in India is the most commonly utilized type of legal entity in India. A company is owned by shareholders (a minimum of two shareholders with an upper limit of fifty). The company is managed by its board of directors (minimum of two directors).

Unlike a branch office, liaison office, and project office, a company is treated under Indian law as an independent legal entity. An application has to be filed with the Registrar of Companies (ROC) for registration and incorporation of the company (see Chapter 8).

47

EXAMPLE: If a multinational company wishes to establish a subsidiary in India it will likely do so as a privately held company. If individual investors wish to establish a stand-alone business to generate income in India they will most likely do so as a company.

EXAMPLE: Suppose a UK company seeks to establish a presence in India by establishing a company there. This company then executes a contract with another Indian party to supply computer chips, but then fails to deliver. In this situation, the Indian purchaser would normally be limited to suing the Indian company directly for breach of contract, and not the foreign holding company.

The procedure and rules to register a company and the official fees are discussed in Chapter 8.

2. Branch Office, Liaison Office, and Project Office

Many times a foreign company will seek to establish a presence in India, but will not want to establish a separate legal entity. For accounting, tax, and other reasons, the foreign company may instead want the Indian office to function as a part of the head office overseas. If that is the case, the foreign company will normally choose to establish a liaison office, branch office, or project office, and not a company. However, there are limitations as to the nature of business that can be carried on in a liaison office, a branch office, or a project office (see below).

Indian law considers each of these three entities as extensions of the head office overseas and not as separate legal entities. The employees of these entities are considered as the employees of the overseas company. The activities of these entities are considered as the activities of their head offices.

Note that foreign investors are required to register and file appropriate documentation with the Registrar of Companies (ROC) within thirty days of setting up a place of business in India, either as a branch office, liaison office, or project office. To see the required government form and the required supporting documents go to www.doylesguideasia.com/india/chapter7/appendixa.

a. Branch Office

Unlike a company, a branch office may only engage in business activities specifically defined by statute. A branch office may only pursue the following activities:

i.   Exporting and importing goods

ii. Rendering professional or consulting services

iii. Carrying out research work in which the parent company is engaged

iv. Promoting technical or financial collaborations between Indian companies and parent or overseas group companies

v.   Representing the parent company in India and acting as buying and selling agents in India

vi. Rendering services in information technology and development of software in India

vii. Rendering technical support for the products supplied by the parent/group companies

viii. Serving as a foreign airline and shipping company

With regard to liability, the branch and company structures also differ. For a company, liability arising from the actions of the business or its employees is generally limited to the Indian company only. The same is not true for a branch, since Indian law treats a branch as merely an extension of its head office overseas.

EXAMPLE: Suppose a foreign company establishes a branch office in India, and the branch office enters into a contract to supply goods and fails to perform. The Indian purchaser would normally have the choice of either suing the foreign company's head office overseas directly *or* its branch office in India. This is because the branch operates as a part of the business overseas, not as a stand-alone business entity.

There are no capital requirements for setting up a branch office. However, the expenses of maintaining the branch office, including the rent and the salaries of the employees, are to be paid out of remittances received into the bank account of the branch office from its overseas head office.

EXAMPLE: An Austrian company wishes to establish a branch office in India. In this situation, the Austrian company would not be subject to any minimum capital requirements; however, the expenses of the branch office, such as salaries, rent, and other office expenses would be required to be paid out of remittances received from its parent company overseas (not from amounts received by the branch office in India).

A foreign investor seeking to establish a branch office in India is required to file an application with the Reserve Bank of India (RBI). To see the appropriate form and the supporting documentation required go to www.doylesguideasia.com/india/chapter7/appendixa.

The approval is normally granted by the RBI within four months.

b. Liaison Office

Just as with a branch office, the liaison office is merely an extension of its head office overseas and is not considered as a separate legal entity. It is also strictly regulated as to the types of activities it may engage in.

A liaison office may only pursue the following activities:

i.   Representing in India the parent company/group companies

ii. Promoting exports and imports from and to India

iii. Promoting technical and financial collaborations between parent/group companies and companies in India

iv. Acting as a communication channel between the parent company and Indian companies

Unlike a branch office or a company, a liaison office is not permitted to earn income.

Also, just as with a branch office, there are no capital requirements for setting up a liaison office. However, the expenses of maintaining the liaison office, including the rent and the salaries of the employees are to be paid out of remittances received into the bank account of the liaison office from its overseas head office.

In order to establish a liaison office in India, prior approval must be obtained from the RBI. To see the required supporting documents which must be submitted go to www.doylesguideasia.com/india/chapter7/appendixa.

The approval is normally granted by the RBI within four months.

c. Project Office

The project office, unlike the company, branch office, or liaison office, may only be established to execute specific projects in India. In order to operate a project office no prior permission is required from the RBI, subject to the project office securing from an Indian company a contract to execute a project in India, plus certain funding requirements. Project funding must be accomplished in one of these ways:

i.   The project is funded by inward remittance from abroad.

ii. The project is funded by a bilateral or multilateral international finance agency.

iii. The project has been cleared by an appropriate government authority.

iv. A company or entity in India awarding the contract has been granted a term loan by a public financial institution or a bank in India for the project.

EXAMPLE: A city just outside of Mumbai has a new project to extend its existing railway lines. The primary contractor for the project is an Indian company which executes a contract for a French company to perform certain engineering services. The primary contractor has been granted a term loan from a major bank in India.

In this situation, the French engineering company would be allowed to operate a project office in India for the duration of its contract with the primary contractor.

The foreign company operating a project office is also required to provide a report to the local RBI office under whose jurisdiction the project office is established. To see the information the report is required to contain go to www.doylesguideasia.com/india/chapter7/appendixb.

A project office may also undertake or carry on any activity relating and incidental to the execution of the project.

EXAMPLE: Suppose a German company establishes a project office to install equipment on the same railway project mentioned above. During the course of the project, it becomes necessary for the German company to also provide specific engineering services related to the project. In this situation, the project office may engage in these engineering services as long as they are deemed related or incidental to the project.

There is no capital requirement for setting up a project office. However, just as with a branch office and liaison office, the expenses of maintaining the project office, including the rent and the salaries of the employees, are to be paid out of remittances received into the bank account of the project office from its overseas head office.

Chapter 8

What Legal Issues Are Associated with the Start-Up of a Foreign-Held Company?

There are several legal and practical issues associated with the legal start-up of a private limited company (company) in India. The start-up process involves registration with the Registrar of Companies (ROC), as well as obtaining other government licenses and approvals that may be required, depending upon the business activities the company seeks to engage in. Note that shelf companies are not readily available in India, so this process must generally be followed each time a new company is formed.

To see the list of information required during the company registration process go to www.doylesguideasia.com/india/chapter8/appendixa.

To see the list of documents required to obtain the company's Tax ID Card or the Permanent Account Number Card go to www.doylesguideasia.com/india/chapter8/appendixb.

To see the list of documents required to obtain the company's VAT Certificate, (applicable for manufacturing companies) go to www.doylesguideasia.com/india/chapter8/appendixc.

1. Promoters

The parties responsible for registering the company with the ROC are referred to as the company's promoters. Indian law requires a minimum of two promoters for a private company. The promoters may be individuals or business entities, and they must be available to sign documentation, as required, during the registration process. In the case of business entities as promoters, such entities are required to authorize an individual to sign on their behalf.

The promoters will be required to be among the company's initial share-holders immediately after the company's registration. Each of the promoters is required to hold a minimum of one share upon the company's registration, such that the aggregate holding of the promoters is not less than 0.1 million Rs. The promoters are generally free to transfer those shares to existing shareholders or third parties, thereafter, if they wish to do so. It is not required for the parties serving as promoters to reside in India.

Promoters' potential legal liability is generally limited to the par value of the shares they will hold after registration is completed. The promoters are also responsible for paying expenses associated with the company's registration. After registration, however, the company may choose to reimburse the promoters for those expenses.

2. Director Registration

The first step in the company registration process is for the promoters to select and register the initial company directors. Directors may be individuals only (no business entities) and are required to obtain a Directors Identification Number (DIN) from the Ministry of Corporate Affairs, which normally can be completed within three to four days of submitting the request online at the Ministry of Corporate Affairs official website. Companies are required to have a minimum of two directors.

3. Company Name

The next step is the name reservation. In order to reserve the name, one of the promoters is required to submit a signed official form online at the official website of the Ministry of Corporate Affairs. To see this form together with an English translation go to www.doylesguideasia.com/india/chapter8/appendixd.

The promoter submitting the name reservation form is required to provide the proposed company name together with at least three alternative names. The ROC will then examine the application according to the following guidelines:

i.   The central government will not approve a name if, in its opinion, the name is undesirable.

ii.   The requested name is identical to or nearly resembles the name of another company, or the name is contained in another party's registered trademark, or in a trademark application under consideration.

iii. The name does not otherwise violate guidelines issued by the central government.

Note that the Ministry of Corporate Affairs has formulated guidelines with regard to the use of key words in a company's name, and if certain key words appear in the name, special minimum requirements for share capital will apply (see Section 5 below).

In the event that the name is approved by the ROC, the promoters are required to submit the incorporation documents with the ROC within sixty days of the date of name approval. The name registration process may normally be completed within seven days.

EXAMPLE: A UK company submits a registration form with the ROC and the requested name is approved. In this situation, the promoters are required to submit the company's final approved registration documents with the ROC within sixty days. If not, the company must reapply to request the name again.

4. Memorandum and Articles of Association

Prior to final registration, the applicant will be required to submit the company's Memorandum and Articles of Association (Charter) to the ROC. The Charter states the company's main objective in seeking incorporation, amount of registered capital, and basic rules the company is required to follow after incorporation is successfully completed.

These rules generally include the frequency with which directors' and shareholders' meetings take place, what constitutes a quorum at meetings, notice requirements for meetings, the numbers required to pass a resolution at a meeting, etc.

To see a sample Charter go to www.doylesguideasia.com/india/chapter8/appendixe.

5. Registered Capital and Paid-Up Capital

With regard to the amounts to be invested in a start-up company in India, the most important concepts to understand are the company's registered capital and paid-up capital.

Registered capital is stated in the company charter (see above) and indicates the total amount that can be invested into the company by the shareholders. Indian law does not normally place minimum requirements with regard to a company's registered capital.

EXAMPLE: A company is registered in India with a registered capital of 500 million Rs. In this situation 500 million Rs. represents the total amount that shareholders of this company may invest (without amending the charter).

The company's paid-up capital refers to the registered value of the shares actually paid in by the shareholders.

EXAMPLE: Same facts as above, but the company shareholders actually pay into the company 250 million Rs. upon the company registration. In this situation, the company's registered capital is 500 million Rs. and paid-up capital is 250 million Rs.

Note that the company's paid-in capital (under normal circumstances) represents the shareholders' total exposure to liability associated with the company. The minimum paid-up capital required by law is 0.1 million Rs.

EXAMPLE: Malaysian investors in India establish an Indian company with a registered capital of 1 million Rs. The investors are required to pay a minimum of 0.1 million Rs. into the company at the time of incorporation. In this situation (under normal circumstances), the Malaysian shareholders total exposure to liability associated with the company is limited to 0.1 million Rs. (which has already been paid in).

The most common requirement with regard to registered capital concerns the use of certain key words in the company name.

The following chart lists the keywords together with the minimum capital requirements:

Keywords	Minimum Registered Capital
Corporation	Rs. 50 Million
International, Globe, Universal, Continental, Intercontinental, Asiatic, Asia, if first word of the company name	Rs. 10 Million
If any of the words above are included in the name other than as first word	Rs. 5 Million
Hindustan, India, Bharat, if first word of the company name	Rs. 5 Million
If any of the three words directly above are included in the name other than as first word	Rs. 0.5 Million
Industries/Udyog	Rs. 10 Million
Enterprise, Product, Business, Manufacturing	Rs. 1 Million

EXAMPLE: A German shoe company named "Intercontinental Shoes" decides to establish a limited company in India and submits a name application form to reserve the name "Intercontinental Shoes Ltd." Among the requirements to use this company name would be that the minimum registered capital of the company be no less than Rs. 10 million.

EXAMPLE: Same facts as above, but the requested name is instead "Shoes Intercontinental Ltd." In this situation, the minimum registered capital would instead be Rs. 5 million.

EXAMPLE: A Danish stationery company establishes a company in India under the company name "Universal Stationery Ltd." Due to the use of the key word "Universal" as the first word of the company name, the registered capital would be legally required to be set at no less than Rs. 10 million. In this situation, the company's registered capital would be Rs. 10 million, and the company's paid-up capital would be no less than 0.1 million Rs. up to the limit of Rs. 10 million.

6. Director Signing Authority

After registration, the names of the company's directors and their authority to sign on behalf of the company remain on file with the ROC.

Directors are designated as either authorized or unauthorized by the company's Board of Directors. Authorized directors are allowed to sign on behalf of the company, unauthorized directors are not.

Many times, as a controlling mechanism, the company will designate that only a combination of two or more directors signing together are authorized to sign on behalf of the company. Also, many companies will designate that a director(s) may sign on behalf of the company only together with the company seal. This makes the physical presence of the company seal another kind of control mechanism.

EXAMPLE: A company is registered in India, and the company's board of directors designates that any two of the four company directors can execute documents involving sums of more than $100,000 US on behalf of the company with the company seal. The company only issues one seal, which resides at the company's registered office in the room of the company's managing director.

In this situation, each time the company directors want to execute a document on behalf of the company involving a sum exceeding $100,000 US, practically speaking, they would be required to go to the managing director in possession of the seal in order to execute such documents.

7. Company Auditor

A company is required to appoint the first auditors within one month of the date of incorporation.

8. Timing

Registration of the company can generally be completed within a week of submitting all required forms and supporting documents either in person or online, as required.

9. Official Fees

The amount of official fees payable to the ROC is calculated based upon the amount of the company's registered capital on a sliding scale as shown below:

Registered Capital	Official Fee
Rs. 10,000 or part thereof above Rs. 10 Million up to Rs. 20 Million	Rs. 50 per Rs. 10,000 increment for registered capital which is set between Rs. 10 Million and Rs. 20 Million
For every further increase of Rs. 10,000 or part thereof above Rs. 5 Million up to Rs. 10 Million	Rs. 100 per Rs. 10,000 increment for registered capital which is set between Rs. 5 Million and Rs. 10 Million
For every further increase of Rs. 10,000 or part thereof above Rs. 0.5 Million up to Rs. 5 Million	Rs. 200 per Rs. 10,000 increment for registered capital which is set between Rs. 0.5 Million and Rs. 5 Million
For every further increase of Rs. 10,000 or part thereof above Rs. 0.1 Million up to Rs. 0.5 Million	Rs. 300 per Rs. 10,000 increment for registered capital which is set between Rs. 0.1 Million and Rs. 0.5 Million
For a company whose authorized capital does not exceed Rs. 0.1 Million	Rs. 4,000

If the Official Fee payable according to the amount of Registered Capital exceeds Rs. 20 million, the total amount of Official Fee for registration of the company is capped at Rs. 20 million.

EXAMPLE: If a company's registered capital is Rs. 1 million, the official fee payable to the ROC at the time of final registration would be as follows:

	Official Fee
Official fee payable for the amount up to Rs. 0.1 Million	Rs. 4,000
Official fee payable for the amount above Rs. 0.1 Million to Rs. 0.5 Million	Rs. 12,000
Official fee payable for the amount above Rs. 0.5 Million (USD 10,416 approx.) to Rs. 1 Million	Rs. 10,000
Estimated other miscellaneous official fees	Rs. 1,200
Total Fees payable to the ROC	Rs. 27,200

10. Other Registrations

After incorporation of the company, the company is required to file the following further registrations:

i. Permanent Account Number (Tax Registration Number)—application to be filed with the nominated agency of the Income Tax Department, Government of India, such as NSDL (National Securities Depository Limited). To see the registration form go to www.doyles guideasia.com/india/chapter8/appendixf.

ii. Tax Deduction and Collection Account Number (TAN)—application to be filed with the nominated agency of the Income Tax Department, Government of India, such as NSDL.

iii. Other government licenses and registrations commonly required, depending upon the company's business activities include

Service Tax Registration for service industries

Excise registration for manufacturing activity

VAT registration for manufacturers, exporters, and dealers

Importer-Exporter Code Certificate for the importing and exporting of goods

The above registrations can normally be completed within fifteen to thirty days from the date of providing all the required information and documents to the relevant government authorities.

11. Opening of Bank Account

Immediately after incorporation, the company is required to open a bank account for conducting its business. Each bank has its own format for the application form; however, listed below are some common requirements:

i.   Signed copy of Certificate of Incorporation

ii.   Signed copy of MOA (Memorandum of Agreement) and AOA (Articles of Association)

iii. Documentary evidence of the registered office address (Form 18 filed with ROC or copy of lease)

iv.   Certified true copy of the PAN Card (Permanent Account Number)

v.   Certified true copy of the board resolution authorizing the opening of the bank account and specifying the names of persons authorized to operate the said account of the company

12. Public Access to Company Details

After the company is incorporated, many details regarding the company's structure are easily available to the public at the government website, including the company's Corporate Identification Number, ROC Code, authorized capital, paid-up capital, date of incorporation, address of registered office, email address, date of last annual general meeting, balance sheet, company status, and the names of directors.

Chapter 9

What Legal Issues Are Associated with Operating as a Foreign-Held Company?

Indian law regulates the types of activities in which foreign-held companies may engage, designating that some activities are completely prohibited and others are allowed as long as certain compliance and/or approval requirements are met.

The government regulates the activities of foreign-held companies such as

i. wholly own subsidiaries of foreign registered companies

ii. branches, representative, and liaison offices of foreign registered companies

iii. joint venture companies registered in India in which a foreign registered company or foreign individual is a shareholder together with a local party

iv. companies registered in India in which a shareholder is an Indian citizen, but not a resident of India

EXAMPLE: A South African company establishes a liaison office in Chennai. This Indian liaison office would be subject to regulation.

EXAMPLE: Swedish investors and Indian investors establish a limited company in which the Swedish investors hold 40% of the shares and the Indian investors 60%. This joint venture company would be subject to regulation.

EXAMPLE: An Indian national residing in the US for the past twenty years seeks to establish a company in India. Even though he is an Indian citizen the company will be subject to regulation because he is no longer a resident in India.

1. Regulated Activities

Regulated activities are those which foreign investors are prohibited from engaging in and those which foreigners are allowed to engage in subject to requirements (see below).

Prohibited activities include retail trading (except single product retailing), atomic energy, lottery, and others (List 1 Activities).

To see a complete list of prohibited activities go to www.doylesguideasia.com/india/chapter9/appendixa.

The activities in which foreigners are allowed to participate, subject to complying with requirements (see below), include banking, finance, intrastate telecommunication, publishing, manufacturing, trading for exports, insurance, construction courier service, and many others (List 2 activities).

To see a full list of permitted activities go to www.doylesguideasia.com/india/chapter9/appendixb.

2. Foreign Investment Approval

Foreign-held companies seeking to engage in List 2 activities require the approval of the Government of India with respect to compliance with the Foreign Direct Investment (FDI) policy. This may be done using one of two methods:

i.   Approval Required—Approval of the Foreign Investment Promotion Board (Board) is required prior to investment.

ii. Automatic Approval—The Board's Approval is not required.

a. Approval Method

Foreign investors not qualifying for automatic approval (see below) are required to submit an application to the Board and obtain approval prior to making their investment.

To see the application form (Form No. FC/IL) go to www.doylesguideasia.com/india/chapter9/appendixc.

To see the checklist of documents to be submitted, along with the form to get the approval, go to www.doylesguideasia.com/india/chapter9/appendixd.

The Board uses the following criteria when reviewing the application:

i.   Whether the application complies with specified investment limits and conditions, if any, related to List 2 activities

ii. Whether the proposal involves technology transfer or collaboration, and if so, the source and nature of the technology to be transferred and the terms of payment of royalty for the technology

The application process normally takes between thirty and forty-five days.

b. Automatic Approval Method

When the automatic approval method is applicable, the foreign investor is not required to obtain the Board's approval; however, the foreign investment is required to be reported to the Reserve Bank of India (RBI) within specified statutory time limits.

The activities and investment limits for the automatic entry route are mentioned in List 2.

To see the activities and investment limits applicable to foreign investors and the automatic approval method go to www.doylesguideasia.com/india/chapter9/appendixb.

3. Reporting Requirements

a. Inward Remittance

After approval or automatic approval (as applicable) the foreign investor will be required to make an inward remittance into India in an amount representing the declared investment made by the foreign investor. Within thirty days of the India-registered company's receipt of this amount, the India-registered company is required to report the remittance to the RBI along with a copy of the Foreign Inward Remittance Certificate and the following information:

i. Name and address of the foreign investors

ii. Date of receipt of the funds and their rupee equivalent

iii. Name and address of the authorized dealer through whom the funds have been received

iv. Details of the Government's approval, if any

To see the form which is required to be submitted go to www.doylesguideasia.com/india/chapter9/appendixe.

EXAMPLE: Danish investors establish a company in India to engage in construction services (List 2 activity) and receive approval from the Board to begin operations. The company's original application to the Board states that the Danish investors will remit Rs.15 million within the first three months of the company's operation. Upon the receipt of these funds, the company will be required to notify RBI within thirty days.

b. Issuance of Shares

Subsequently, on allotment of shares by the India-registered company against the inward remittance, this information has to be reported to the RBI within thirty days from the date of such allotment on Form FC—GPR inter alia with the following information:

i. Name and address of the India-registered company

ii. Name and address of the foreign investor

iii. Description of main business activity

iv. Particulars of the shares issued

v. Total inflow on account of allotment of shares

vi. Post allotment pattern of shareholding.

EXAMPLE: A UAE company incorporates a subsidiary in India. After the completion of the incorporation process, when the new shares are allotted to the UAE company, the Indian subsidiary of the UAE company will be required to report the allotment to the Regional RBI office in the jurisdiction where the Indian company is incorporated.

To see the required form go to www.doylesguideasia.com/india/chapter9/appendixf.

Chapter 10

What Is the Process to Obtain a Work Permit?

All foreigners seeking to work in India on a long term basis are required to obtain a work permit, referred to in India as an Employment (E) Visa (Employment Visa) from the Indian Embassy or High Commission in their country of residence.

The procedure and requirements to obtain a work permit in India are less defined than in many other countries, and presiding officials have wide discretion in deciding who qualifies. The following, however, is a description of the general process and requirements.

1. Application Procedure

Indian law generally allows skilled professionals and people immigrating to India to fill a specific position with an Indian employer to obtain an Employment Visa. The foreign employee is required to secure the Employment Visa prior to entering India.

EXAMPLE: A Dutch national accepts an offer of employment from an Indian registered company and enters India for the purpose of work before receiving an Employment Visa. Using these facts, in order to obtain an Employment Visa, the Dutch national would be required to leave India and initiate the Employment Visa process in his home country (see below).

The following documents are required to be submitted by the foreign employee to the Indian Embassy or High Commission in his country of residence:

i.   A completed visa application form

ii.   A current valid passport

iii. Recent passport photographs

iv.   Proof of employment

    v.   Terms and conditions of employment

    vi. Position title and job description on the letterhead of the Indian company

    vii. Letter of recommendation from the Indian company employing the foreigner

    viii. Proof of registration of employer's organization in India

The Indian Embassy or High Commission receiving the application may also require additional supporting documents. The processing time for the Employment Visa application will depend upon the policy and procedures of the Embassy or High Commission in the particular country.

2. Employment Visa Period

Employment Visas are typically issued for a period of one year and may be renewed in one-year increments for up to five years at the discretion of the Foreigners Regional Registration Officer (FRRO) in India. The availability of annual renewals depends upon the specifics of the situation and normal practices in the region within India where the extension application is filed.

3. Intra Company Transfers

Employment Visas may also be applied for by high level or crucial employees of a foreign company who are needed to work in that foreign company's office in India.

EXAMPLE: A Korean national who has worked for a Singaporean company as the CFO of its Thailand office for the past five years learns that he will be transferred to work in the Singapore company's office in Mumbai. In this situation, the Korean may qualify to receive an Employment Visa as an internal transfer.

There are no set requirements to receive an Employment Visa as an internal transfer, and they are granted on a case by case basis; however, in general, it is preferred that the applicant have a four-year degree, and the official may take into account the availability of local staff to fill the position.

4. Dependents

Spouses and children of the Employment Visa holder may qualify to receive an X Visa to reside (not work) in India. The dependents are required to obtain the X Visa (to be issued by the Indian Embassy or High Commission in their own country) prior to entering India.

The following supporting documents are required to be submitted together with the X Visa application for the spouse of a foreign employee:

i.   Passport and visa copies of the spouse who is to be employed in India

ii.   Recent photographs

iii. Current passport

iv.   Marriage certificate

v.   Visa application form

5. Registration of Foreign Nationals

All foreigners holding a visa for a period of more than 180 days (except those covered under special categories) are required to register with the relevant District Foreigners Registration Officer (FRD) or Foreigners Regional Registration Officer (FRRO) within fourteen days of their first arrival in India (except for nationals of specific countries, in which case the period may be as short as twenty-four hours or seven days). Note that each local FRD or FRRO may have different registration requirements.

EXAMPLE: A foreign employee from the UK arrives in India on September 1st with an Employment Visa valid for one year. That foreign employee would be required to register with the local FRRO by September 14th.

A foreigner holding an Employment Visa is required to appear in person before the FRRO and present the following documents:

i.   Copy of employment contract or appointment letter

ii.   Terms and conditions of appointment

iii. Job description from employer/company

iv.   Arrival report, issued by the prescribed authority

v.   Properly completed application form

vi.   Photocopy of main pages of passport

vii. Recent passport photographs

viii. Details of proof of residence in India

Foreigners may also be required to provide the FRRO with an HIV test from a World Health Organization recognized institution.

At the end of the registration process the foreign applicant will be issued a residence permit, which will usually have the same validity period as the Employment Visa. Registration is required to be done only once during the validity of the Employment Visa, irrespective of the number of times the foreigner leaves and re-enters India. Only if the foreigner re-enters India on a new visa will he be required to register again.

EXAMPLE: A Norwegian national enters India with an Employment Visa, and within fourteen days registers with his local FRRO and receives a residence permit. If he leaves and returns to India during the validity period stated in his Employment Visa he will not be required to re-register with the FRRO. However, if in the future he changes jobs and has to obtain a new Employment Visa, he will be required to re-register with the FRRO.

Note that only children above the age of sixteen are required to register with the FRRO.

EXAMPLE: Same facts as above except the Norwegian Employment Visa holder is accompanied by his fifteen-year-old son who has already secured an X visa. In this situation, the son would not be required to register with the FRRO until he turns sixteen.

Chapter 11

What Investment Incentives Are Available to Foreign Investors?

The Indian government encourages specific types of business projects in India by granting qualifying projects various incentives. These incentives include tax incentives, import duty exemptions and reductions, as well as other incentives, as set forth below.

This chapter discusses two incentive programs implemented by the Indian government:

Special Economic Zones and Export Oriented Units.

1. Special Economic Zones

Special Economic Zones (SEZ) are areas within India designated by the government to give investors who establish businesses (referred to as units) in those areas the following investment incentives:

i.   Income tax holidays and extended carry forward of losses.

ii. Exemption from excise duty on the procurement of goods, including raw materials from a DTA used for setting up the SEZ unit. DTA refers to the whole of India, including territorial waters; however it does not include areas within SEZs).

iii. Duty free import of raw materials, capital goods, spare parts, etc.

iv. Duty free exports.

v.   Duty draw back on goods and services purchased from the DTA.

vi. Exemption from Central Excise Tax on goods brought from the domestic market.

vii. Exemption from Service Tax on services provided to SEZ units.

viii. Exemption from Central Sales Tax.

ix. No import license required.

x.   Allowed to operate as a 100% foreign-held company (with only a few exceptions).

To see a list of SEZs go to www.doylesguideasia.com/india/chapter11/appendixa.

a. SEZ Tax Incentives

i. Tax Exemptions on Income from Exports

The following tax incentives are available to SEZ units for a period of up to fifteen years on income derived from exports (normal corporate tax rate is 30%):

i.   100% tax exemption on the profits derived from exports during the first five consecutive years

ii. 50% tax exemption on profits from exports during the next five consecutive years

iii. Tax exemption equal to an amount not exceeding 50% of the profits (subject to special considerations) during the remaining five years

Such incentives become available to the SEZ unit starting from the year in which the unit begins to manufacture or produce items or to provide services.

EXAMPLE: A US computer company establishes a call center in India inside an SEZ. In this situation, the project (referred to as a unit) would receive the following tax incentives for a period of fifteen years, commencing from the year the call center begins operation:

Years 1 to 5   100% tax exemption

Years 6 to 10   50% tax exemption

Years 11 to 15   a tax exemption equal to an amount not exceeding 50% of the profits (subject to special considerations)

Note that the above tax incentives apply only to the unit's income derived from the goods or services exported. For the company's income derived from domestic sales, normal tax rules would apply.

EXAMPLE: Suppose a unit located in an SEZ realizes total income of INR 100 million in one year. Of this INR 100 million, INR 80 million represents revenue from export sales and the remaining INR 20 million represents proceeds from the sale of goods to customers in India. In this situation, the unit would qualify for the above tax incentives only with respect to the INR 80 million from export sales. For the remaining INR 20 million, normal tax rules would apply.

ii. Customs Duty Exemptions

SEZ units are allowed exemption from Customs Duty on imports of raw materials, capital goods, and spare parts. Such units are also allowed exemption from Customs Duty on goods exported by them to any place outside India.

iii. Central Excise Duty Exemption

SEZ units are granted exemption from Central Excise Duty on goods sourced from within the DTA.

Normally, goods sold by manufacturers located in the DTA to purchasers in the DTA are subject to Central Excise Duty. However, the goods supplied by parties in a DTA to a SEZ unit are treated as "deemed exports," and therefore, such goods are exempt from Central Excise Duty.

EXAMPLE: Suppose an SEZ unit buys goods from a supplier in the DTA. Normally, Central Excise Duty would be applicable to such supplies; however, in this situation, because the purchaser is located in an SEZ, no Central Excise Duty is applicable.

iv. Service Tax Exemption

The services provided by a supplier in the DTA to SEZ units are exempt from Service Tax. The normal rate of Service Tax in India is 10.3%.

EXAMPLE: A factory located in an SEZ contracts with a sourcing company located in the DTA to provide services, which would normally be taxable at 10.3%. However, because the recipient of the services is located in an SEZ, the service tax would not be applicable.

v. Central Sales Tax (CST) Exemption

CST of 2% is normally applicable on the sale and purchase of goods between parties from different Indian states. However, purchases made by units in an SEZ are exempt from CST.

EXAMPLE: A factory located in an SEZ in the State of Maharashtra orders raw materials from a supplier located in the DTA in the State of Gujarat. CST would not apply to this transaction since the purchaser of raw materials is an SEZ unit.

b. Additional Benefits

SEZ units are also afforded the following two benefits:

i.   SEZ units may pay managerial remuneration up to a limit of INR 24 million per annum to its managing director, whole-time director, manager, and managerial personnel without approval from the government.

Normally, if a company intends to pay management personnel over INR 4.8 million, it must obtain prior approval from the government. If the company operates in an SEZ, however, this rule does not apply.

ii.   A foreign person may be appointed as managerial personnel even if he does not satisfy the requirement of being a resident in India for at least twelve months prior to his appointment (see Chapter 10).

EXAMPLE: A Frenchman is hired by a company located in an SEZ to be its managing director. Normally, in this situation, the Frenchman would be required to reside in India a minimum of one year prior to being legally allowed to accept the position of managing director or other managerial position, i.e. whole-time director or manager. However, in this situation, because the company is located in an SEZ, the rule does not apply.

c. SEZ Requirements

Investors seeking to establish a unit in an SEZ are required to submit an application with the Development Commissioner. To see the application form go to www.doylesguideasia.com/india/chapter11/appendixb.

The Development Commission will then forward the application to the Approval Committee. In order to be approved, the application must meet the following criteria:

i.   The project must meet positive Net Foreign Exchange earnings requirements.

ii.   There must be adequate space and other infrastructure support available for the project.

iii. The investor agrees to comply with the environmental and pollution control standards.

iv.   The investor submits proof of residence in India, namely, a passport, ration card, driver's license, voter identity card, or any other proof, plus an audited balance sheet for the last three years and income tax returns.

v.   The proposal fulfills the sector specific requirements.

The Approval Committee will normally approve or reject the application within fifteen days of its receipt; however, in the event that the application is required to be submitted to the Board of Approval, the consideration period is forty-five days.

After approval of the proposal by the Approval Committee or Board of Approval (as applicable), the Development Commissioner will then issue a Letter of Approval. The Letter of Approval sets forth the items to be manufactured, service activities, including trading or warehousing, and the projected annual report and Net Foreign Exchange Earnings for the unit's first five years of operations.

The Letter of Approval is valid for a period of five years starting from the date operations begin. At the end of that five-year period, the investor will be required to apply to renew the Letter of Approval with the Development Commissioner for an additional five-year period.

2. Export Oriented Unit

The Export Oriented Unit program seeks to attract projects that earn income through the sale of exports.

An Export Oriented Unit may be set up for manufacturing and providing services such as related repairing, reconditioning, remaking, and re-engineering services for export (no trading activities). The following are some of the incentives available to investors qualifying as an Export Oriented Unit:

i.   Exemption from Central Excise Duty in the procurement of capital goods, raw-materials, consumables spare parts, etc. from the Domestic Tariff Area

ii. Exemption from Customs Duty on the import of capital goods, raw materials, consumables, spare parts, etc.

iii. Reimbursement of Central Sales Tax paid on domestic purchases

iv. Secondhand capital goods, without any age limit, allowed to be imported duty free

v.   No import license requirement

The primary requirement of an Export Oriented Unit is that it achieves what is referred to as Positive Net Foreign Exchange Earning (NFE). NFE is calculated over five-year periods starting from the commencement of production according to the document (referred to as a legal undertaking) executed by the Export Oriented Unit and the Development Commissioner.

Normally, only projects with a minimum investment of INR 10 million in the project's production facility building and machinery are considered for Export Oriented Unit status; however, projects with less investment are sometimes considered.

To see the applicable form go to www.doylesguideasia.com/india/chapter11/appendixc.

Applications for establishing manufacturing EOU units are submitted to the Units Approval Committee, which is required to rule on the application within fifteen days of submission.

Applications for establishing a service Export Oriented Unit are submitted to the Board of Approval. However, there is no set time frame for processing applications submitted to the Board of Approval.

Other applications (which require an Industrial License) are required to be ruled on within forty-five days.

On approval, the Development Commissioner issues a Letter of Permission/Letter of Intent which is valid for a period of three years (renewable), during which time operations should begin. Once the unit begins production, the Letter of Permission/Letter of Intent issued is valid for a period of five years.

Chapter 12

What Legal Issues Are Associated with Foreign Ownership of Land?

A foreigner is not allowed to own land, buildings, and other immovable property in India except in specific situations as set forth below.

1. Ownership for Non-Business Purposes

A foreign individual may purchase land and/or immovable property in India for non-business purposes if at the time of purchase that foreign individual qualifies as a resident of India. This rule, therefore, makes the legal definition of resident in this situation quite important.

In order for a foreigner to qualify as an Indian resident, he is required to have resided in India for more than 182 days during the preceding financial year (financial year is defined here as April 1st to March 31st) while being employed or carrying on a business in India.

EXAMPLE: A Japanese businessman working in New Delhi seeks to purchase land and a house in India. The Japanese man resided in India during the previous financial year for a total of 254 days while working for an Indian company. In this situation, the Japanese businessman would qualify as a resident and be permitted to make the purchase.

Further, a foreign national may also be treated as a resident in India if he comes to India for any other purpose (other than employment or business), and the circumstances indicate his intention to stay in India for an indefinite period.

EXAMPLE: A US national moves to Chennai for an indefinite period for the purpose of retirement and seeks to buy a condominium there. In this situation, the US national may purchase the condominium if he can establish that it is his intention to live in India for an indefinite period.

Land and immovable property may also be acquired by a foreign individual by way of inheritance from a resident of India.

EXAMPLE: An Indian man who owns a house and land in Mumbai dies with a will leaving the house and land to his friend who lives in the UK and has UK nationality. The UK national could inherit the house and land in Mumbai under the will without qualifying as a resident of India.

Note that when the above described foreign nationals own land and/or immovable property in India and then sell that land and/or immovable property and receive the proceeds of the sale from the purchaser, they may only remit those sale proceeds outside India after obtaining permission from the Reserve Bank of India (RBI) to do so.

EXAMPLE: Same facts as above, but shortly after receiving title, the UK national seeks to sell the land and house and send the sale proceeds to the UK. In this situation, in order to transfer the sale proceeds outside India, he would be required to first obtain approval from the RBI.

Indian law also grants rights to own land to individuals who are not Indian citizens, but have family ties in India. These persons are referred to as Persons of Indian Origin or PIOs. Such persons have to register themselves as PIO with the Indian Mission in their country of residence.

EXAMPLE: The son of an Indian national who grew up in the US and has US citizenship moves to Hyderabad and seeks to buy land and a house. Such person may do so as a PIO (without qualifying as an Indian resident).

The requirement to obtain RBI approval before remitting the sales proceeds from the sale of land and/or immovable property outside India does not apply to PIOs.

EXAMPLE: Same facts as above, and the son of the Indian national later sells the land and house and receives the sale proceeds from the purchaser and wishes to remit the sale proceeds to the US. In this situation, he may do so without obtaining permission from the RBI.

A PIO may use local financing to buy a residence. Local financing is not available for the other categories of persons.

2. Ownership for a Business Purpose

Foreign registered companies with branch offices and project offices in India engaging in specified business activities are allowed to acquire land and immovable property for the purpose of pursuing those business activities.

For branch offices, these specified activities are as follows:

i. The import/export of goods

ii. Professional and consulting services

iii. Research work for the parent company overseas

EXAMPLE: A Canadian import/export company establishes a branch office in India for exporting Indian made handcrafts and importing certain consumer goods into India. The Canadian company then seeks to purchase office space in which to operate. This should be permissible under the law with no prior approval required from the government.

Foreign registered companies with project offices in India are also allowed to purchase land and/or immovable property in India for the purpose of carrying out their designated projects.

EXAMPLE: A Dutch company is awarded a project in India and establishes a project office to carry out the project. The company may purchase the land and buildings necessary or incidental to carrying out that project with no prior approval required from the government.

Any foreign company acquiring land and/or immovable property to engage in the above business activities is required to file a declaration with the RBI. To see the declaration form go to www.doylesguideasia.com/india/chapter 12/appendixa.

The financing of the purchase of land and/or immovable property is required to be done either by remitting funds from outside India through normal banking channels or by using existing funds in the purchaser's account(s) with an authorized Indian bank. Financing the purchase locally is not permitted.

EXAMPLE: A branch office of a Spanish company which qualifies to purchase land and/or immovable property in India for a business purpose seeks to purchase a warehouse. In this situation, the branch would be required to finance the purchase either by remitting the purchase price from outside of India or by using existing funds the branch has with an authorized India bank. The branch would not be allowed to finance the purchase locally.

If a foreign company owns land and/or immovable property in India and then sells the property to a third party and receives the proceeds from the sale, the company may only remit those sales proceeds outside of India after it obtains prior approval to do so from the RBI.

EXAMPLE: A Swedish company with a project office in India purchases land and buildings, and after three years, the Swedish company sells the land and buildings. In order for the Swedish company to transfer such sales proceeds outside India, it must first obtain permission from the RBI to do so.

3. Land Ownership by Indian Subsidiaries of Foreign Companies

In contrast to the rules applicable to non-Indian registered foreign companies with branch offices and/or project offices in India, Indian law does *not* place restrictions on foreign owned Indian registered companies seeking to purchase land and immovable property in India.

EXAMPLE: A Singaporean company registers a wholly owned subsidiary in India, and that subsidiary purchases land for the purpose of leasing the land to third parties. This purchase would be permissible under the law. However, the subsidiary would be subject to restrictions as to the types of business activities it would be allowed to legally pursue as stated in Chapter 9.

4. Leases

The conditions and restrictions associated with the purchase of land and/or immovable property by foreign individuals for a non-business purpose (see Section 1 above) and by foreign registered companies with a branch office and/or project office in India for a business purpose (see Section 2 above) are equally applicable to leases for a period exceeding five years.

EXAMPLE: An Austrian man seeks to enter into a lease agreement for land and a house for ten years to use as a residence. In order to proceed with this arrangement, the Austrian would be required to qualify as an Indian resident (see Section 1 above).

EXAMPLE: A French company with a branch office in India seeks to lease office space for a period of seven years. In order to be allowed to do so, the branch office must engage in one of the three activities stated in Section 2 — the export/import of goods, professional or consulting services, or research work for the parent company.

Leases of land and immovable property by foreign individuals and foreign registered companies for a period of five years or less are not regulated by the RBI.

EXAMPLE: A German man who has never been to India enters into a lease agreement for land in Hyderabad for a period of five years. This should be permissible under the law.

EXAMPLE: A Canadian company with a liaison office in India enters into a lease agreement to rent space in a warehouse in New Delhi for five years. This should be permissible under the law.

5. Title Search

Every prospective purchaser of land and/or immovable property in India should perform a thorough title search of the property prior to purchase.

Such title search will help the prospective purchaser ascertain or confirm

i.   the status of the title and rights of the seller

ii. the property boundaries

iii. whether there are mortgages, liens, or other encumbrances recorded on the title

iv. whether there are leases recorded on the title

v.   whether the land is subdivided

as well as other relevant information.

The title search may be performed at the local sub-registrar office of the district where the property is located. Note that the status of the property title is normally open for public inspection.

6. Documentation

Transferring the title of land and/or immovable property requires that a conveyance/sale deed be executed by the purchaser and the seller be properly registered with the jurisdictional sub-registrar for the area where the property is situated.

Leasing land and/or immovable property for a period of more than eleven months requires that a lease deed be executed by the parties and properly registered with the jurisdictional sub-registrar.

Indonesia

Capital City	Jakarta
Major Financial Center	Jakarta
Population (projected 2010)	233 million
Location	Southeastern Asia, archipelago between the Indian Ocean and the Pacific Ocean
Major Languages	Indonesian
Legal System	Civil law
Square Miles	735,355 sq mi
Gross Domestic Product (projected 2010)	USD 504 billion
Major Exports	Oil and gas, plywood, textiles, rubber, palm oil
Currency	Rupiah (IDR)
U.S. Dollar Exchange Rate (as of November 2009)	USD 1 = IDR 9545
Euro Exchange Rate (as of November 2009)	EUR 1 = IDR 14100

Section Author
Renato M. Leuterio
Senior Partner-Advisor
Grant Thornton Hendrawinata
Email: rl@gthendrawinata.com
Website: http://www.gtindonesia.com

Chapter 13

Should Our Business Establish as a Company Limited or Representative Office?

One of the first issues faced by prospective investors in Indonesia is choosing the appropriate type of legal structure through which to operate their business. The most commonly used of the structures available are company limited and representative office.

When choosing the structure that is appropriate for your business you should consider a number of factors, including

i.   capital requirements
ii. the intended business activities to be pursued
iii. liability issues
iv. tax treatment

1. Company Limited

The private company structure (company) in Indonesia is similar to a Limited Liability Company (LLC) structure in the US and is the most utilized type of legal entity in Indonesia.

A company is owned by shareholders (minimum two) and managed by directors (minimum one). The liability of each of the shareholders is generally limited to the total par value of their shares. The shareholders' direct participation in company affairs is normally quite limited. It is the directors who are responsible for managing company affairs and who owe various fiduciary duties to the shareholders and the company (duty of care, duty of loyalty, etc.).

Unlike a representative office, a company limited is treated under Indonesian law as a stand-alone legal entity.

EXAMPLE: If a multinational wishes to establish a subsidiary in Indonesia it will likely do so as a privately held company. If individual investors wish to establish a stand-alone business to generate income in Indonesia, they will most likely do so as a company.

EXAMPLE: Suppose a multinational establishes a wholly owned subsidiary in Indonesia as a company limited. That new company limited then executes a contract with another Indonesian company to supply garments, but then fails to supply those garments. In this situation, the Indonesian purchaser would generally be limited to suing the Indonesian subsidiary for the breach of contract, not its headquarters overseas.

2. Representative Office

Many times, however, foreign investors will not want to operate as a company limited. This is most likely to be true when a multinational company seeks to establish a presence in Indonesia, but does not wish to establish a separate legal entity. For accounting, tax, and other reasons, the multinational company may instead want the Indonesian office to function as a part of the head office overseas. If that is the case, the multinational will normally choose to establish a representative office, not a company limited.

The representative office's structure is very different from the company limited's. Unlike a company limited, the representative office is not allowed to earn income. A representative office merely serves as an extension of its head office overseas. It is not a stand-alone legal entity. A representative office is also strictly regulated to perform only specific activities designated by statute on behalf of its head office overseas.

Indonesian law designates two categories of representative offices, national representative offices and regional representative offices, each with its own list of permissible activities.

National representative offices may engage only in the following activities:

i.   Introducing and promoting the goods which are manufactured overseas

ii.   Giving information or directives on the export and import of the goods

iii. Conducting market research and supervising the sales and marketing of the products in Indonesia

iv.   Connecting the foreign principal with domestic companies

v.   Concluding contracts with domestic companies in the name of the foreign company to export goods

Regional representative offices may engage only in the following activities:

i.   Controlling the activities, already conducted in the region, of the foreign company

ii.   Fostering the communication and coordination of the different activities within the region

iii. Making preparations relating to the establishment and business development of foreign investment in Indonesia

It is also required that the regional representative office's head office must already be engaged in business in at least one other country in addition to Indonesia and the home country of its head office.

EXAMPLE: A construction supplies company with its headquarters in Sweden seeks to establish a representative office in Indonesia. It has no other office or branch in Asia. In this situation, the Swedish company would not qualify to establish a representative office in Indonesia.

EXAMPLE: Same facts as above, except the Swedish company operates a branch office in Singapore and otherwise qualifies to operate a representative office in Indonesia. In this situation, the Swedish company would qualify.

In addition, both national representative offices and regional representative offices are specifically prohibited from engaging in the following activities:

i.   Conducting direct sales

ii.   Managing a company that is either an affiliate, subsidiary, or branch of the principal company

iii. Importing products

iv.   Making any transactions with companies or people in Indonesia either for export, import, or domestic trading

v.   Owning or maintaining production facilities or operational activities

vi.   Accepting orders or participating in tenders

vii. Issuing bills of lading

viii. Carrying out direct trading activities in Indonesia in the form of securing contracts, selling or entering into transactions, either at the initial or final settlement stage, for example, submission of bids, signing contracts, claim settlements, etc.

3. Capital Required

The rules governing the amount of investment required for a company limited are presented in Chapter 14.

There is no minimum capital requirement for setting up a representative office.

4. Registration and Official Fees

The procedure to register a company limited is presented in Chapter 14, and the procedure to register a representative office is presented in Chapter 15.

If the foreign company is required to register the representative office with the Ministry of Trade, the foreign company is required to pay 5 million Rupiah as a bank guarantee to the Bank of Indonesia. Note that this amount will be returned to the foreign company, if, in the future, the office is dissolved.

If the foreign company is required to register the representative office with the Ministry of Public Works, the registration fee depends upon the type of activities the representative office plans to pursue.

If the representative office will be providing consulting services the registration fee is $5,000 US.

If the representative office will be providing construction services the registration fee is $10,000 US.

Chapter 14

What Legal Issues Are Associated with the Start-Up of a Foreign-Held Company?

There are several legal and practical issues associated with operating as a Foreign-Held Company (company). The process involves registration with the Indonesia Investment Coordinating Board (Board), obtaining the company's Tax Identification Number and VAT Code, if required (from the Indonesian Taxation Authority), as well as obtaining other government licenses and approvals that may be required, depending upon the business activities the company seeks to engage in. Note that shelf companies are not readily available in Indonesia, so this process must generally be followed each time a new company is formed.

Basically, there are two ways to set up a company. The foreign investor can either establish a company that is a 100 % foreign owned company or form a joint venture with an Indonesian company.

See the form and list of documents required during the company registration process at www.doylesguideasia.com/indonesia/chapter14/appendixa.

See the list of documents required to obtain the company's Tax Identification Number at www.doylesguideasia.com/indonesia/chapter14/appendixb.

See the list of documents required to obtain the company's VAT Code (if required) at www.doylesguideasia.com/indonesia/chapter14/appendixc.

1. Timing

Applications to register a foreign-held company are processed by the Board and can normally be accomplished in two weeks, depending on a number of factors. These factors include the types of business activities the company is to pursue, the speed with which the investor supplies required information and documents, and the availability of the parties who are required to sign various documents.

After registration is approved, it normally takes approximately another seventy days to prepare and submit the other required documents, such as the company's Articles of Association, Domicile Letter, Tax Identification Number, VAT Code (if required), and the Company Certificate, as well as to obtain approval from the Department of Law and Human Rights.

2. Filings

All documents associated with the company's registration must be submitted to and approved by the Board.

All documents associated with the registration of the company's Tax Identification Number and VAT Code (if required) must be submitted to the District Tax Office in Jakarta, or, if the company office is to be located outside Jakarta, to the District Tax Office of the province where the office will be.

3. Company Name

The first step of the company registration process is the name reservation. In order to reserve a name, the company is required to submit a signed name application to any notary public in Indonesia. (A notary public is the only one who has access to the Board's company name database.)

If the applicant's intended company name is in conflict with another name, then it will be rejected, and the applicant will be required to submit a new name.

The name reservation is valid for one month, so within that time the company registration should be completed for the Board, otherwise the name reservation will lapse, and the name will have to be reserved again.

The investors should, therefore, not invest in marketing materials containing the company's intended name until after the BKPM's (Board's) approval of a company name. This sounds like common sense, but many people make this mistake.

4. Authorized Capital

Authorized capital refers to the total financial responsibility of the company's shareholders with respect to the company. Each individual shareholder may make this investment in the company by using either cash or in-kind in the form of either tangible or intangible assets. If non-cash assets are to be contributed, the shareholder(s) contributing such assets as capital should have the non-cash assets properly appraised during the company's registration process. Each shareholder is required to pay into the company 100% of their shares' par value.

EXAMPLE: Suppose a company's authorized capital is set at US $200,000, payable in cash. If that is the case, US $200,000 would be required to be actually paid into the company by the shareholders upon final registration of the company. The amount of capital actually paid into the company by the shareholders is referred to as the company's "paid-up" or "paid-in" authorized capital.

Note that Indonesian law stipulates that the company's debt to equity ratio may not exceed three to one, meaning that the company is not allowed to borrow more than three times the amount of its equity.

EXAMPLE: Suppose a company is established in the manufacturing sector and its registered capital is designated at US $200,000. According to the above rule, this company may not borrow more than US $600,000, unless the company's registered capital first increases accordingly.

5. Minimum Capital

The Board has not set a minimum amount of total investment capital or equity required for a foreign investment to be approved. However, in practice, the Board will usually approve applications with a minimum paid-up capital of between US $100,000 and US $200,000 for a foreign-held company investing in a single line of business or single location of investment.

6. Articles of Association

The company is required to notarize its Articles of Association (articles) through a notarial deed. The notarial deed contains the articles prepared in the Indonesian language. The articles are required to be registered with and approved by the Ministry of Law and Human Rights.

The articles state basic rules the company is required to follow after incorporation is successfully completed. They are required to contain the following information:

i.   The name and domicile of the company

ii.   The purposes and objectives, as well as the business activities of the company

iii. The period of incorporation of the company

iv.   The amount of authorized capital, issued capital, and paid-up capital

v.   The number of shares, shares classification if any, including the number of shares for each classification, the rights attached to each share, and nominal value of each share

vi.   The number of members of the Board of Directors and the Board of Commissioners and their names and titles

vii. The determination of the place and procedures for holding a general meeting of shareholders

viii. The procedures of appointment, replacement, and dismissal of the members of the Board of Directors and the Board of Commissioners

ix.   The procedure for profit utilization and dividend distribution

7. Bank Accounts

Immediately after registration is complete, most companies will want to open a corporate bank account.

Requirements to open a corporate bank account vary from bank to bank, but generally, the company will be required by the bank to provide its Tax Registration Number, as well as other relevant documents. See a sample list of the documents and information which may be requested by the bank. at www.doyles guideasia.com/indonesia/chapter14/appendixd.

Note that if any of the signatories for the bank account are foreigners, many banks will require that each of the foreign signatories submit a valid work permit (see Chapter 16) prior to opening the account.

Chapter 15

What Legal Issues Are Associated with Establishing a Representative Office?

It is common for foreign investors seeking to enter the Indonesian market for the first time to establish a representative office as a first step, then later register as a company limited (see Chapter 14) when they decide to expand their presence in Indonesia.

For the activities which a representative office of a foreign company registered outside of Indonesia may engage in, see Chapter 13.

As discussed in Chapter 13, a representative office in Indonesia may be classified as either a national representative office or a regional representative office, with each having its own registration procedures and requirements.

1. National Representative Office

The government agency responsible for the registration of a national representative office (NRO) depends upon the intended activities of the office.

The following are the business sectors which a foreign registered company may engage in as a national representative office, presented together with the government agency designated to process the registration application:

Business Sectors	Government Agency Responsible
Bilateral Trade	Ministry of Industry and Trade
Construction	Ministry of Public Works
Mining Activities	Ministry of Mining
Banking	Ministry of Finance

Indonesian law requires that a NRO is required to appoint one local or foreign individual to act as its legal representative and that this individual may be held personally liable if the head office overseas is found by a court to have violated Indonesian law. The legal representative is also responsible for receiving service of process for all court proceedings in which the company is a party.

EXAMPLE: A Swiss registered company establishes a national representative office in Indonesia and designates a German national as its legal representative. Later the head office in Switzerland is charged with smuggling goods into Indonesia. In this situation, if the company is found guilty, the German national may also be found criminally liable for the illegal action.

Note that a NRO is required to be located in Jakarta or in one of the provincial capitals of Indonesia.

a. Bilateral Trade

Foreign registered companies seeking to establish a NRO in order to engage in activities related to bilateral trade must first register with the Ministry of Industry and Trade (MIT).

The first step of the registration process is for the foreign registered company seeking to register as a NRO to prepare and submit the following three letters to the MIT:

i.   Letter of Intent, stating the company's intention to establish a national representative office.

     To see the required format for the letter go to www.doylesguideasia.com/indonesia/chapter15/appendixa.

ii. Letter of Appointment, appointing the legal representative.

     To see the required format for the letter go to www.doylesguideasia.com/indonesia/chapter15/appendixb.

iii. Letter of Statement, stating that the legal representative will follow Indonesian law.

     To see the required format for the letter go to www.doylesguideasia.com/indonesia/chapter15/appendixc.

These three letters must be stamped by a notary public and approved by the Indonesian Embassy in the head office's home country. Upon granting approval, the Indonesian Embassy where the three letters are submitted will also issue a Letter of Notification to the MIT stating approval to open the NRO. The foreign company will then submit these four letters to the MIT.

Note that the permit for operation is issued by the MIT in the name of the legal representative himself, not the foreign company. Therefore, if in the future the foreign company decides to replace the legal representative, the replacement person will be required to obtain a new license (also to be issued in his own name not in the name of the company).

EXAMPLE: A Norwegian company establishes a NRO in Indonesia to engage in bilateral trade. Initially, the company designates a German individual to act as the office's legal representative; therefore, the permit for operation is issued by the MIT in the German's name for a period of three years. After six months the Norwegian company decides to replace the German with a Canadian. In this situation, the Canadian would be required to apply for and receive a new permit, to be issued in the Canadian's name.

This permit is usually valid for a period corresponding to the period stated in the approved Letter of Appointment (see above) with a maximum period of three years.

Also, in order to obtain the permit, if a foreign individual is designated as the office's legal representative that foreign individual will be required to name an Indonesian individual or an Indonesia-held business to act as the office's co-sponsor (also referred to as surety).

EXAMPLE: A Swedish company establishes a national representative office and designates an Israeli national as its legal representative. In this situation, the Israeli national will be required to name a willing Indonesian individual or Indonesian company to act as the office's co-sponsor or surety.

b. Construction

Foreign companies seeking to engage in construction activities in Indonesia as a NRO are required to apply for and obtain a license from the Ministry of Public Works (MPW) prior to commencing operations.

The MPW's criteria for granting such licenses is that the company must have good financial standing and good technical skills, as well as a minimum of three years experience in construction. The MPW will normally rule on the application within two weeks of submission.

If granted, the license will be valid for a period of three years and is renewable.

If the office is successful in obtaining a license and then later is awarded a construction project in Indonesia, the NRO will then be required to form a joint operation with an Indonesian company in order to participate in the project.

EXAMPLE: A Korean registered company establishes a NRO for the purpose of seeking out new construction projects to participate in. After a time, the NRO is named as the primary contractor to construct a shopping mall in

Jakarta. Before starting the project, the foreign company would be required to seek out and form a joint operation with a local company to carry out the construction.

c. Mining Activities

Foreign companies seeking to establish a NRO in order to seek out projects and business partners in the oil and gas industry are required to apply for and receive a license from the Directorate General for Oil and Gas of the Ministry of Energy and Mineral Resources (MOE) prior to commencing operations.

Applications are usually processed by the MOE within two to three months and, if approved, the license will be valid for a period of one year and is renewable.

The foreign company is required to prepare and submit a letter of appointment and letter of intent in the same form as used by a NRO to engage in bilateral trade (see above). These two letters must be stamped by a notary public and approved by the Indonesian Embassy in the head office's home country. Upon granting approval, the Indonesian Embassy where the two letters are submitted will also issue a Letter of Reference to the MOE stating approval to open a NRO.

To see a list of the supporting documents to be submitted together with the application go to www.doylesguideasia.com/indonesia/chapter15/appendixd.

d. Banking

Foreign banks seeking to establish a NRO are required to submit an application for and obtain a license from the Board of Governors of Bank Indonesia.

Note that Bank Indonesia will only grant a license to foreign banks with sufficient assets and that are listed among the world's top three hundred banks in terms of asset size (as listed in the Banker's Almanac).

Foreign banks are required to submit an application letter stating the reason for opening the office, signed by a director of the foreign bank and addressed to the Board of Governors of Bank Indonesia.

The application letter should be accompanied by the following documents:

i.   Copy of a document setting forth the total assets of the bank, showing that the bank ranks among the top three hundred banks in the world in terms of asset size

ii. Letter of Assignment from the head office to the person to be designated as the legal representative in Indonesia

iii. Curriculum Vitae of the person to be designated as the legal representative

iv. Letter stating that the person to be designated as the legal representative will work exclusively for the bank (will hold no position with another company)

v. Letter stating that there is no objection from the banking authority in the country where the head office is located to open a representative office in Indonesia (to be presented to Bank Indonesia within thirty days of the date that the application is originally submitted)

Note that in addition to receiving the application, Bank Indonesia will also interview the person to be designated as the legal representative.

Within thirty days of the date that a complete application is submitted, Bank Indonesia will either issue a letter of approval of the application or a letter of objection to the foreign company applicant, depending upon the outcome of its review.

2. Regional Representative Office

The Indonesian Investment Coordinating Board (Board) is the government agency responsible for issuing regional representative office (RRO) licenses.

To see the supporting documents required to be submitted together with the application go to www.doylesguideasia.com/indonesia/chapter15/appendixe.

The normal processing time of an application for a RRO is about two weeks. If the application is approved, the license will be issued for an indefinite period and is not limited to a specific representative.

EXAMPLE: A French company establishes a RRO and designates a Greek national as the RRO's legal representative. After two years of operation the company seeks to replace the Greek national as the legal representation with a Norwegian national. In this situation, neither the RRO nor the Norwegian national will be required to reapply for the license with the Board.

Chapter 16

What Is the Process to Obtain a Work Permit?

Obtaining a work permit for the first time in Indonesia can be a lengthy, fairly involved process. The applicant will be required to locate and prepare an extensive list of documents and applications to multiple government offices.

1. General Requirements

Indonesia has relatively high requirements for those companies seeking to employ foreigners, the most substantial of which are listed below.

One relatively unique requirement of companies seeking to employ foreigners is that they are required to provide necessary education and training programs for Indonesian employees who are expected to eventually replace the foreign employees.

This normally involves the Indonesian employer taking steps such as seeking out Indonesian employees who have the educational background to perform the position currently held by the foreigner and having the foreign workers transfer technology and expertise to those Indonesian employees.

This continues until such a time when Indonesian employees have the necessary qualifications required to occupy the position currently occupied by foreign workers.

Note that this requirement does not apply to foreign workers who occupy the position of director and/or commissioner.

Another relatively unique requirement is that companies seeking to employ foreigners are subject to a special tax. This tax is payable to the Department of Manpower and is equal to $100 US per foreign employee per month ($1200 US per employee, per year) payable one year in advance. Proof of such prepayment will be a supporting document to receive a work permit (see below).

EXAMPLE: A German held company in Indonesia employees five foreigners. In this situation, the tax payable to the Department of Manpower would be calculated as follows:

5 foreign employees x $1,200 US = $6,000 US.

This amount would be payable each year in advance.

Note that the ratio between the number of foreign workers and local workers in a company is set per industry by the Indonesian Investing Co-ordinating Board (see below) and the Department of Manpower and is subject to change.

EXAMPLE: An Indonesian finance company seeks to employ foreigners with specific financial expertise. The applicable ratio of Indonesian employees to foreign employees in this situation would be three Indonesian employees for every one foreign employee.

2. Foreign Labor Utilization Plan

In order for a company in Indonesia to employ foreigners, the company must first submit a Foreign Labor Utilization Plan (Utilization Plan) to the Indonesian Investment Coordinating Board (Board) for approval. The approval process normally takes about seven business days.

The Utilization Plan sets forth the proposed number of foreigners and a description of the positions, as well as the proposed salaries for the positions and other terms of employment.

The Utilization Plan may be approved for a maximum period of five years and may be extended by the Board for an additional maximum period of five years (for a total potential maximum period of ten years). To see a sample of the Foreign Labor Utilization Plan go to www.doylesguideasia.com/indonesia/chapter16/appendixa.

EXAMPLE: A French engineering company participating in an infrastructure project in Indonesia requires seven foreign engineers in order to complete the project. In order to obtain seven work permits for the foreign engineers, the company will be required to first submit a Utilization Plan proposal for Board approval, setting forth that seven foreign workers are necessary, their job descriptions, salaries, and other related details.

In addition to approval by the Board, the Utilization Plan must also be approved by the Department of Manpower.

3. Limited Stay Visa

After the Utilization Plan has been approved, a letter of recommendation (TA-01) issued by the Department of Manpower (recommendation letter) is required. It will serve as a supporting document to receive a Limited Stay Visa. The application process to obtain the recommendation letter normally takes about seven business days.

Based on the recommendation letter, the Directorate General of Immigration will communicate with the Indonesian embassy/consulate in the applicant's home country to request the embassy issue the Limited Stay Visa and stamp it in the foreigner's passport. After it is issued, the Limited Stay Visa allows the foreigner to enter Indonesia and proceed with the work permit/visa application process.

Within seven days of arrival in Indonesia, the foreigner is required to go to the Immigration Office, report his arrival into Indonesia, submit his passport (with the Limited Stay Visa stamp) and embarkation card, and complete necessary paperwork. Failure to do this will constitute a violation of the immigration regulations, which may result in fines and being required to appear in court, etc.

4. Limited Stay Permit Card (KITAS)

After the above process is completed, the foreign applicant will be issued a Limited Stay Permit Card (also commonly referred to as the KITAS card) for himself and each of his dependents, valid for one year.

After receiving the KITAS card, the foreigner will also receive a Blue Foreigner's Registration and Change Book (Blue Book). The Blue Book is similar in size to a passport and tracks changes in the foreigner's immigration status. All subsequent changes of the foreigner's address, marital status, newborn children, etc. are required to be reported to the Immigration Office and recorded in the Blue Book within a timely period.

The KITAS card and Blue Book allow the foreigner to live in Indonesia for one year and may be renewed annually, up to two times.

5. Exit/Re-Entry Permit

Whenever the foreigner holding a KITAS card plans to temporarily leave Indonesia, he must apply for an exit/re-entry permit from the Immigration

Office. The application takes one day and requires the foreigner to write a letter requesting authorization to leave Indonesia. The permit is stamped in the foreigner's passport and designated as either single or multiple.

A single exit/re-entry permit means that the foreigner can only leave and re-enter the country one time during the period stated in the permit.

A multiple exit/re-entry permit allows the foreigner to leave and re-enter Indonesia as many times as needed during the period stated in the permit.

Note that it is advisable for the foreign permit holder to always have a valid multiple re-entry permit stamped on the passport, just in case of the need for an emergency departure, such as illness of a family member back home, etc.

6. Work Permit Rules

After completing the procedures mentioned above, the company must subsequently submit an application to obtain the Foreign Manpower Working Permit (work permit) for the foreigner.

To see the application and list of supporting documents required go to www.doylesguideasia.com/indonesia/chapter16/appendixb.

Note that for positions other than directors (there are no specific work permit rules applicable to foreigners applying for a work permit to fill a director position), a foreigner's expertise must be clearly proven, as the policy of the government is to limit the employment of foreigners to only those "experts" who can significantly contribute to national development. It must also be proven that an Indonesian cannot fill the position.

Deportations of foreigners for violating the terms of their work permit are common. One common offense cited is that the foreigner is working in a position other than what is stated in the work permit.

EXAMPLE: A foreigner's work permit states that the foreigner's title is Production Manager of the company, but the foreigner's business card states the foreigner is the Marketing Manager. In this situation, these facts constitute grounds for deportation of the foreigner, due to failing to comply with the scope of work stated in the work permit.

Another problem encountered by work permit holders is if their actual place of work in Indonesia differs from the place of work stated in their work permit.

EXAMPLE: A foreigner's work permit states he is to work out of the company's Jakarta office, but the foreigner actually works out of the company's Bali office. In this situation, the foreigner would also face possible fines, deportation etc.

7. Work Permit Term

Work permits are normally valid for a period of one year and are renewable.

8. Dependent Visa

The foreign employee's spouse, children (up to age seventeen), and other dependent family members may accompany the foreign employee as his dependents under a dependent visa, as long as the above rules are complied with. The validity period of the dependent visa is the same as the foreign employee's visa.

The dependent visa only allows the dependent family members to stay with the working spouse/parent and does not entitle them to work in Indonesia.

EXAMPLE: A Canadian citizen comes to work in Indonesia and obtains the proper visas, work permit, etc., and his spouse accompanies him as his dependent. This should be permissible; however, if in the future the spouse wishes to work in Indonesia, she would be required to follow the applicable procedures and qualify to obtain a work permit and other necessary authorizations as stated above.

Chapter 17

What Investment Incentives Are Available to Foreign Investors?

The Indonesian government encourages specific types of business projects by offering investors in those projects incentives. The incentives available to a given project (if any) depend upon the project's intended activities, location, and amount of investment, as well as other factors.

This chapter discusses the incentives available and the applicable requirements.

Note that the investment incentives described below are granted for a fixed period of time, and after the expiration of that period of time, the incentives no longer apply, and the project is subject to ordinary rules and regulations.

EXAMPLE: A project is granted a corporate income tax reduction for a period of six years, starting from the date operations begin. Upon the expiration of that six-year period, the project would be subject to normal corporate income tax rules going forward.

Also, note that the tax exemptions and reductions only apply to income derived from the promoted activity, not to the company's income in general.

EXAMPLE: A joint venture between Indonesia and UK investors engages in the production of industrial chemicals and earns income from this activity. The joint venture also earns income from other unrelated activities not promoted by Indonesian tax law. In this situation, the joint venture's income derived from the production of industrial chemicals would be fully exempt from income tax; however, income derived from its other activities would be subject to normal tax rates.

The incentives are awarded at the time the Indonesia Investment Coordinating Board (Board) approves the project (see Chapter 14).

EXAMPLE: Korean investors establish a company to engage in oil refining. At the time that they apply for Board approval of the project, they also request tax and other incentives.

1. Tax Incentives

Qualifying private limited companies operating in Indonesia engaging in specific promoted activity groups may receive tax incentives for their income derived from those activities.

These promoted activity groups include textile industries, pulp, paper and paper board industries, geothermal exploitation, operation of an oil refinery, production of industrial chemical materials, food crops development, horticulture cultivation, industrial group food processing, production of cement, and many others.

To see a complete list of these promoted activities go to www.doylesguide asia.com/indonesia/chapter17/appendixa and www.doylesguideasia.com/indonesia/chapter17/appendixb.

Note that the exact same incentives are available to the activities stated in the Appendix A list and the Appendix B list.

a. Income Tax Reduction

The Indonesian government grants an income tax reduction equaling as much as 30% of the total amount of investment in the project. This tax reduction may be spread out during the project's first six years of operation, starting in the first year of operation.

EXAMPLE: German investors establish a pulp and paper mill in Indonesia with a total investment of 100 million Rp. In this situation, the project may deduct a total 30 million Rp. from its income tax payable over a period of six years, starting in the project's first year of operation.

The government also grants a net income tax deduction equal to 5% of the investor's investment in fixed tangible assets, including land, buildings, and machines, to be used for the project's main business activities. This tax reduction is available for six years, starting in the year the tax reduction was awarded.

EXAMPLE: A German company invests US $1 million in purchasing land, buildings, and machines to be used in the project. The income tax reduction available for this project would be calculated as follows: 5% (rate of tax deduction) x US $1,000,000 (total investment in fixed assets) = US $50,000 (amount of tax reduction each year for six years, starting in the year the tax reduction was awarded).

b. Extended Carry Forward Loss

Normally carry forward loss in Indonesia is limited to ten years. Qualifying companies engaging in promoted activities, however, may have the normal carry forward loss period extended by one year in the following situations:

i.   Project engages in the promoted business activity group (see above) and is located in an industrial estate and bonded zone.

ii. Project hires at least five hundred Indonesian employees for five consecutive years.

iii. Project requires a minimum of Rp.10,000,000,000 investment for costs or to develop economic and social infrastructure in a business location.

iv. At least 5% of the total investment in the project over a five-year period is used for domestic research and development costs for product development or production efficiency.

v.   70% of the total raw materials or products used by the project are domestically sourced by the project's fourth year of production.

EXAMPLE: An Austrian company establishes a food processing facility in Indonesia. In its first year of operation it operates at a loss of Rp.15 million. In the event that this company does not qualify under any of the above criteria, the company would only be allowed to carry forward this loss (to offset tax on future profit) for ten years. If, however, the company qualifies under any of the above criteria, the company would be allowed to carry forward the loss for eleven years.

c. Accelerated Depreciation

The Indonesian government also grants projects engaging in promoted activities accelerated amortization and depreciation of up to ten years on buildings and non-buildings.

To see further details go to www.doylesguideasia.com/indonesia/chapter17/appendixc.

2. Reduction of Import Duties

Foreign-held companies engaging in investment projects which are approved by the Board, are granted certain incentives with regard to the payment of import duties. The projects include existing foreign-held companies expanding existing projects by restructuring, diversifying, expanding, modernizing, and/or rehabilitating equipment in order to increase the project production capacity by more than 30%, or by diversifying its products.

These projects are granted a customs duty cap rate of 5% (if the normal customs duty rate for the imported items is already less than 5%, then the normal rate will apply) in the following situations:

i.   The importation of capital goods, namely machinery, equipment, spare parts, and auxiliary equipment is for a period of two years, starting from the date that the special import duty rate was granted.

EXAMPLE: French investors establish a company in Indonesia for the purpose of producing liquid dyes used in the production of paint and receive Board approval for the project. The company then imports machinery into Indonesia to produce the dyes. The normal customs duty for the machinery is 6.3% of the machinery's value. In this situation, the customs duty for the importation of the machinery would be 5% of the machinery's value.

EXAMPLE: Same facts as above, but the normal customs duty rate for the machinery is 3.2%. In this situation, the customs duty rate would remain 3.2%.

ii. Goods and materials or raw materials imported are used as materials or components to produce finished goods. Under this requirement, the imported goods must be used within two years of the date of their importation into Indonesia.

EXAMPLE: Same facts as above and the company also imports certain raw materials from India used to produce the dye. The normal customs duty rate for the raw material is 5.4%. In this situation, the customs duty rate for the importation of the raw materials would be 5% of their value, as long as the materials are used within two years of their importation.

3. Export Manufacturing

There are many incentives available to projects to manufacture products for export. Some of these incentives are as follows:

i.   Duty drawback of import duties is paid on the importation of goods and materials needed to manufacture products for export.

EXAMPLE: A US company registers a company in Indonesia for the purpose of producing clothing for export and receives Board approval for the project. One of the raw material items used to produce the clothing is imported from Thailand. The normal Indonesian customs duty rate for the item is 4.2% of the item's value. In this situation, the company will be required to pay the duty upon the item's importation into Indonesia; however, when the finished item in which the raw material from Thailand was used is later exported, the company would be allowed to draw back (in essence receive a refund) of the duty originally paid.

    ii. Exemption from Value Added Tax and Sales Tax is given on luxury goods and materials purchased domestically, to be used in the manufacture of the exported products.

    iii. Importing company is free to import any raw materials required, regardless of the availability of comparable products from sources from within Indonesia.

EXAMPLE: Same facts as above, and a similar raw material later becomes available from a producer in Indonesia. In this situation, the company would be allowed to continue to import the raw material from Thailand, despite the fact that a comparable raw material is now available in Indonesia.

4. Bonded Zones

A Bonded Zone refers to an area especially designated for the activities of processing goods and materials, construction designing, engineering, sorting, performing preliminary inspections, performing final inspections, and packing of imported goods and materials originating from other areas within the Indonesian Customs Territory (includes Indonesia and outlaying areas), which are carried out primarily for export purposes.

Companies located in a Bonded Zone qualify to receive incentives which include

    i. exemption from import duty, excise tax, income tax, and Value Added Tax on luxury goods and capital goods and equipment, (including raw materials for the production process)

    ii. exemption of Value Added Tax and Sales Tax on luxury goods shipped to the Bonded Zones for the purpose of further processing by their subcontractors outside the bonded zones or the other way around, as well as among companies within these areas

5. Land Rights

The applicable rules concerning foreign ownership of land are presented in Chapter 18.

Chapter 18

What Legal Issues Are Associated with Foreign Ownership of Land?

The general rule is that foreigners are not allowed to own any interest in land in Indonesia.

This restriction is disappointing to many foreign investors who ideally would like to own the land occupied by their business premises or individual home; however, the above rule is quite clear. Foreigners seeking to acquire an interest in land, therefore, normally use one of the two strategies discussed below.

1. Using a Nominee

One way foreign investors seek to acquire an interest in land is through an Indonesian nominee. In this situation, the foreign individual or company seeks out an Indonesian national or an Indonesian-held company to purchase the land on their behalf. This option is generally in compliance with Indonesian law.

EXAMPLE: A medium-sized Japanese furniture producer with an office in Indonesia seeks to purchase land and build a factory. The Japanese company then seeks out an Indonesian national to act as its nominee, and the Indonesian national purchases the land on the Japanese company's behalf.

EXAMPLE: A UK national seeks to purchase a house and land in a beach side community. The UK national locates an Indonesian company to act as its nominee and purchase the land on his behalf.

In order to effect these transactions the documents described below must be executed by the foreign purchaser and the Indonesian nominee.

a. Loan Agreement

The normal way the nominee arrangement is structured is that the foreign purchaser and the Indonesian nominee execute a loan agreement stating that the foreign purchaser is lending the nominee an amount representing the purchase price of the land.

In the agreement, the Indonesian nominee acknowledges that the foreigner has lent the purchase price to the nominee for the express purpose of purchasing the property.

Note that the foreign purchaser may pay the land seller directly without first transferring the purchase price to the nominee.

EXAMPLE: A Canadian individual intends to purchase a beach house and land in Jakarta and seeks out an Indonesian national to act as a nominee in order to make the purchase. Among the documents to be executed would be a loan agreement whereby the Canadian loans the nominee an amount representing the purchase price. The Canadian should be able to pay the seller directly without having to pay the purchase price through the nominee.

b. Statement Letter

In the Statement Letter the nominee acknowledges the loan from the foreigner (see above) and the foreigner's intention to own the land.

c. Right of Use Agreement

In the Right of Use Agreement, the nominee grants the foreign purchaser the exclusive right to possess and use the land for an indefinite period.

d. Power of Attorney

The Power of Attorney is irrevocable and gives the foreigner complete authorization to sell, mortgage, lease, or otherwise transfer the land to third parties.

2. Using the Foreign Company Limited

The most common land-related rights which may be transferred to a foreign company (PMA), according to Indonesia law, are leasehold rights, building rights, and right of use.

a. Leasehold (Hak Guna Usaha/HGU)

In Indonesia, leasehold refers to the right to use state-owned land for agriculture—specifically plantation farming, fishing, or cattle raising.

EXAMPLE: A Spanish company seeks to acquire rights to a palm oil plantation owned by the government. In this situation, the Spanish company would most likely structure this through a leasehold.

This leasehold right may be granted for a maximum period of ninety-five years and simultaneously renewed in advance for a period of an additional sixty years. The lease may then be further renewed for an additional thirty-five years.

EXAMPLE: Same facts as above and the Spanish company obtains a ninety-five year lease to use the land until the end of the ninety-fifth year, but does not renew the lease after that period. In this situation, all rights to the land would then revert back to the government.

Such leasehold can be used as collateral or transferred to another party with government approval.

EXAMPLE: A US company enters into a ninety-five year renewable lease of state-owned cattle raising land, and the lease contract states that the US company's interests under the agreement are fully transferrable. In this situation, the US company may assign its leasehold rights to any third party upon obtaining government approval to do so.

b. Building Rights (Hak Guna Bangunan/HGB)

Another right associated with land which may be transferred to a foreign company is the right to construct and own buildings. Such a right may be granted for a maximum period of eighty years and simultaneously renewed in advance for an additional fifty years. It may be further renewed for thirty years.

EXAMPLE: A Swedish company seeks to acquire rights to a piece of land in an industrial estate in Indonesia and build a factory. In this situation, the Swedish company would need to acquire building rights in order to construct the factory.

Similar to leasehold rights, building rights can be used as collateral or transferred to another party and generally granted to tenants in industrial estates.

EXAMPLE: Same facts as above, but the Swedish company seeks financing of the construction of the factory with an Indonesian bank. Among the assets which the Swedish company may choose to use to collateralize the loan are the building rights the Swedish company has obtained.

c. Right of Use (Hak Pakai/HP)

The right to use and/or harvest farm land directly owned by the state or a private company may be given for seventy years and simultaneously renewed in advance for forty-five years, and it may be further renewed for twenty-five years. This right can also be used as a mortgage. In addition, it can also be transferred to another party through government approval.

Land rights as intended above may be granted and extended all at once in advance of any investment activity, with the following broad conditions:

i.   Such investment is for the long term and associated with the structural change of the Indonesian economy into a more competitive one.

ii. Such investment is made with a level of investment risk and with the expectation of a long-term return on investment.

iii. Such investment does not require extensive land area.

vi. Such investment uses state-owned land rights.

v.   Such investment does not interrupt the sense of impartiality in the community, as well as public interest.

The granting and the simultaneous renewal of land rights in advance as set forth above may be cancelled by the government if such investment company abandons, inflicts damage to public interest, uses the land in violation of the stated purposes and objectives set forth when the land rights were granted, or violates any applicable laws.

EXAMPLE: A Korean company obtains a seventy-five year lease of property to operate a shrimp farm. In year six, the Korean company abandons the premises, never to return. In this situation, the government may cancel the leasehold contract and re-enter the premises.

EXAMPLE: Same facts, but instead of abandoning the premises, the shrimp farm starts polluting the surrounding water supply through the waste water generated by the farm. In this situation, the government may cancel the leasehold contract and re-enter the premises.

Foreign individuals are allowed to own a separate house or apartment constructed on a piece of land if such land is so designated by the government, and the right to own the house or apartment is specifically granted in an agreement with a landowner.

EXAMPLE: A South African individual who has resided in Indonesia for a number of years, leases a plot of land outside Jakarta from the government. The terms of the lease state that he will own all structures built on the property.

Shortly after execution, the South African builds a house and begins to live there. Under these facts, as long as the land plot is not located in an area where ownership of residential buildings by foreign individuals is prohibited, the South African would be allowed to own the house.

Malaysia

Capital City	Kuala Lumpur
Major Financial Center	Kuala Lumpur
Population (projected 2010)	28 million
Location	Southeastern Asia, peninsular between Thailand and Singapore, and Malaysian Borneo bordering Indonesia, and Brunei
Major Languages	Malay (official), English, Chinese dialects, Tamil, Telugu, Malayalam
Legal System	Common law
Square Miles	127,355 sq mi
Gross Domestic Product (projected 2010)	USD 221 billion
Major Exports	Electronic equipment, petroleum and liquefied natural gas, chemicals, palm oil, wood and wood products, rubber, textiles
Currency	Ringgit (MYR)
U.S. Dollar Exchange Rate (as of November 2009)	USD 1 = MYR 3.4275
Euro Exchange Rate (as of November 2009)	EUR 1 = MYR 5.0605

Section Authors

Azmi Mohd Ali, Senior Partner
Azmi & Associates
Email: azmi@azmilaw.com.
Website: http://www.azmilaw.com

Azlin Azhar (Ms), Partner
Azmi & Associates
Email: azlin@azmilaw.com

Chapter 19

Should Our Business Establish as a Limited Company, Representative Office, Branch Office, or Regional Office?

One of the first issues faced by prospective investors in Malaysia is choosing the appropriate type of legal structure through which to operate their business. Generally, the following are the most common structures adopted by foreign investors doing business in Malaysia:

i. Private limited company

ii. Branch office

iii. Representative office

iv. Regional office

1. Limited Company

The private limited company (company) is the most commonly adopted structure for doing business in Malaysia.

A company is owned by shareholders (minimum two, except for a wholly-owned subsidiary which may have the holding company as its sole shareholder) and managed by directors (minimum two). The liability of each of the shareholders is generally limited to the total par value of their shares. The shareholders' direct participation in company affairs is normally quite limited. It is the directors who are responsible for managing company affairs and who owe various fiduciary duties to the shareholders and the company (duty of care, duty to act honestly, etc.).

Unlike a branch office, representative office, and regional office, a limited company is treated under Malaysian law as a stand-alone legal entity.

EXAMPLE: If a multinational wishes to establish a subsidiary in Malaysia it will likely do so as a privately held company. If individual investors wish to establish a stand-alone business to generate income in Malaysia, they will most likely do so as a company.

EXAMPLE: Suppose a multinational establishes a wholly owned subsidiary in Malaysia as a company limited. That new limited company then executes a contract with another Malaysian company to supply construction materials, but then fails to supply those materials. In this situation, the Malaysian purchaser would generally be limited to suing the Malaysian subsidiary of the multinational for the breach of contract, not its headquarters overseas.

2. Branch, Representative Office, and Regional Office

Many times, however, foreign investors will not want to operate as a limited company. This is most likely to be true when a multinational company seeks to establish a presence in Malaysia, but does not wish to establish a separate legal entity. For accounting, tax, and other reasons, the multinational company may instead want the Malaysia office to function as a part of the head office overseas. If that is the case, the multinational will normally choose to establish a representative office, branch office, or regional office, not a limited company.

Malaysian law treats each of these three entities as extensions of the head office overseas, not as separate legal entities. The employees are the employees of the overseas company. Their activities are the activities of the head office.

Among the legal requirements to establish a branch office is that it will be required to appoint a legal agent, who is either an individual residing in Malaysia or a Malaysian registered company.

EXAMPLE: A German company establishes a branch office in Malaysia and appoints a Malaysian national as its legal agent. The German company is later sued in Malaysian civil court by a third party. In this situation, the Malaysian court may view the address of the legal agent as the German company's address in Malaysia for purposes of effecting service of process, notices, etc.

There is no requirement for a legal agent for a representative office or a regional office.

a. Branch

In many ways the branch structure is very similar to that of the limited company. Both are allowed to earn income in Malaysia, and similar tax rules apply to both. Also, the rules governing the activities of a branch are the same as the rules governing the activities of a foreign-held limited company.

It is with issues concerning liability where the branch and limited company structures fundamentally differ. For a limited company, liability arising from the actions of the business or its employees is generally limited to the Malaysian company only. The same is not true for a branch. Malaysian law treats a branch as merely an extension of its head office overseas.

EXAMPLE: Suppose that the multinational establishes a branch, and the branch enters into a contract to supply computer related services and fails to perform. The Malaysian purchaser could then sue the head office of the multinational directly.

b. Representative Office and Regional Office

The representative office and regional office structures are very different from those of the branch office and limited company. Unlike a branch or limited company, representative offices and regional offices are not allowed to earn income. Just as with a branch, representative offices and regional offices merely serve as extensions of their head offices overseas. They are not standalone legal entities. They are also strictly regulated to performing specific functions, designated by the Malaysian Ministry of International Trade and Industry, on behalf of their head offices overseas.

A representative office and a regional office are allowed to carry out the following activities:

i.   Planning or coordinating business activities

ii.   Gathering and analysis of information or undertaking feasibility studies on investment and business opportunities in Malaysia and the region

iii. Identifying sources of raw materials, components, or other industrial products

iv.   Undertaking research and product development

v.   Acting as a coordination center for the corporation's affiliates, subsidiaries, and agents in the region

Representative offices and regional offices are specifically prohibited from engaging in the following activities:

   i.   Engaging in any trading (including import and export), business, or any form of commercial activity.

   ii.   Leasing warehousing facilities. Any shipment, transshipment, or storage of goods shall be handled by a local agent or distributor.

   iii.   Signing business contracts on behalf of the foreign corporation or providing services for a fee.

   iv.   Participating in the daily management of any of its subsidiaries, affiliates, or branches in Malaysia.

   v.   Conducting any business transactions or deriving income from its operations.

3. Capital Required

The rules governing the amount of investment required for a limited company are set forth in Chapter 20.

The rules governing the amount of investment required for a Malaysian branch of an overseas company are presented below.

A representative office and a regional office are not subject to any minimum capital requirement or any equity condition; however, they must both be completely funded for all staff salaries, rent, and other operating expenses to be paid from sources outside Malaysia.

4. Branch Registration and Official Fees

The procedure to register a company and the relevant official fees are presented in Chapter 20.

A Malaysian branch of an overseas company to be located in Kuala Lumpur is required to register with the Companies Commission of Malaysia (CCM) before commencing operations. If the branch is to be located outside Kuala Lumpur, then the overseas company has the option of either registering with the CCM in Kuala Lumpur or with the local office of the CCM in the state in which the branch is to be established.

The following documents are required to be submitted to the CCM to establish a branch of an overseas company:

i.   The foreign company's certified true copy of its certificate of incorporation, or registration in its place of origin, or a document of similar effect

ii. The foreign company's certified true copy of its charter statute or Memorandum and Articles of Association

iii. A list of directors of the foreign company

iv. A memorandum of appointment or power of attorney authorizing one or more persons residing in Malaysia to accept on behalf of the foreign company, service of process and any notices required to be served on the branch/foreign company

v.   The statutory declaration by the agent of the foreign company

The approval process normally takes one day only, provided that the application and all relevant documents are in order and the applicant otherwise qualifies.

The official fees associated with registration of a branch depend on the authorized share capital of the overseas head office.

Head Office Share Capital (RM Equivalent)	Applicable Official Fee
Up to RM 100,000	RM 1,000
RM 100,001–RM 500,000	RM 3,000
RM 500,001–RM 1 Million	RM 5,000
RM 1,000,001–RM 5 Million	RM 8,000
RM 5,000,001–RM 10 Million	RM 10,000
RM 10,000,001–RM 25 Million	RM 20,000
RM 25,000,001–RM 50 Million	RM 40,000
RM 50,000,001–RM 100 Million	RM 50,000
RM 100,000,001 and above	RM 70,000

Pursuant to the Economic Stimulus Package announced by the CCM in March 2009, the official fees for the above registration will be reduced up to 15% as follows:

Head Office Share Capital (RM Equivalent)	Registration Fees from 1 Apr 09 to 31 Mar 2010	Percentage of Reduction
Not exceeding RM 100,000	RM 900	10%
RM 100,001–RM 500,000	RM 2,550	15%
RM 500,001–RM 1 Million	RM 4,250	
RM 1,000,001–RM 5 Million	RM 6,800	
RM 5,000,001–RM 10 Million	RM 8,500	
RM 10,000,001–RM 25 Million	RM 17,000	
RM 25,000,001–RM 50 Million	RM 34,000	
RM 50,000,001–RM 100 Million	RM 42,500	
Exceeding 100 million	RM 59,500	

This reduction will be effective from 1 April 2009 until 31 March 2010 only.

EXAMPLE: Suppose a Canadian company wishes to establish a branch in Malaysia. The Canadian company's authorized share capital is the Malaysia Ringgit equivalent of RM 35 million. In this case the applicable official fee would be RM 34,000.

Also, note the following:

i.   If the foreign company establishing the branch has no share capital and is engaged in trade, commerce, or industry, including transportation, the maximum official fee applicable is RM 70,000.

ii. If the foreign company establishing the branch does not have a share capital (and does not engage in any of the activities described above) the official fee applicable is RM 1,000.

5. Representative Office and Regional Office Registration

An application for the establishment of a representative office and a regional office (excluding banking, financial, and tourism services) should be submitted by hand to the Director-General of the Malaysian Industrial Development Authority (MIDA), Manufacturing Services Division, 1st Floor, Plaza Central, Jalan Stesen Central 5, Kuala Lumpur 50470 Kuala Lumpur, Malaysia; Tel:

(603)2267-3633; Fax: (603)2273-4216; Email: services@mida.gov.my; Website: www.mida.gov.my.

The following documents and information are required:

i. Form RE/RO-1, which can be obtained from MIDA's official website located at www.mida.gov.my.

ii. A certified true copy of the Certificate of Incorporation of the parent company.

iii. Other relevant information that can support the company's application, such as the company profile and brochure.

iv. If there are expatriates to be appointed, certified true copies of their passports, their curriculum vitae, and their certified academic qualifications.

The registration approval process can normally be completed within four weeks, provided that the application and all relevant documents are in order.

Chapter 20

What Legal Issues Are Associated with the Start-Up of a Foreign-Held Company?

There are several legal and practical issues associated with the legal start-up of a private limited company (company). The start-up process involves registration with the Companies Commission of Malaysia (CCM), as well as obtaining other government licenses and approvals that may be required, depending upon the business activities the company seeks to engage in. Shelf companies are available in Malaysia and will be discussed in the last section of this chapter.

To see the list of information required during the company registration process go to www.doylesguideasia.com/malaysia/chapter20/appendixa.

1. Promoters and Subscribers

The parties responsible for registering the company with the CCM are referred to as the company's promoters. The promoters (minimum one) must be individuals (not business entities), and they must be available to sign documentation, as required, during the registration process and incur the initial company expenses for the incorporation process.

The subscribers are the parties responsible for subscribing to the first shares of the company and may either be individuals or business entities.

Malaysian law requires a minimum of two subscribers, and the subscribers may or may not have acted as company promoters.

Each subscriber is required to hold a minimum of one share upon the company's registration; however, they are generally free to transfer those shares to any party, thereafter, if they wish to do so. A subscriber's liability is normally limited to the par value of the share(s) held upon incorporation.

2. Reservation of Company Name

The first step of the company registration process is the name reservation. In order to reserve the name, the applicant or its representative is required to submit a signed name reservation form to the CCM.

To see the name reservation form go to www.doylesguideasia.com/malaysia/chapter20/appendixb.

Note that the company name must have the words Sendirian Berhad (which means private limited) as part of its name or the abbreviation Sdn Bhd.

The registrar will then examine the application in order to ensure that no similar company names have previously been reserved and that the names submitted do not violate any ministerial rules.

Note that names such as International, Chartered, Pioneers, Bumiputra, ASEAN, UNESCO, or a person's name that is not the name of a director will not be approved by the CCM for incorporation unless consent of the Minister of Domestic Trade and Consumer Affairs has been obtained.

The registrar has considerable discretion with regard to his consideration of the company names requested. Many times, the first name is rejected for violating one of the two rules stated above, and the applicant will be required to resubmit the form requesting a different name. It is advisable to submit several alternative names simultaneously to the CCM to save time, just in case the first proposed name is rejected.

The applicant should, therefore, not invest in marketing materials containing the company's intended name until an approval from the CCM confirming that the requested name has been obtained.

To see a sample of the supporting documents required to be submitted to the CCM go to www.doylesguideasia.com/malaysia/chapter20/appendixc.

3. Memorandum of Association

After the name is reserved, the company's Memorandum of Association (MOA) must be submitted together with other required documents. To see a sample of a company MOA go to www.doylesguideasia.com/malaysia/chapter20/appendixd.

The MOA sets forth the reserved company name, the company's objectives, the intended amount of share capital, and other relevant information.

Each of the subscribers must sign the MOA and write in their own handwriting the number of shares each of them has agreed to take.

4. Articles of Association

The applicant will also be required to submit the company's Articles of Association (Articles) to the CCM. The Articles state basic rules the company is required to follow after incorporation is successfully completed.

These rules generally include the frequency with which directors' and shareholders' meetings take place, what constitutes a quorum at meetings, notice requirements for meetings, the number required to pass a resolution at a meeting, etc.

To see a sample company Articles go to www.doylesguideasia.com/malaysia /chapter20/appendixe.

5. Directors

The company is required to have a minimum of two directors, each of whom must maintain their primary residence in Malaysia. Directors must be individuals (not business entities).

EXAMPLE: A Korean investor registers a company in Malaysia, and the new company has five directors. The law requires that a minimum of two of the five directors maintain their primary residence in Malaysia at all times.

It is quite common, as a controlling mechanism, for a company to designate the authority of a director to sign on behalf of the company, whether alone, (for example by the managing director) or together with another director. Also, many companies will impose a requirement that in order to execute documents on behalf of the company, the company seal must be affixed to the document, together with the signatures of two directors or a director together with the company secretary. This makes the physical presence of the company seal another kind of control mechanism.

Note that, unlike shareholders, directors incur legal obligations and substantial liability associated with the actions of the company. A person should carefully take into consideration the substantial liability associated with being a company director before agreeing to be appointed and serve as one.

6. Address

It is the normal situation in Malaysia for the company to maintain an official registered office and a separate business address. The registered office address is usually the address of the appointed company secretary. The business address of the company is the address where the actual place of business of the company is located.

EXAMPLE: A Belgian company establishes a subsidiary in Malaysia to produce wooden furniture and establishes a factory in Penang, Malaysia, but its company secretary resides in Kuala Lumpur, Malaysia. In this situation, the company may choose to have its official registered office address in Kuala Lumpur, while having its primary business address in Penang.

7. Share Capital

The minimum authorized capital of a company in Malaysia is RM 1,000, of which a minimum of RM 2 must be fully paid up (representing the issued and paid-up capital).

The minimum authorized share capital required for a foreign-held company is discussed in Chapter 21.

8. Official Fees

The registration fee for the incorporation of a company in Malaysia varies from RM 1,000 to RM 70,000, depending on the chosen authorized share capital of the company based on the following schedule.

Authorized Share Capital	Applicable Registration Fee
Up to RM 100,000	RM 1,000
RM 100,001–RM 500,000	RM 3,000
RM 500,001–RM 1 Million	RM 5,000
RM 1,000,001–RM 5 Million	RM 8,000
RM 5,000,001–RM 10 Million	RM 10,000
RM 10,000,001–RM 25 Million	RM 20,000
RM 25,000,001–RM 50 Million	RM 40,000
RM 50,000,001–RM 100 Million	RM 50,000
RM 100,000,001 and above	RM 70,000

However, pursuant to a recent announcement by the CCM, the above official fees have been temporary reduced as follows:

Authorized Share Capital	Registration Fees from 1 Apr 09 to 31 Mar 2010	Percentage of Reduction
Not exceeding RM 100,000	RM 900	10%
RM 100-001–RM 500,000	RM 2,550	15%
RM 500,001–RM 1 Million	RM 4,250	
RM 1,000,001–RM 5 Million	RM 6,800	
RM 5,000,001–RM 10 Million	RM 8,500	
RM 10,000,001–RM 25 Million	RM 17,000	
RM 25,000,001–RM 50 Million	RM 34,000	
RM 50,000,001–RM 100 Million	RM 42,500	
Exceeding 100 million	RM 59,500	

Please note that this reduction will be effective from 1 April 2009 until 31 March 2010 only. This registration fee must be paid to the CCM upon the final submission of the application to incorporate the company.

9. Timing

Registration of the company can normally be accomplished in three to seven days, depending on whether all the documents required for incorporation are complete and comply with applicable regulations.

10. Filings

After company registration is completed, other various statutory filings are required to be submitted to the CCM within one month from the date of incorporation. These filings are fairly routine. To see a list of these filings go to www.doylesguideasia.com/malaysia/chapter20/appendixf.

11. Public Access to Company Details

After the company is successfully registered, many details regarding the company's structure are easily available to the public at the CCM. These details include the company's list of shareholders and directors, registered capital, details of company charges, balance sheet for the preceding year, etc.

12. Purchase of Shelf Companies

As an alternative to incorporating a new company (as outlined above), the applicant may wish to purchase a shelf company. A shelf company is a company which has already been registered by formation agents for the purpose of sale to third parties.

The transfer of ownership of a shelf company is accomplished via a transfer of shares from the initial subscribers to the purchasers of the company.

EXAMPLE: A Taiwanese company has submitted a bid for a telecommunication contract in Malaysia, and the terms of the bid state that the bidder must establish a company in Malaysia very shortly after winning the bid or risk forfeiture. The Taiwanese company wins the bid. In this situation, in order to save time, the Taiwanese company may elect to purchase a shelf company.

In order for the purchasers of the shelf company to change the existing company name, Malaysian law requires that they complete and file the required name reservation forms (see Section 2 above).

After the name reservation is completed, the former name of the company is required to appear beneath the new name (usually with the phrase "formerly known as XYZ Sdn Bhd") on all documents, business letters, statements of account, invoices, official notices, publications, bills of exchange, promissory notes, endorsements, checks, orders, receipts, and letters of credit of, or purporting to be issued or signed by or on behalf of, the company for a period of not less than twelve months from the date of the change.

EXAMPLE: Same facts as above, except that after the purchase of the shelf company, the Taiwanese investors want to change the company name from XYZ Sdn Bhd to ABC Sdn Bhd. After submitting the necessary name change documentation with the CCM, the company would be required to include the former company name (XYZ Sdn Bhd) on all related company documents for a period of twelve months from the date of the change.

Chapter 21

What Legal Issues Are Associated with Operating as a Foreign-Held Company?

The Malaysian government regulates foreign investment within the country through guidelines and policies issued by regulating authorities such as the Ministry of International Trade and Industry (MITI), the Economic Planning Unit (EPU), the Central Bank of Malaysia (CBM), the Malaysian Securities Commission (MSC), and others as set forth below.

1. Definition of Foreign

Normally, any project within Malaysia designated as "foreign" requires registration and approval from the designated government agency (see Section 4 below).

Under Malaysian law, the definition of foreign is quite broad and includes any company incorporated outside of Malaysia and any company whose head office or principle place of business is not in Malaysia.

EXAMPLE: A Singapore registered company operates a representative office in Malaysia. That representative office would be legally classified as a foreign entity.

EXAMPLE: A company with headquarters in London incorporates a subsidiary in Malaysia. The Malaysian subsidiary would be legally classified as foreign.

Also meeting the definition of "foreign" is any Malaysian registered company which is legally classified as a foreign interest.

The definition of foreign interest includes foreign nationals (including foreign nationals who have permanent residence in Malaysia) and local companies and local institutions in which foreigners hold more than 50% of the voting rights in that local company or local institution.

EXAMPLE: A US investor registers a company in Malaysia together with a Malaysian investor in which the US investor holds only 25% of the total company shares, and the Malaysian investor 75% of the shares, but the US investor controls 65% of the voting rights through provisions of the shareholders' agreement and company articles. In this situation, the Malaysia registered company would be classified as a foreign interest and therefore, subject to regulation.

EXAMPLE: Same facts as above, but the shareholding of the US company is 40%, and the company holds only 40% of the total company voting rights. In this situation, the company would not be legally classified as a foreign interest.

2. Bumiputera Requirements

In Malaysia, certain legal rights and privileges are reserved for those Malaysian nationals who qualify as ethnic Malay or aboriginal, also referred to as Bumiputera. These rights and privileges sometimes affect the requirements imposed on foreign investors in Malaysia.

Historically, Malaysian law has imposed the following minimum shareholding quotas on Malaysian registered companies with foreign shareholders (unless special permission was otherwise granted by the government):

30% minimum Bumiputera shareholding

40% Malaysian (non-Bumiputera) shareholding permissible

30% maximum foreign shareholding permissible

In 2009, the government substantially reduced and even revoked the Bumiputera quota for most situations. Note, however, that Bumiputera quotas may still be applicable (or at least a factor) when a company with foreign shareholders requests registration approval, depending upon the area of investment, the region within Malaysia the investment is to be made, the amount of investment to be made, and the policy of the controlling government agency, as well as other factors.

3. Nominee Shareholders

Generally, nominee shareholders are individuals or companies that agree to hold shares on behalf of the true owner(s) of the shares. Under this arrangement, typically the nominee shareholder and the true owner execute an agreement stating that the nominee shareholder agrees to hold the shares in name only. The true owner retains all rights of ownership and control (voting rights, rights to transfer, rights to receive dividends, etc.) of the shares.

Contractual arrangements between foreign investors and Malaysian parties in the form of nominee agreements, voting agreements, etc. are legally enforceable and common place in Malaysia. Investors should note, however, that these arrangements are enforceable only against the other party to the contract and are not binding on the company itself.

EXAMPLE: A Canadian company executes a contract whereby a local individual agrees to hold 30% of the shares of a Malaysian registered company on the Canadian company's behalf as its nominee, with the local individual's name to appear on all registration documents. The Malaysian individual later breaches the contract by refusing to transfer dividends received from the Malaysian company to the Canadian company as set forth in the contract. In this situation, the Canadian company would be limited to only pursuing a legal claim against the Malaysian individual for breach of contract but would have no direct recourse against the Malaysian company.

4. Registration

Unlike many other countries, Malaysia does not have a central registration authority for foreign investment, but rather uses a system whereby specific governmental agencies are responsible for different areas of foreign business.

Each of these agencies has its own procedures, requirements, and approval criteria. The chart below lists the government agencies responsible for specific sectors of foreign investment and the normal processing time for registration approval. (See next page.)

Investment Sector	Responsible Agency	Processing Time (approx.)
manufacturing	MITI (http://www.miti.gov.my)	12 days
finance and banking	CBM (http://www.bnm.gov.my)	2 to 12 months depending on situations
hotel management	Ministry of Tourism (http://www.motour.gov.my)	1 to 3 weeks
construction	Construction Industry Development Board (http://www.cidb.com.my)	1–14 days
consumer marketing consulting	Ministry of Domestic Trade, Co-operatives and Consumerism (http://www.kpdnkk.gov.my)	22 days
*real estate	EPU and the relevant State Agencies (http://www.epu.gov.my)	10 days to 2 weeks

* For the rules applicable to foreign ownership of land see Chapter 24.

Chapter 22

What Is the Process to Obtain a Work Permit?

This chapter summarizes the authorizations and application procedures required for foreigners to work in Malaysia.

1. Employment and Visit Pass

The standard authorization required for a foreigner to work and live in Malaysia is either an Employment Pass or a Visit Pass, depending upon the situation.

An Employment Pass is applicable when the foreigner is to hold a key position in the company, such as a management position or other high level position. There are three requirements for a foreign employee seeking an employment pass:

i.   The position is approved by a designated government agency (see below).

ii. The applicant has an employment contract to work in Malaysia for a minimum of two years.

iii. The applicant is required to have a salary of no less than RM5,000 per month.

The Employment Pass has a maximum validity period of five years; however, the common practice within the Immigration Department is to grant employment passes for a period of only two years and make them renewable.

A Visit Pass is applicable to foreigners holding positions below the level of professional administration. Visit Passes have a maximum validity period of one year and are renewable.

EXAMPLE: A German individual is to be employed as the Managing Director at a Malaysian manufacturing company. His contract of employment is for five years, his salary is RM8,000 per month, and he is approved for the post by MIDA (see below). Using these facts, the German would qualify for an Employment Pass (rather that a Visit Pass).

EXAMPLE: Same facts as above, but the German's salary is to be RM4,000 per month. Using these facts, he would not qualify for an Employment Pass; therefore, he would be required to apply for a Visit Pass instead.

EXAMPLE: A Swedish national seeks to work for the same company to be employed as a welder for a period of one year with a salary of RM3,000 per month. Using these facts, the Swedish national would apply for a Visit Pass rather than an Employment Pass.

2. Reference Visa

Note that nationals of certain countries are required to obtain a Reference Visa (RV) in order to enter Malaysia for purposes of employment.

To obtain the RV requires two steps:

i.   The employer company in Malaysia must request approval from the Immigration Department, which normally takes between fourteen and thirty days.

ii. The foreign employee (who has not yet entered Malaysia) then goes to any Malaysian embassy or mission to request the RV, using the approval documents as supporting documentation.

To see a list of the countries whose citizens are required to obtain an RV prior to their arrival into Malaysia go to www.doylesguideasia.com/malaysia/chapter22/appendixa.

3. Dependents

The following persons qualify to receive a Dependent's Pass: the spouse, the children of the foreign employee under twenty-one years of age, and legally adopted children (if the foreign employee is married).

The Dependent Pass application may be submitted to the Immigration Department either at the same time as the application for an Employment Pass or after the Employment Pass application has already been approved. The supporting documents required to apply for a Dependent Pass are as follows:

i.   Cover letter from the expatriate's company (for all dependents)

ii. DP11 Form (for all dependents)

iii. Two passport sized photos (for all dependents)

iv. Proof of marriage (for spouse)

v.   Children's birth certificates (for children)

Note that dependents of a foreign employee with a Visit Pass are not eligible to receive a Dependent Pass, but they may qualify for other types of passes (i.e. Long Term Social Visit Pass), depending upon the circumstances.

4. Required Documentation for the Employment Pass and Visit Pass

The foreign employee is required to submit the following documents together with an application to the Immigration Department:

i.   A letter from the company introducing the foreigner as its representative

ii. Completed Form DP11 with a photograph of the foreign employee attached

iii. Offer and acceptance letter or employment contract or personal bond (for Visit Pass only)

iv. Photocopy of the latest passport of the foreign employee

The following documents may also be required by the Immigration Department (as applicable):

i.   Approval letter from the Malaysian Industrial Development Authority (MIDA), Bank Negara Malaysia/Central Bank of Malaysia (BNM), or Malaysia Securities Commission (SC), whichever is applicable. However, for applications processed by the Expatriate Committee (EC) or the Multimedia Development Corporation (MDC), their approval letter is not required to be submitted to the Immigration Department.

ii. For upper level employees, the employer company's corporate information printout from the Companies Commission of Malaysia and generally, forms 9, 24, and 49.

iii. The foreign employee's resume and a photocopy of certificate, diploma, or degree for MIDA approval of posts other than key posts.

iv. Release letter from a previous employer when switching from previous employer in Malaysia to new employer in Malaysia.

5. Application Process

The process for the foreign employee to be employed and be given either an Employment Pass or Visit Pass (collectively known as Authorization) involves two steps: receiving initial approval from the designated government agency (depending upon the area of employment) and applying to the Immigration Department.

a. Initial Approval

Malaysia uses a system whereby the government agency designated to initially process the employment application depends upon the foreign applicant's area of employment. Under this system, each designated agency has its own application requirements and procedures.

EXAMPLE: The application for the employment of a foreigner in the area of product manufacturing would be submitted to the Malaysian Industrial Development Authority (MIDA).

EXAMPLE: The application for the employment of a foreigner in the area of finance would be submitted to the Bank Negara Malaysia (BNM).

A company in Malaysia seeking to employ a foreigner is required to submit an application for an employment pass and supporting documents with the designated government agency as stated below:

Area of Employment	Government Agency	Est. Processing Time
Manufacturing and related services sectors	Malaysia Industrial Development Authority	7 working days to 4 weeks
Information technology sector	Multimedia Development Corporation	3 working days
Financial, insurance, and banking sectors	Bank Negara Malaysia	7 working days
Securities and futures markets	Securities Commission	3 days
Biotechnology industry	Malaysian Biotechnology Corporation	7 to 10 days
Other sectors	Expatriate Committee	7 days

i. Manufacturing Sector Employment

Malaysian companies which have already been registered or are in the process of being registered seeking to employ a foreigner to work in the area of manufacturing are required to submit an application for Authorization with MIDA.

If the employer is a company which is currently in the process of being registered with MIDA, the company promoter(s) are required to submit an application for the foreign employee's Authorization at the same time as the application to register the company.

If the employer is a company which has already been registered, the company is required to submit an application and supporting documents with the Immigration Department, which will then facilitate the Authorization application process with MIDA.

ii. IT Sector Employment

Companies qualifying for MDC (Multimedia Development Corporation) status may employ foreign workers (without maximum limit) subject only to approval from the MDC.

The foreign employee must have one of the following qualifications:

Five or more years of professional work experience in multimedia, information and communication technology (ICT), or a field that is a heavy user of multimedia

A university degree (any discipline) or a diploma in multimedia or ICT from a technical college, plus two or more years of professional work experience in multimedia, ICT, or a field that is a heavy user of multimedia

A master's degree or higher in any discipline

iii. Financial Sector Employment

Applications for Authorization are required to be submitted by the employer to either the BNM or the Malaysian International Financial Center, depending upon where the foreigner is to work: a commercial bank, investment bank, Islamic bank, or insurance company.

If the foreigner is to work for a Takaful, an Islamic insurance concept which is grounded in Islamic banking transactions, observing the rules and regulations of Islamic law operators, international Islamic banks, and international Takaful operators, prior approval will be required from the BNM.

iv. Securities Sector Employment

Companies seeking to employ foreigners in the field of securities must file an application to employ foreigners and supporting documents with the SC (Securities Commission) for approval. Upon such approval, the company will need to apply for the Employment Pass or Visit Pass from the Immigration Department.

v. Biotechnology Sector Employment

Those companies qualifying for Bio Nexus Status wishing to hire foreign staff are required to submit applications by hand to the Malaysian Biotechnology Corporation. The application will then be submitted and processed by the EC (Expatriate Committee) of the Ministry of Home Affairs.

vi. Other Work Areas

The EC is also responsible for processing Authorization applications in employment areas other than those administrated by MIDA, MDC, SC, and BNM (see above).

Companies seeking to employ foreigner(s) outside these areas are required to submit an application by hand or by post to the EC.

Note that the following minimum registered paid-up capital requirements (see Chapter 20) will apply to the employer company:

RM150,000 for 100% local (Malaysian) owned

RM200,000 for local and foreign owned

RM250,000 for 100% foreign owned

b. Approval from the Immigration Department

After receiving initial approval from the designated government agency, the application for the Employment Pass or Visit Pass is sent to the Immigration Department. Normally, this application to the Immigration Department will be done by the company employing the foreigners.

The Immigration Department requires that the expiration date of the foreigner's passport must be at least eighteen months after the date of the Authorization application; otherwise the application will not be approved. Also, the expiration on the passport may not be before the expiration date of the Authorization.

EXAMPLE: On the date of submitting the application for a Visit Pass the expiration date on a foreigner's passport is four months from that time. In this situation, the Immigration Department will not issue a Visit Pass.

EXAMPLE: An Australian national applies for an Employment Pass. As of the date of the application, the expiration date on his passport is in two years. In this situation, he may qualify to receive an Employment Pass; however, the period of the Employment Pass will not exceed two years.

6. Official Fees

The official fee for an Employment Pass is RM200 per annum payable to the government for all positions (other than certain key posts approved by MIDA, in which case the fee payable is RM300 per annum).

Official fees for Visit Pass applications vary depending upon the government agency where the application is made. To see a list of these fees go to www.doylesguideasia.com/malaysia/chapter22/appendixb.

Chapter 23

What Investment Incentives Are Available to Foreign Investors?

The government agencies responsible for encouraging and attracting specified types of business activities and projects in Malaysia include the Malaysian Industrial Development Authority and the Ministry of Finance. The incentives available from each and their criteria for granting such incentives are set forth below.

1. Malaysian Industrial Development Authority (MIDA)

MIDA is the main government agency in charge of encouraging specified types of manufacturing and service projects in Malaysia.

In order for a project to qualify to receive the incentives offered by MIDA, the project must engage in one or more of the activities promoted by MIDA at the time. To see a complete list of the promoted activities go to www.doyles guideasia.com/malaysia/chapter23/appendixa.

Note that MIDA promotes specific types of activities in Malaysia and not the company itself.

EXAMPLE: Suppose a company registered in Malaysia has a project to produce auto parts for export, and MIDA approves promotion for the project and grants a partial tax exemption. The company begins to receive income from the sale of auto parts to overseas buyers. The company also engages in the activity of providing consulting services which are not promoted by MIDA. In this situation, the income the company receives from producing auto parts for export (promoted activity) would receive the partial tax exemption, but with the income received from providing consulting services (non-promoted activity) normal tax rates would apply.

There are various financial and non-financial incentives offered by MIDA with respect to promoted activities; following are the three main incentives:

i.   Pioneer Status

ii. Investment Tax Allowance

iii. Bio Nexus Status

a. Pioneer Status

Projects receiving Pioneer Status are entitled to partial tax exemption, i.e. paying tax on only 30% of the project's annual statutory income.

EXAMPLE: A Japanese company establishes a subsidiary in Malaysia to produce computer components, and the project applies for and obtains Pioneer Status from MIDA to pursue this project. In Year One of the project, the company realizes a statutory income of RM1000 generated from the activity. In this situation, only 30% of the Japanese project's total statutory income for the year (RM300) would be taxable. (The rate of corporate income tax in Malaysia for the year 2009 was 25% of the annual net profits.)

This partial tax exemption lasts for a period of five years, commencing from the date production begins as determined by the Ministry of International Trade and Industry (MITI).

EXAMPLE: Same facts as above, and the project is granted the partial tax exemption for a period of five years. At the beginning of Year Six (counting from the project starting date as determined by MITI) the partial tax exemption would cease and normal tax rules would apply.

Note that in order to encourage investors to locate their project specifically in the state of Sarawak, projects granted Pioneer Status located in that state will receive a 100% exemption on statutory income for a period of five years.

EXAMPLE: Same facts stated above, but the project is located in the state of Sarawak. In this situation, the Japanese project would receive a 100% exemption on statutory income instead of 30% as stated above.

Also, note that for strategic projects in hi-tech industries with heavy capital investments and high R&D content or intensive linkages, a 100% tax exemption may be granted for a period of five years. Intensive linkages in this context refer to a connection of a series of rigid mechanical/technical links that are involved in the creation of a certain technological device/equipment.

EXAMPLE: A Korean company has a long term project to produce electronic components in which the company is required to invest the equivalent of $150 million to build the factory in Malaysia and begin operations. In this situation, if the project qualifies for Pioneer Status as a high tech industry, it would qualify to receive a 100% tax exemption on its statutory income for a period of five years.

Basically, to qualify for pioneer status, the company must prove to be carrying on manufacturing activities which are promoted by MIDA.

The form and procedure to apply for pioneer status can be accessed through the following links:

1. http://www.mida.gov.my/en_v2/uploads/images/e-Services_Portal/
   Forms_and_Guidelines/Manufacturing/manufacturing1/ICA1-7-9-
   Guidelines.doc

2. http://www.mida.gov.my/en_v2/uploads/images/e-Services_Portal/
   Forms_and_Guidelines/Manufacturing/manufacturing1/ICAJA1%20-
   %20100309.rtf

b. Investment Tax Allowance

The Investment Tax Allowance (ITA) is offered by MIDA for long term projects with large capital investments.

Note that MIDA has broad discretion to award a wide range of incentives to a project granted ITA, depending upon its individual qualifications. For a complete list of incentives available under ITA, go to www.doylesguideasia.com/malaysia/chapter23/appendixb.

Among the incentives normally granted to projects qualifying under ITA is a tax deduction based upon the project's total capital expenditure.

A project receiving ITA may use an amount representing 60% of its total qualifying capital expenditure in the project as a tax deduction against 70% of its annual statutory income. The remaining 30% of the project's annual statutory income is taxed at the normal tax rate.

EXAMPLE: A South African company has a long term project to produce various types of construction equipment in Malaysia and obtains ITA incentives from MIDA for the project. The South African company's total capital expenditure in the project is RM1000. In this situation, the total income tax deduction the project may use over the life of the project would be RM600 (the amount representing 60% of the total qualifying capital investment).

The project may receive the benefit of this tax deduction each year until such time as the total amount of tax savings granted is fully used.

EXAMPLE: Same facts as above, and in Year One the project utilizes RM450 of its total RM600 tax deduction (calculated based upon 70% of its total statutory income in that year), and in Year Two it utilizes the remaining RM150. In Year Three normal tax rules would apply (due to the fact that all of the project's total tax savings have already been used in Year One and Year Two).

A project receiving ITA located in the state of Sarawak may use an amount representing 100% of its qualifying capital expenditure in that project as a tax deduction against 100% of the project's statutory income each year.

EXAMPLE: Same facts as above, but since the project is located in the state of Sarawak, the project would be allowed to use all of its RM1000 of qualifying capital expenditure as a tax deduction against 100% of the project's statutory income.

Applications for Pioneer Status and ITA incentives must be submitted to MIDA at

MIDA Headquarters
Malaysian Industrial Development Authority (MIDA)
Block 4, Plaza Sentral
Jalan Stesen Sentral 5
Kuala Lumpur Sentral
50470 Kuala Lumpur
Malaysia
Tel: 603-2267 3633
Fax: 603-2274 7970
Email: investmalaysia@mida.gov.my

To see a sample application go to www.doylesguideasia.com/malaysia/chapter23/appendixc.

c. Bio Nexus Status

MIDA grants certain special incentives for projects engaging in the biotechnology industry that qualify for Bio Nexus Status, which are described in points (i) through (viii) below.

i. An exemption from tax on 100% of statutory income for either a period of ten consecutive years from the first year the company derived statutory income from a new project or five consecutive years from the first year the company derived statutory income from an existing project.

ii. A tax exemption of 100% of the statutory income derived from a new project or expansion of a project equal to 100% of qualifying capital expenditure in the project for a period of five years.

EXAMPLE: A US company engages in a biotechnology project in Malaysia and is granted Bio Nexus Status. The company invests $25 million in the project over five years. In this situation, the project may be granted a 100% exemption of statutory income; however, the total amount of tax savings the project can realize would be capped at $25 million. After that amount has been reached, the normal tax rules would apply unless MIDA has stated otherwise (see below).

   iii. A concessionary tax rate of 20% on statutory income from qualifying activities for ten years upon the expiration of the tax exemption period.

EXAMPLE: Same facts as above, and the project is granted a 20% concessionary rate (the corporate tax rate for the year 2009 is 25% of annual net profits) after the tax exemption expires. In this situation, after the $25 million in total tax savings has been reached, the 20% concessionary tax rate would apply for an additional five year period.

   iv. Tax exemption on dividends distributed by a Bio Nexus Status company. (Where the recipient of the dividend is a company, the tax rate on dividends in Malaysia is 25%; however, if the company has adopted the single tier system, the tax on dividends is exempted effective from the year 2008.)

   v. Exemption of import duty and sales tax on raw materials/components, machinery, and equipment.

   vi. Double deduction on expenditures incurred for R&D.

   vii. Double deduction on expenditures incurred for the promotion of exports.

   viii. Tax incentives for a period of ten years on buildings used solely for biotechnology activities.

MIDA also has the authority to grant incentives to investors in Bio Nexus Status project companies. Investors in these companies may be entitled to the following tax incentives:

   i. A company or an individual that carries on business in Malaysia investing in a Bio Nexus Status company is eligible for a tax deduction equivalent to the total investment made as seed capital.

   ii. A Bio Nexus Status company undertaking a merger and acquisition with a biotechnology company is eligible for exemption of the stamp duty for its share purchase. This exemption is valid until 31 December 2011.

Applications should be submitted to the Malaysian Biotechnology Corporation (BiotechCorp), at the following address:

Malaysian Biotechnology Corporation Sdn Bhd
Client Support Services Division—Evaluation & Funding
Level 21, Menara Naluri
161, Jalan Ampang
50450 Kuala Lumpur
Tel : 603-2116 8585
Fax : 603-2116 5432
www.biotechcorp.com.my

For the latest updates, please refer to MIDA at their website: www.mida.gov.my.

2. Free Zones

Free zones are administrated by the Malaysian Ministry of Finance and are designated as either free commercial zones or free industrial zones. Generally, locating in a free zone entitles a company to certain benefits in the form of exemption from customs checks.

a. Free Commercial Zones

Companies which operate within Free Commercial Zones (FCZ) are subject to greatly reduced customs formalities.

The scope of activities permitted in a FCZ includes trading (except retail trading), breaking bulk (separation of goods), grading (evaluation of product quality), repacking, relabeling, and transit.

Currently there are thirteen FCZs located at the North, South, and West Port of Port Klang, Port Klang Free Zone, Pulau Indah MILS Logistic Hub (Selangor), Butterworth, Bayan Lepas (Penang), Kuala Lumpur International Airport, Rantau Panjang, Pengkalan Kubor (Kelantan), Stulang Laut, Johor Port, and Port Tanjung Pelepas (Johor).

b. Free Industrial Zone

The activities permitted in Free Industrial Zones (FIZ) are limited to manufacturing related activities.

Companies located in a FIZ are granted reduced customs formalities, as well as the duty free import of raw materials, component parts, machinery, and equipment specifically required in the manufacturing process.

Companies seeking to locate in a FIZ must qualify under the following criteria:

i.   A minimum of 80% of the company's goods produced must be for export.

ii. The raw materials/components used in production must be predominantly imported.

Currently there are sixteen FIZs located at Pasir Gudang, Tanjung Pelepas (Johor), Batu Berendam I, Batu Berendam II, Tanjung Kling (Melaka), Telok Panglima Garang (Selangor), Pulau Indah (PKFZ), Sungai Way I, Sungai Way II, Ulu Kelang (Selangor), Jelapang II, Kinta (Kedah), Bayan Lepas I, II, III, Bayan Lepas IV, Seberang Perai, and Sama Jaya (Pulau Pinang).

Chapter 24

What Legal Issues Are Associated with Foreign Ownership of Land?

Generally, foreign individuals and foreign companies are not allowed to own land in Malaysia unless the exceptions described below apply.

1. Residential Property

Foreign individuals and foreign companies are allowed to own houses and the land upon which the houses sit, residential condominium units, and apartment units (units) which have a purchase price of RM500,000 or more without having to request any special permission from the Malaysian government.

EXAMPLE: A Belgian investor wishes to buy land and a villa in Penang, Malaysia for a purchase price of RM800,000. This should be permissible under the law.

EXAMPLE: A US company seeks to purchase five condominium units in Kuala Lumpur, each valued at RM500,000 for its executives working there to live. This should be permissible under the law (subject to the rule stated below concerning ratios of ownership).

Note, however, that there are significant conditions associated with this right to buy residential units, as described below.

a. Financing

Foreign purchasers of units are allowed to finance only 60% to 80% of the value of the unit domestically through a Malaysian bank or finance company.

EXAMPLE: A Swiss investor wishes to purchase five condominium units on Langkawi Island, Malaysia with the purchase price of each set at RM500,000.

Using these facts, the Swiss investor will only be able to locally finance between 60% and 80% of the value of the five units. He would be required to finance the remaining amount through other means or use cash.

b. Ownership Ratio

Certain legal rights and privileges are reserved for Malaysian nationals who qualify as ethnic Malay or aborigine, also referred to as Bumiputera. These rights and privileges sometimes affect a foreigner's ability to purchase a unit.

Generally, foreigners may purchase as many units as they wish, provided that a minimum percentage of Bumiputera ownership (typically 10%) is maintained.

EXAMPLE: A foreigner wishes to purchase a condominium unit in a building from a Bumiputera owner; however, the sale would cause the total Bumiputera ownership of the building to fall below 10%. In this situation, the foreigner's purchase of the condominium would not be allowed.

EXAMPLE: Same facts as above, but the condominium seller is a Malaysian citizen who is an ethnic Chinese (i.e. not a Bumiputera). In this situation, the foreigner's purchase of the condominium would be allowed because it would not affect the Bumiputera ownership ratio.

2. Purchases Requiring EPU Approval

Bumiputera ownership requirements also affect the purchase of non-residential land and immovable property by foreigners.

a. Non-Residential Property

Malaysian law places restrictions on the following parties doing transactions involving land and immovable property:

i.   Foreign individuals (including permanent residents)

ii.   Foreign registered companies

iii. Malaysian registered companies in which foreigners hold more that 50% of the total company voting rights

The restrictions generally apply to two types of transactions:

i.   Any *direct* purchase of land and/or immovable property valued at RM20 million or more, resulting in the dilution in the ownership of the property held by a Bumiputera party(ies) and/or government agency

ii.   Any *indirect* purchase of property valued at more than RM20 million
      by a non-Bumiputera interest through the purchase of shares, which
      results in a change of control of that company owned by a Bumiput-
      era party(ies) and/or Malaysian government agency, where such prop-
      erty makes up more than 50% of that company's total assets

For transactions in which these restrictions apply the foreign investor must obtain prior approval for the acquisition from the Economic Planning Unit (EPU).

EXAMPLE: A Japanese registered company seeks to purchase an office in Kuala
Lumpur currently owned by a Bumiputera individual for the purchase price of
RM150 million. In this situation, the Japanese company would be required to
obtain prior approval from the EPU before going forward with the purchase.

EXAMPLE: Same facts as above, but the purchase price is RM10 million. In
this situation, no EPU approval would be required (however, other government approvals may be required in some situations).

EXAMPLE: A Malaysian registered company with Singaporean shareholders
holding 60% of the total voting rights seeks to acquire 100% of the shares of
another Malaysian registered company which is currently held by Bumiputera
shareholders and owns a hotel. The purchase price for the shares is RM55 million. For this transaction, the purchasing company would be required to obtain prior approval from the EPU prior to going forward with the purchase.

Note that for the purchase of non-residential property by a foreign individual the EPU may (or may not) require the foreign individual to make the
purchase through either a new or existing Malaysian registered company, rather
than allowing the foreign individual to make the purchase in his own name.

EXAMPLE: A Dutch citizen wishes to purchase a non-residential property in
Kuala Lumpur from a Malaysian citizen who is an ethnic Indian. In this situation, the EPU may allow the Dutch citizen to make the purchase himself, or
the EPU may require the Dutch citizen to make the purchase through a new
or existing Malaysian company (see shareholding and paid-up capital requirements below).

In the event that the EPU requires the foreign individual to make the purchase through a Malaysian company, the company must have at least 30% Bumiputera shareholding interest and have a registered capital of no less than
RM250,000.

EXAMPLE: Same facts as above, and the EPU requires that the Dutch citizen make
the purchase through a Malaysian registered company. In this situation, the
Malaysian registered company would be required to have a minimum of 30% of
the shares held by Bumiputera and a registered capital of no less than RM250,000.

b. Exemptions

Foreign interests may acquire the following types of properties through a locally incorporated company without approval from the EPU (however, certain other regulations may still be applicable):

i.   Acquisition of residential units valued at RM500,000 (see Section 1)

ii.   Transfer of property to a foreigner based on family ties (only allowed among immediate family members)

iii. Acquisition of commercial unit valued at RM500,000 and above

iv.   Acquisition of agricultural land valued at RM500,000 and above or of land which is at least five acres in area for any one the following purposes:

   • Agricultural activities on a commercial scale using modern or high technology

   • Agro-tourism projects

   • Agricultural or agro-based industrial activities for the production of goods for export

v.   Acquisition of industrial lands valued at RM500,000 and above

EXAMPLE: A Malaysian national wishes to sell a condominium unit to his sister who grew up in Canada. She is a Canadian citizen (not a Malaysian citizen). The purchase price of the condo unit is RM150,000. This sale and purchase would be permissible without prior approval from the EPU.

Note that although the transactions under items (iii), (iv), and (v) do not require EPU approval, these purchases must be made through a Malaysian registered company (with a minimum 30% of the shares held by Bumiputera shareholders and have a minimum registered capital of RM250,000), and the EPU must be notified before the title of the property is transferred.

EXAMPLE: A US investor wishes to purchase agricultural land in Malaysia for RM5 million for the purpose of establishing a shrimp farm to produce shrimp for export. In order to be allowed to do so without having to obtain prior approval from the EPU, the US investor would first be required to register a company in Malaysia and designate that company as the party to purchase the land. Also, a minimum of 30% of the shares of such Malaysian company must be Bumiputera owned, and the registered capital of the company must be at least RM250,000. In addition, prior to transferring title, the purchaser must advise the EPU of the planned purchase.

Although the EPU is the main government body responsible for granting approvals for non-residential purchases of land and immovable property in

Malaysia, additional approval may also be applicable, depending upon the state in Malaysia where the land and/or immovable property is located.

3. Restrictions on Foreign Interests

Foreign interests are not allowed to acquire the following types of properties:

i. Residential and non-residential units of less than RM500,000 in value

ii. Residential units under the category of low and low-medium cost as determined by the State Authority

iii. Properties built on Malay reserved land

iv. Properties allocated to Bumiputera in any property development project as determined by the State Authority

4. Title Search

Any purchaser interested in purchasing land and/or immovable property in Malaysia should conduct a thorough title search prior to closing. By conducting a title search, the prospective purchaser can obtain information concerning the ownership, encumbrances, registered leases, and interests registered on the property title.

5. Leases

Malaysian law requires that all leases of land and/or immovable property for terms of more than three years be registered on the property title. The maximum lease period allowed is generally ninety-nine years (however, specific rules apply in some cases).

EXAMPLE: A UK individual wishes to lease land and a house in Johor Baharu, Malaysia for a period of four years from a Malaysian company. In this situation, Malaysian law requires that the parties register the lease on the title.

Leases for terms of three years or less are not subject to any registration requirement.

EXAMPLE: Same facts as above, but lease period is for three years. In this situation, there would be no requirement to register the lease on the title.

Foreign interests are generally allowed to lease land and/or immovable property in Malaysia, subject only to restrictions which may be imposed by the government on certain tracts of land. If the land is subject to such restrictions, it should be stated on the property title.

After registration, the lease appears on the property title, which places subsequent purchasers of the property on notice of the existence of the leaseholder's rights to the property.

EXAMPLE: Suppose a foreign individual leases a tract of land for a period of thirty years and registers the lease with the local Land Office. The owner then sells the land to a third party purchaser without mentioning the existence of the lease to the purchaser. In this situation, the third party purchaser would purchase the land subject to the pre-existing rights of the foreign tenant. The tenant would, therefore, be free to continue to have rights over the land (as set forth in the lease agreement) during the remaining lease term.

Philippines

Capital City	Manila
Major Financial Center	Makati City
Population (projected 2010)	94 million
Location	Southeastern Asia, archipelago east of Vietnam
Major Languages	Filipino, English (both official)
Legal System	Combination of civil and common law
Square Miles	115,831 sq mi
Gross Domestic Product (projected 2010)	USD 166 billion
Major Exports	Electrical machinery, clothing, food and live animals, chemicals, timber products
Currency	Philippines Pesos (PHP)
U.S. Dollar Exchange Rate (as of November 2009)	USD 1 = PHP 47.68
Euro Exchange Rate (as of November 2009)	EUR 1 = PHP 70.21

Section Authors

Tadeo F. Hilado
Partner
Angara Abello Concepcion
 Regala & Cruz
Email: tfhilado@accralaw.com
Website: http://www.accralaw.com

Joselito M. Bautista
Senior Associate
Angara Abello Concepcion
 Regala & Cruz
Email: jmbautista@accralaw.com
Website: http://www.accralaw.com

Chapter 25

Should Our Business Establish as a Corporation, Branch, Representative Office, or Regional Office?

A foreign investor may establish a business presence in the Philippines either as a corporation, branch office, representative office, regional operating headquarters, or regional headquarters.

In choosing the type of entity which would be most appropriate, the foreign investor should consider the following factors:

i.   Allowed activities for the entity

ii. Minimum capital requirements

iii. Liability issues

iv. Tax treatment

1. Corporation

The structure of a corporation in the Philippines is similar to the Limited Liability Company (LLC) structure in the United States in that the corporation becomes a legal entity separate and independent from the foreign investor or any parent company.

A corporation registered in the Philippines is allowed to undertake any business activity not otherwise reserved to Philippine nationals by Philippine laws. The business activities restricted to Philippine nationals are presented in Chapter 27.

EXAMPLE: If a foreign company wishes to establish a presence in the Philippines, it will most likely do so as a corporation. If individual investors wish to establish a stand-alone business to generate income in the Philippines, they will also most likely do so as a corporation.

EXAMPLE: Suppose a Swedish company establishes a wholly owned subsidiary corporation in the Philippines. That new corporation then executes a contract with a local company to supply auto parts, but then fails to supply those parts. In this situation, the purchaser would generally be limited to suing the Philippine subsidiary for the breach of contract, not its parent company in Sweden.

2. Branch Office, Representative Office, Regional Headquarters, and Regional Operating Headquarters

In some circumstances, however, a foreign company may not want to establish a separate legal entity. Reasons for this may range from optimizing accounting, administration, and management arrangements with affiliated businesses to tax planning reasons. In these situations, a foreign company may choose to instead establish a branch office, representative office, regional headquarters, or regional operating headquarters in the Philippines.

If this is the case, the foreign company is required to appoint a resident agent who may either be an individual residing in the Philippines or a corporation organized and registered in the Philippines and lawfully transacting business in the Philippines. The resident agent is responsible for receiving any court or legal summons or documents on behalf of the foreign company.

a. Branch Office

A branch office may earn income in the Philippines; however, its activities will be limited to those activities in which a foreign-held company in the Philippines may legally engage (see Chapter 27).

EXAMPLE: Suppose that the foreign company does not want to establish a corporation, but does want to engage in activities in the Philippines that would generate income. In this situation, the foreign company would most likely establish a branch office.

Philippine law treats all liabilities of the branch as the liabilities of its head office overseas.

EXAMPLE: A Dutch company establishes a branch in the Philippines, and the branch is later served a summons stating that the Dutch company is being sued in a Philippine court. In this situation, the Dutch company would be responsible for this claim in all respects.

EXAMPLE: Suppose a multinational company establishes a branch in the Philippines, and the branch enters into a contract with a local Philippine company to provide services but fails to perform. In this situation, the Philippine company could then sue the head office of the multinational company directly.

b. Representative Office

A representative office (sometimes referred to as a liaison office) of a foreign registered company may interact directly with the Philippine customers of its head office overseas but is not allowed to earn income. The representative office must also be fully subsidized by its head office.

A representative office may generally engage in the following activities:

i.   Disseminate information

ii. Promote the head office's products

iii. Perform quality control on the head office's products

A representative office does not have a legal identity separate from its head office overseas; therefore, (just as with a branch office) the head office is liable for all the liabilities of its representative office. Normally, however, the representative office will not incur significant liabilities in the Philippines due to the limited activities permissible (see above).

c. Regional Headquarters and Regional Operating Headquarters

A Regional Headquarters (RHQ) is an administrative branch office of a foreign registered company engaged in international trade and acts as a supervising, communicating, and coordinating center for such foreign company's subsidiaries, branches, or affiliates in the Asia-Pacific Region and other foreign markets.

EXAMPLE: A UK company with offices throughout Asia seeks to establish an office in the Philippines. The intention is for this new office's activities to be limited to only coordinating activities between the other offices in Asia. In this situation, the UK company would likely establish a RHQ in the Philippines.

The RHQ may not earn income. It is allowed to operate only as a cost center, and may not participate in the management of any subsidiary or branch office the multinational may have inside the Philippines, or solicit or market any of the head office's goods or services in the Philippines.

EXAMPLE: Same facts as above, but the UK company also has a branch office in the Philippines which sells goods in the Philippines. If the UK company establishes a RHQ, it would be prohibited from managing the branch office in the Philippines or promoting the head office's goods there.

Because the RHQ does not earn income from sources within the Philippines and does not participate in managing any subsidiaries or branch offices located inside the Philippines, it is exempt from corporate income tax. It is also exempt from VAT and from all local government licenses, fees, and charges which are normally applicable, except for real property tax on land improvements and equipment which remain applicable. The RHQ also enjoys tax and duty free importation of equipment and materials necessary for training and conferences.

In contrast, the Regional Operating Headquarters (ROHQ) of a foreign company *is* allowed to earn income by performing qualifying services for its affiliates, subsidiaries, or branches located in the Philippines, in the Asia-Pacific Region, and in other foreign markets. These qualifying services include the following:

i.   General administration and planning

ii.   Business planning and coordination

iii. Sourcing/procurement of raw materials and components

iv.   Corporate finance advisory services

v.   Marketing control and sales promotion

vi.   Training and personnel management

vii. Logistics services

viii. Research and development services and product development

ix.   Technical support and maintenance

x.   Data processing and communication

xi.   Business development

The ROHQ is required to declare each of its affiliates, branches, and subsidiaries in which it will provide these services to the Securities and Exchange Commission (SEC) and is not to provide services to any other party who has not been so declared.

EXAMPLE: A Japanese car maker maintains multiple service centers for its customers all over the Philippines. The head office in Japan decides to establish a new office in the country to source certain spare parts for these service centers, and the intention is for the service centers to pay the new office for this service. In this situation, the Japanese company would likely establish the new entity as a ROHQ.

The ROHQ is *not* allowed to (either directly or indirectly) solicit or market any goods and services either on behalf of its head office or its branches, affiliates, subsidiaries, or any other company. ROHQs are also prohibited from engaging (either directly or indirectly) in the sale or distribution of goods or services of its head office, or the head office's branches, affiliates, subsidiaries, or any other company.

EXAMPLE: Same facts as above, but the Japanese company also wants the new office to market and sell the Japanese company's cars to the general public. In this situation, the marketing and selling of cars to the general public would not be permitted if the new entity was established as a ROHQ.

Note that a ROHQ is subject to Philippine corporate income tax and VAT, but is exempt from all kinds of local taxes and other government fees and charges, except real property tax on land improvements and equipment which remain applicable.

3. Capital Required

The amount of paid-in capital required for a corporation and the assigned capital required for a branch office, representative office, regional headquarters, or regional operating headquarters are discussed in Chapters 26 and 27.

4. Registration and Official Fees

Prior to transacting business in the Philippines, foreign-held corporations, branch offices, representative offices, regional headquarters, and regional operating headquarters are required to obtain a license to do business from the SEC. The procedure to obtain licenses applicable for each is discussed in Chapter 26.

The filing fee payable for registering a corporation is equal to one fifth of one percent of the corporation's stated authorized capital stock or the subscription price of the subscribed capital stock, whichever is higher, but not less than PhP1,000.

There is also a legal research fee payable to the SEC equal to one percent of the above described filing fee and an additional fixed fee of PhP510 payable to the SEC for registering the Articles of Incorporation and Bylaws.

EXAMPLE: Suppose an Australian investor registers a corporation with its authorized capital stock set at PhP10,000,000. The government filing fee would be calculated as follows:

PhP20,000	Filing Fee
PhP200	Legal Research Fee
PhP510	Articles and Bylaws
PhP20,710	**Total**

The filing fee payable for establishing a branch office is one percent of the actual inward remittance by the head office overseas but shall not be less than PhP2,000. There is also a legal research fee payable to the SEC of one percent of the filing fee.

EXAMPLE: A Norwegian company establishes a branch office in the Philippines and sets the assigned capital at PhP10,000,000. The filing fee would be calculated as follows:

PhP100,000	Filing Fee
PhP1,000	Legal Research Fee
PhP101,000	**Total**

The filing fee for establishing a representative office is one tenth of one percent of the actual inward remittance from the head offices overseas but shall not be less than PhP2,000. There is also a legal research fee payable to the SEC of one percent of the filing fee.

EXAMPLE: An Australian company establishes a representative office in the Philippines and sets its assigned capital at PhP1,500,000. The filing fee is calculated as follows:

PhP1,500	Filing Fee
PhP15	Legal Research Fee
PhP1,515	**Total**

The filing fee payable for establishing a RHQ is a fixed fee of PhP5,000.

The filing fee payable for establishing a ROHQ is one percent of the actual inward remittance of the head office overseas but shall not be less than one percent of the Philippine currency equivalent of US $200,000 at the time of remittance. There is also a legal research fee payable to the SEC of one percent of the filing fee.

EXAMPLE: A Canadian company establishes a ROHQ in the Philippines and remits PhP10,000,000 into the Philippines for its operation. The filing fee is calculated as follows:

PhP100,000	Filing Fee
PhP1,000	Legal Research Fee
PhP101,000	**Total**

Chapter 26

What Legal Issues Are Associated with the Start-Up of a Foreign-Held Company?

There are many legal and practical issues associated with registering a foreign-held corporation in the Philippines. The start-up process for a foreign-held corporation in the Philippines includes several steps:

i. Registering the corporation with and obtaining a business license from the Philippine Securities and Exchange Commission (SEC) (see Chapters 25 and 27)

ii. Registering with and obtaining a tax identification number from the Bureau of Internal Revenue (BIR)

iii. Registering as an employer with the Social Security System, the Home Development Mutual Fund, and the Philippine Health Insurance Corporation

iv. Registering with the Local Government Unit (LGU) to obtain a permit to do business at the corporation's principal office and/or place of operation

v. Registering with several other government agencies where certain activities require special permits

To see the list of documents and information required to register with the BIR go to www.doylesguideasia.com/philippines/chapter26/appendixa.

To see the list of documents and information required to obtain a business permit go to www.doylesguideasia.com/philippines/chapter26/appendixb.

Shelf companies are not common in the Philippines; therefore, this procedure must be followed each time a foreign business is established.

1. Incorporators

A corporation is formed by incorporators of not less than five but not more than fifteen individuals of which a majority must be residents of the Philippines. For purposes of complying with the residency requirement, Philippine law considers all Philippine citizens who reside in the Philippines and foreigners who hold any Philippine visa which is valid for at least one year as residents of the Philippines.

EXAMPLE: Italian and Filipino investors seek to register a corporation and designate five individuals to be the incorporators. Three of the five promoters reside in the Philippines (two Italians and one Filipino) and the other two in Italy. This would be permissible under the law.

Each incorporator is required to subscribe to at least one share upon the corporation's registration; however, third parties (other individuals and/or businesses) are allowed to be among the corporation's initial shareholders as well.

An incorporator's liability is similar to that of a shareholder, which is limited to his capital contribution in the corporation.

Also, note that upon incorporation, the corporation is required to appoint the corporation treasurer and such person is required to open the Treasurer-in-Trust account (see Section 12 below).

2. Timing

Registration of a corporation with the SEC normally takes approximately one to three weeks, depending on the type of business which the corporation will engage in and the availability of documents and information required from the incorporators.

Post-incorporation registrations with the BIR, LGU, and others (see above) normally take an additional four to six weeks.

3. Filings

All required documents and applications associated with the registration of a corporation are required to be filed with the main office of the SEC in Metro Manila, or if the principal office is located at an area where an extension office of the SEC exists, at such SEC extension office.

4. Company Name

The first step in the corporation registration process is to reserve the corporation name. Name reservation is accomplished by submitting the name reservation form stating the proposed name and two alternatives with the SEC, together with the payment of the registration fee.

Name registration is also available over the internet at www.sec.gov.ph; however, note that if the name is reserved over the internet, such registration will not be effective until after payment of the registration fee is made to the SEC.

To see the name reservation form go to www.doylesguideasia.com/philippines/chapter26/appendixc.

The name reservation process normally takes approximately one to three days.

Names requested which are deceptive or confusingly similar to an existing business name will not be approved. The approved name will be reserved for a maximum of 120 days at one time and may be renewed upon expiration. Upon final registration of the corporation the approved name will be permanently reserved for the corporation.

Note that many times, the name reservation process delays the corporation registration because the names submitted will be similar to a name previously registered and, therefore, not be allowed. Therefore, when possible, the incorporators should request names which are unique in character.

5. Signatures

After reservation of the name, the incorporators prepare the Articles of Incorporation and Bylaws (Articles) of the corporation (see below).

Each of the incorporators is required to sign the Articles. This may cause logistical problems if the incorporators are located in different parts of the world, since each will be required to sign the same document.

Also, note that if the Articles are signed by the Incorporators while they are outside the Philippines, Philippine law requires that the Articles be notarized and authenticated by a Philippine consul in the country where each incorporator is present at the time he signs the Articles.

EXAMPLE: Five investors seek to register a corporation in the Philippines, and each acts as an incorporator. During the corporation registration process, the Articles are distributed to the five incorporators for signature, and one of the incorporators is in Mexico. In this situation, such incorporator would be required to have his signature on the document notarized and authenticated at the Philippine Embassy or consul in Mexico.

In most cases, this logistical problem is solved by designating Philippine-based individuals to act as incorporators, who will thereafter assign the shares to the ultimate shareholders of the corporation.

6. Principal Office

A corporation is required to provide the exact address in the Philippines where its principal address is to be located.

When applying for BIR registration and business permit registration, the applicant will be required to submit one of the following as proof of the location of the corporation's principal office:

i.   Proof of ownership of the office space

ii. A lease contract

iii. A certificate by the owner of the office premises confirming his permission for the applicant to use the office space as its place of business

7. Articles of Incorporation and Bylaws

The Articles set forth the basic corporation information such as the number of directors on the board, the requirements for director and shareholder meetings, what constitutes a quorum, as well as other relevant information.

A standard form of the Articles is available at the SEC. Most applicants use such standard form to avoid delays in the examination and evaluation by the SEC.

8. Capital Stock

The capital stock is the amount stated in the Articles to be subscribed and paid in by the shareholders, either in cash or non-cash assets (including labor and services). This may be contributed by the shareholders either at the time of registration or afterwards, provided that at least 25% of the shareholders' subscription is paid at the time of such subscription (see below).

Note that under Philippine law, all or a portion of the corporation's issued capital may be purchased using services rendered by a subscriber(s) to the corporation in good faith as consideration. In such cases, the value of the services must be ascertainable and based on the fair market value of the services. Future services are not allowed as consideration for share subscription.

EXAMPLE: An engineer constructs a building to be owned by the corporation. Instead of paying the engineer in cash, the directors of the company and the engineer may agree that the engineer receives newly issued shares as payment for those services. This is permissible under the law.

If the consideration for the shares issued to a shareholder is to be paid using a non-cash asset, its value must be equal to the value of the stocks issued. In such cases where non-cash assets are to be contributed, the shareholder will need approval of the valuation by the SEC.

EXAMPLE: Korean investors register a corporation in the Philippines and set its capital stock at PhP12million fully paid up. In the event that the corporation's initial shareholders wish to fund all or a portion of the capital stock using non-cash assets, they must receive advance approval from the SEC of the non-cash assets valuation in order to do so.

Note that Philippine law requires that at least 25% of the subscription of the capital stock be paid at the time of incorporation.

EXAMPLE: Chinese investors establish a corporation in the Philippines and subscribe to PhP10million of capital stock. In this situation, the corporation's initial shareholders would be required to pay into the company a minimum of PhP2.5million.

9. Minimum Capital

The minimum paid-in capital requirements applicable to foreign-held corporations are discussed in Chapter 27.

Also, note that higher paid-up capital requirements are applicable to corporations which participate in sectors such as commercial banks, insurance companies, investment houses, retail trade, and other specific industries.

10. Directors

Directors (minimum five, maximum fifteen) are responsible for the management of the corporation and owe fiduciary duties to the shareholders. Each director is required to hold at least one share of the corporation. Also, note that a majority of directors must be residents of the Philippines.

11. Filing Fees

The official filing fees payable to the SEC are discussed in Chapter 25.

12. Bank Accounts

As part of the incorporation process, the corporation is required to open a Treasurer-in-Trust account in the same bank where the paid-in capital is deposited.

A Treasurer-in-Trust account is established by the initial treasurer of the corporation by opening a bank account in his own name, in trust for the corporation, to which the paid-in capital will be remitted thereafter.

The bank will then be required to issue a certificate of deposit, which will be required to be submitted to the SEC as proof that the corporation has deposited the required amount in a bank.

Upon issuance of the SEC registration, the corporation may convert the Treasurer-in-Trust account into a regular savings or current account.

13. Public Access to Company Details

Note that after corporate registration is complete, details of the corporation such as the shareholders list, list of directors, Articles, corporation address, etc. will be kept on file by the SEC and accessible to the public.

14. Documentary Stamp Tax

At the conclusion of the registration process, the SEC will issue the Certificate of Incorporation. At such time the corporation will be required to pay a stamp tax equivalent to P1.00 for each P200, or fractional part thereof, of the corporation's subscribed capital stock. The payment of the stamp tax is due on the fifth day of the following month after the incorporation.

EXAMPLE: Swedish investors establish a corporation in the Philippines and subscribe to the capital stock of PhP20million. The SEC issues the corporation's Certificate of Incorporation on June 3rd. The stamp tax payable by the corporation would be calculated as follows:

PhP20million capital stock/200=PhP100,000 stamp tax payable.

Such amount would be payable by July 5.

Chapter 27

What Legal Issues Are Associated with Operating as a Foreign-Held Company?

For purposes of this chapter, a foreign company is defined as one formed, organized, or existing under any laws other than those of the Philippines. A corporation is also considered foreign if more than 40% of its capital is held by foreigners.

EXAMPLE: A company established in the US and owned by US citizens is considered a foreign company.

EXAMPLE: A Japanese company and a local Philippine company establish a joint venture company in the Philippines in which the Japanese company holds 45% of the shares, while the Philippine company holds the remaining 55%. This joint venture company would be classified as a foreign company.

This chapter discusses the rules applicable to foreign companies doing business in the Philippines.

1. License to Do Business Requirement

Foreign companies establishing either a subsidiary corporation, branch office, representative office, regional operating headquarters, or regional headquarters are required to obtain a license to do business from the Securities and Exchange Commission (SEC) prior to commencing operations (see Chapter 25).

2. Regulated Activities

Philippine law regulates the activities which foreign companies may engage in. There are certain activities which are reserved only to domestic companies wholly owned by citizens of the Philippines, and to companies which are considered as "Philippine nationals." In general, a company is considered a "Philippine national" if it is organized under the laws of the Philippines, and at least 60% of its capital stock outstanding and voting rights are held by citizens of the Philippines.

The list of business activities with the percentage of allowable foreign participation is set forth in www.doylesguideasia.com/philippines/chapter27/appendixa.

3. Capitalization Requirements

Generally, corporations registered in the Philippines which have foreign shareholdings exceeding 40% of the total shares (which have voting rights) and that meet the definition of a domestic market enterprise, are required to have a minimum paid-up registered capital of no less than US $200,000 or the equivalent thereof.

A domestic market enterprise is an enterprise that produces goods for sale or provides services to the domestic or local market entirely, or whose export sales consistently fail to represent at least 60% of total annual sales.

EXAMPLE: A UK company establishes a subsidiary corporation in the Philippines to produce thumb tacks; 55% of the thumb tacks produced are exported annually, while the remaining 45% are sold locally. In this situation, the corporation would be legally classified as a domestic market enterprise, and the subsidiary corporation would be required to have a paid-up registered capital of no less than US $200,000.

EXAMPLE: Several German investors and a Philippine investor enter into a joint venture agreement to establish a corporation in the Philippines which will produce furniture. They are committed to exporting 100% of their production abroad. In this situation, the joint venture corporation would not be required to have a minimum registered capital of US $200,000.

EXAMPLE: A US company establishes a corporation in the Philippines to engage in call center services, with 70% of its customers based abroad and the remaining 30% based locally. In this situation, the corporation would not be classified as a domestic market enterprise, and the minimum US $200,000 capital requirement would not apply.

Note, however, that Philippine law provides that corporations legally classified as foreign and falling under the legal classification of a domestic market enterprise, may have the minimum registered capital requirement reduced from US $200,000 to US $100,000, if the corporation utilizes advanced technology (as determined by the Philippine Department of Science and Technology) or employs a minimum of fifty direct employees.

EXAMPLE: Japanese investors establish a company in the Philippines which falls under the legal classification of a domestic market enterprise. The company then employs 150 workers. In this situation, the company will be required to have a minimum registered capital of US $100,000.

EXAMPLE: Swiss investors establish a domestic market enterprise company in the Philippines to perform product research and development. If the Philippine Department of Science and Technology determines that this corporation utilizes advanced technology, the company's minimum registered capital is US $100,000.

In general, foreign companies are not allowed to engage in retail trade activities, except where the foreign company

i.   has paid-up capital of at least US $2,500,000, provided that the investment per store is not less than US $830,000 or

ii. specializes in high end or luxury products, provided that the paid-up capital per store is not less than US $250,000.

4. Nominee Shareholders

Generally, nominee shareholders are individuals or companies that agree to hold shares on behalf of the true owner(s) of the shares. In a typical nominee arrangement, the nominee shareholder and the true owner will execute an agreement which provides that the nominee shareholder agrees to hold the shares in the nominee's name only, but the true owner retains all rights of ownership and control (voting rights, rights of transfer, receiving dividends, etc.) of the shares.

However, under Philippine law, any similar type of arrangement which aims to circumvent legal restrictions on the foreign ownership of shares in a corporation is prohibited, and both the guilty foreign and Philippine parties may be subjected to a fine of not less than five thousand pesos and imprisonment of not less than five or more than fifteen years. This law is referred to as the Anti Dummy Law.

EXAMPLE: A French investor seeks to establish a wholly owned corporation in the Philippines for the purpose of purchasing land in the Philippines. The French investor then enters into an arrangement with a Philippine party for the Philippine party to hold the shares of the corporation on the French investor's behalf, as a way of enabling the corporation to acquire land. In this situation, both the foreign investor and the Philippine party would be guilty of violating the Anti Dummy Law and would be subject to fine and/or imprisonment.

Chapter 28

What Is the Process to Obtain a Work Permit?

Foreigners seeking to work in the Philippines are generally required to obtain a working visa and an alien employment permit prior to starting work.

This chapter discusses the requirements and application procedures to obtain a working visa and employment permit.

1. Entry to the Philippines

Foreigners seeking to visit and subsequently work in the Philippines may be admitted under either of the following procedures:

"Restricted" nationals, which include nationals from the People's Republic of China and India, are required to obtain an entry visa from the Philippine embassy or consulate in their country of nationality or place of residence prior to their entry to the Philippines.

Foreigners who are not classified as "restricted" by the Department of Foreign Affairs (DFA) may enter the Philippines without a visa and are granted upon arrival an authorized stay of twenty-one days. Such period of stay may, upon request, be extended to one to two months at one time, but not to exceed an aggregate period of one year.

2. Visa Conversion

Following their arrival in the Philippines, foreigners may apply for the conversion of their visa status from that of a temporary visitor to any of the several categories of working visas (see below). When a foreigner applies for visa conversion, he will not be required to leave the Philippines, and in the meantime, may work pending the approval of the working visa and alien employment permit, subject to obtaining a Special Work Permit (SWP) from the Bureau of Immigration (BI).

However, note that the DFA prohibits certain nationalities (e.g. Indians and Chinese) from converting their temporary visitor's visas into working visas. Instead, the DFA requires the employer in the Philippines to apply for a working visa for its prospective foreign employee prior to the foreign employee's entry into the Philippines.

EXAMPLE: A UK national arrives in the Philippines without a visa for the purpose of employment with a Philippine corporation. In this situation, the UK national would be able to apply for a working visa without having to leave the country.

EXAMPLE: Same facts as above, but instead the employee is a Chinese national. In this situation, the Philippine corporation would be required to apply for the working permit on the Chinese national's behalf prior to his arrival into the Philippines.

3. Special Working Permit

Foreigners planning to work in the Philippines for a period of less than six months may apply for a Special Working Permit (SWP) in order to allow them to work in the Philippines without the need to obtain a working visa.

A SWP is valid for a period of three months and is renewable for the same period of time. A person with a SWP is required to maintain a valid tourist visa while in the Philippines. Holders of SWPs are exempted from securing an Alien Employment Permit from the Department of Labor and Employment (see below).

The processing time for a SWP is two weeks.

4. Working Visas

For foreigners who will be working in the Philippines for more than six months, the most common types of working visas applied for are the pre-arranged employment visa, treaty trader visa, PEZA/BOI visa, and the multiple entry special non-immigrant visa.

The factors which determine which working visa is the most appropriate for the foreign employee in a given situation include the structure of the employer corporation and its activities, the corporation's location, and the nationality of the foreign employee, as discussed below.

a. Pre-Arranged Employment Visa

The Pre-arranged Employment Visa, (also known as the 9g visa), is the most common type of working visa and is available to foreigners employed in any lawful occupation where a valid employer-employee relationship exists.

Examples of professions in which foreign employees potentially qualify to receive a Pre-arranged Employment Visa include professors and teachers working in educational institutions, doctors and nurses working in hospitals, scientists working in research facilities, and foreign professionals and employees working at banks and industrial, agricultural, and other business enterprises.

The documents required when applying for a Pre-arranged Employment Visa at the BI are as follows:

i.   General Application Form (BI Form No. MCL-07-01)

ii. Completed and notarized letter from the employer requesting to employ the foreigner

iii. Applicant's Alien Employment Permit (see section below) certified by the Philippine Department of Labor

iv. Foreigner's BI Clearance Certificate

v.   Photocopy of the identification page of the foreigner's passport and admission stamp showing that the foreigner is authorized to stay in the Philippines for at least twenty calendar days after the date of filing the visa application with the BI

The employer in the Philippines is required to submit the above listed documents on the employee's behalf and pay the applicable filing fees. The BI is technically supposed to rule on the application within one month of the time of filing of the application, but the actual period may be longer.

If the application is approved by the BI, the Pre-arranged Employment Visa will be stamped in the foreigner's passport.

In the event that the foreign employee's spouse and/or unmarried minor children are to accompany the foreign employee to the Philippines, the following documents are required to be submitted to the BI, together with the foreign employee's application, in order to receive a 9g visa for the dependent(s):

i.   Copy of marriage certificate of the foreign employee and spouse, which shall be certified or authenticated by the Philippine Embassy or Consulate in or nearest to the place where the marriage ceremony occurred, submitted together with an English translation (if prepared in a language other than English)

    ii. Copy of birth certificates of minor, unmarried children, certified or authenticated by the Philippine Embassy or Consulate in or nearest to the dependent's place of birth, submitted with an English translation (if prepared in a language other than English)

    iii. Photocopy of the identification page of the passport of the foreign employee's accompanying spouse and/or dependents and admission stamp showing an authorized stay of at least twenty calendar days after the date of filing with the BI

Note that Pre-arranged Employment Visa holders are also required to secure an Alien Certificate of Registration ID Card (ACR I-Card). The ACR I-Card is a microchip-based credit card-sized identification card issued to registered foreigners containing personal information such as name, age, date and place of birth. The ACR I-Card must be presented every time the foreigner travels in and out of the Philippines.

b. Treaty Trader Visa

The Treaty Trader Visa, (also known as the 9d visa), is only available to citizens of Japan, the US, and Germany.

The Treaty Trader Visa is issued to foreigners who seek to enter the Philippines solely for the purpose of developing and directing the operations of a business in the Philippines, in which either the foreign applicant or his employer outside the Philippines has already invested or is actively in the process of investing a substantial amount of capital.

EXAMPLE: A German investor makes a substantial investment in a corporation in the Philippines and seeks to move to the Philippines to manage the corporation. Using these facts, if the German investor otherwise qualifies, he would be eligible to receive a Treaty Trader Visa.

EXAMPLE: Same facts, but the investor is from Ireland. The investor would not qualify for a Treaty Trader Visa as only citizens of Japan, the US, and Germany qualify to receive such visa.

Note that it is required that the foreigner's employer must be a foreign person or organization of the same nationality as the foreign employee, and the foreigner must be assigned to the Philippine company where the investment is made.

EXAMPLE: A Japanese company makes a substantial investment in a Philippine corporation and seeks to send a US national to manage the corporation. In this situation, the US individual would not qualify for a Treaty Trader Visa as the nationalities of the employer and the employee are different.

The documents required for a corporation in the Philippines to apply for the Treaty Trader Visa on behalf of the foreign employee are as follows:

i. Notarized letter from the employer requesting that the foreign employee be allowed to enter the Philippines for the purpose of employment

ii. General Application Form duly completed by the applicant and notarized (BI Form No. MCL-07-01)

iii. If the employer is a corporation or partnership in the Philippines, one certified copy of the corporation's Certificate of Registration issued by the Securities and Exchange Commission, Articles of Incorporation, By-Laws, and General Information Sheet

iv. If the employer is a single proprietorship in the Philippines, one certified copy of the Certificate of Registration of the Business Name issued by the Department of Trade and Industry

v. Certified copy of the corporation's latest Income Tax Return and Audited Financial Statements, stamped "RECEIVED" by the Bureau of Internal Revenue

vi. Photocopy of identification page and visa stamp page of the employee's passport

vii. Original notarized contract of employment or Corporate Secretary's Certificate of Election of the employee as a corporate officer, with details of exact compensation and period of employment

viii. BI Clearance Certificate of the employee

If the applicant is to be accompanied by his spouse and/or unmarried minor children, the following documents will also be required to be submitted to the BI:

i. Copy of marriage certificate of the foreign employee and spouse, certified or authenticated by the Philippine Embassy or Consulate in or nearest to the place where the marriage ceremony took place, with an English translation (if prepared in a language other than English)

ii. Copy of birth certificates of minor, unmarried children, certified or authenticated by the Philippine Embassy or Consulate in or nearest to the country of birth, submitted with an English translation (if prepared in a language other than English)

iii. Photocopy of the identification page of the passports of the foreign national's spouse and/or children and admission stamp showing an authorized stay of at least twenty calendar days after the date of filing

The applicable time frame and procedure to obtain the Treaty Trader Visa from the BI are the same as the time frame and procedure applicable to obtain a Pre-arranged Employment Visa (see previous section).

Note that Treaty Trader Visa holders are also required to secure an ACR I-Card.

c. PEZA and BOI Visas

The PEZA and BOI Visas (also known as 47a2 visas), are issued to foreign nationals employed as officers or those holding supervisory, technical, or advisory positions with Philippine corporations which are registered with the Philippine Economic Zone (PEZA) or the Board of Investments (BOI). This visa can also be issued to foreign employees temporarily assigned to work on government projects.

EXAMPLE: Australian investors establish a corporation in the Philippines which is registered for incentives with the BOI and employs a UK national to be the corporation's managing director. In this situation, the UK national would likely apply for a BOI visa.

The following are the documents required to be submitted to the PEZA or BOI (as applicable), in order to apply for either a PEZA Visa or BOI Visa:

i.   Valid passport of the foreign employee and his dependents

ii.   PEZA or BOI application form

iii. Department of Justice (DOJ) application form

iv.   PEZA or BOI endorsement

v.   Declaration by the employer of the number of foreign and Filipino employees

vi.   Copy of the employment contract

vii. Original Marriage Certificate for dependent spouse of the foreign employee, if applicable

viii. Birth certificate(s) of dependent child(ren) of the foreign employee, if applicable

ix.   Affidavit of support and guaranty of return fare for foreign employee's dependents by the employer, if applicable

x.   Signed curriculum vitae of the foreigner

xi.   Organizational chart of the corporation

xii. Affidavit of support in favor of foreigner

After the above described documents are found to be in order and the filing fee paid, the application is then forwarded to the Department of Justice (DOJ) for endorsement.

If approved by the DOJ, the application and supporting documents are then forwarded to the BI for issuance of the visa. The application is then forwarded to the PEZA or BOI (as applicable) for further processing before notifying the foreign employee that the application has been approved.

BOI Visa holders are required to secure an ACR I-Card while PEZA Visa holders are exempted from securing the ACR I-Card.

d. Multiple Entry Special Non-Immigrant Visa

The multiple entry special non-immigrant visa, also known as the EO 226 visa, (multiple entry visa) is available to foreign personnel of offshore banking units or regional or area headquarters of multinational companies, and their respective spouses and minor dependents under twenty-one years of age. A multiple entry visa is valid for one year and may be extended upon meeting certain conditions.

The requirements for a multiple entry visa are as follows:

i.   Notarized letter request by a responsible officer of the company intending to engage the foreign national applicant

ii. Notarized and completed general application form

iii. Photocopy of the relevant pages of the applicant's passport containing the latest arrival or updated stay

iv. Copy of the company's Certificate of Registration issued by the Securities and Exchange Commission

v.   Notarized contract of employment

vi. Certification from the employer

vii. BI Clearance Certificate

Multiple entry visa holders are exempted from the requirement of securing the ACR I-Card.

5. Alien Employment Permit

An Alien Employment Permit (AEP) is issued by the Philippine Department of Labor and Employment (DOLE) and authorizes foreign nationals to engage in lawful employment or remunerated activity in the Philippines.

An AEP is required for foreigners who are issued the Pre-arranged Employment Visa, a Treaty Trader Visa, and the PEZA and BOI Visas.

The general rule is that all foreign nationals allowed to work in the Philippines are required to apply for and obtain an AEP before starting work, subject to the following exceptions:

i.   All members of the diplomatic service and foreign government officials accredited by and with a reciprocity arrangement with the Philippine government

ii. Officers and staff of international organizations of which the Philippine government is a member and their lawful spouses

iii. Foreign nationals elected as members of the Governing Board of any company, who do not occupy any other position, and have only voting rights on the Governing Board of the corporation

iv. Owners and representatives of foreign investors whose companies are accredited by the Philippine Overseas Employment Administration, who come to the Philippines for a limited period and solely for the purpose of interviewing Filipino applicants for employment abroad

v.   Foreign nationals who come to the Philippines to teach, present and/or conduct research studies in universities and colleges as visiting, exchange, or adjunct professors under formal agreements between the universities or colleges in the Philippines and foreign universities or colleges, or between the Philippine government and the foreign government, provided that the exemption is on a reciprocal basis

vi. Resident foreign nationals

vii. All other foreign nationals granted exemption by law

Note that pre-arranged employment visa applicants may work upon the filing of the AEP application.

Applications for an AEP are submitted to the DOLE Regional Office having jurisdiction over the intended place of work. The following documents are required to be submitted to the DOLE:

i.   Completed application form

ii. Photocopy of passport, with visa

iii. Contract of Employment/Appointment or Board Secretary's Certificate of Election

iv. Photocopy of Mayor's Permit to operate business

v.   Photocopy of current AEP (if renewal application)

The AEP is normally issued one week after the application is completed and government fees paid. The AEP will normally be valid for one year, but in any event, for not more than five years.

A foreign national whose application for AEP has been denied, cancelled, or revoked will not be allowed to re-apply unless he provides proof that the grounds for denial, cancellation, or revocation have been corrected.

Chapter 29

What Investment Incentives Are Available to Foreign Investors?

The agencies of the Philippine government responsible for attracting specific types of investments include the Board of Investments (BOI), Philippine Economic Zone Authority Subic Bay, Metropolitan Authority, and the Clark Development Corporation. Each of these agencies may grant investment incentives if the foreign investor engages in specific areas of promoted activities and/or locates its project in designated areas.

Below is a description of the investment incentives made available by each agency, as well as the corresponding application procedures.

1. Board of Investments

Qualifying foreign investors investing in promoted activities (see below) may apply with the BOI to receive various incentives.

Investors seeking to receive BOI promotion are required to submit a completed application and supporting documents and pay the filing fee.

To see the application go to www.doylesguideasia.com/philippines/chapter 29/appendixa. The application normally takes one to two months and, if successful, the BOI will issue a Certificate of Registration to the applicant.

a. Tax Exemptions

The BOI has authority to grant qualifying companies income tax exemptions for the following periods:

i.   Six years for new projects granted pioneer status (see below)

ii. Six years for projects locating in less developed areas, regardless of status (pioneer or non-pioneer) or type of project (new or expansion) (see below)

iii. Four years for new projects granted non-pioneer status

iv. Three years for expansion and modernization projects

These tax exemption periods are to commence on the project's target starting date or the project's actual starting date, whichever occurs first (but in no case prior to the date of BOI approval).

EXAMPLE: A French company establishes a presence in the Philippines and applies for and receives pioneer status (see below) with the BOI. In its application to the BOI, the French company states the target starting date for the project as May 1st. The application was approved by the BOI on February 1st, and its actual starting date is July 1st in the next year. Using these facts, the French company's tax holiday would begin on May 1st.

i. Pioneer Status

Pioneer status is available to projects whose final products involve substantial use and processing of domestic raw materials from the Philippines:

i. The project manufactures, processes or produces, (not merely assembles and/or packages) goods, products, commodities, or raw materials which have not been or are not being produced in the Philippines on a commercial scale.

ii. The project uses a design, formula, scheme, method, process or system of production that transforms any element, substance, or raw materials into another raw material or finished goods which is new and untried in the Philippines.

iii. The project pursues agricultural, forestry, and mining activities and/or services, including the industrial aspects of food processing.

iv. The project produces non-conventional fuels or manufacturing equipment which utilizes non-conventional sources of energy; or uses or converts to coal or other non-conventional fuels or sources of energy in its production, manufacturing, or processing operations.

When considering applications for pioneer status, the BOI takes into consideration the risks and magnitude of investment by the investors engaged in any of the above activities.

EXAMPLE: A joint venture between an Australian company and a Philippine company develops a multimillion dollar project in the Philippines to produce crude palm oil by using local raw materials, and they apply with the BOI for Pioneer status. Using these facts, the project will likely be granted pioneer status by the BOI and, therefore, qualify for a six-year tax exemption.

ii. Investment in Less Developed Areas

The Philippine government encourages investment in the country's less developed areas and poorest provinces (Less Developed Areas) by granting tax incentives to those who will invest there.

To see a complete list of all the provinces in the Less Developed Areas go to www.doylesguideasia.com/philippines/chapter29/appendixb.

New projects (whether pioneer, non-pioneer, or those located in Less Developed Areas) which qualify under any one of the following three criteria may receive bonus years for income tax exemption, not to exceed an aggregate of eight years:

i.   The project meets the prescribed ratio of capital investment in equipment to number of workers as set by the BOI (not to exceed US $10,000 per one worker).

EXAMPLE: A Korean company establishes a factory in Sulu province to produce auto parts and pursues the eight-year maximum tax exemption with the BOI. The BOI states that in order to qualify for the eight-year tax exemption, the project will be required to have the ratio of its investment in capital equipment to number of factory workers at US $10,000 for every one worker. The project will employ twenty factory workers. In this situation, the amount of investment in capital equipment required for the project to qualify to receive the tax exemption for eight years would be US $200,000.

ii.   The project utilizes indigenous raw materials in the Philippines at a percentage set by the BOI, which will be at least 50% of the total cost of raw materials during the promotion period.

EXAMPLE: A Swiss food producer establishes a factory in Ifugao province and seeks to obtain the maximum tax exemption available by the BOI for the project. The BOI states that in order to receive an eight-year maximum tax exemption, a minimum of 70% of its total cost of raw materials used in production must be from indigenous materials.

iii. The project has an annual net foreign exchange savings or earnings of at least US $500,000 per year during its first three years of operation.

EXAMPLE: A Japanese producer of office supplies establishes a factory in Aurora province and has revenue exceeding US $1.1 million (all earned from export sales) in each of its first three years of operation. In this situation, the project would likely qualify for a eight-year tax exemption.

Enterprises registered with the BOI may also receive the benefit of customs duty exemptions for specified imported items. These items include required supplies and spare parts, not locally available at reasonable prices, sufficient quantity, and comparable quality. They also include those items imported tax and duty-free by a registered enterprise with a bonded manufacturing warehouse.

b. Additional Tax Deductions

An additional income tax deduction representing 50% of the wages paid to skilled and unskilled project workers may also be granted by BOI if the project meets the prescribed ratio of investment in capital equipment to the number of project workers, and the project is not related to mining or forestry.

This incentive may not be granted simultaneously with an income tax holiday.

EXAMPLE: A Dutch investor registers a corporation and establishes a factory to produce vacuum cleaner parts just outside of Manila. The BOI advises that in order for the project to receive an additional income tax deduction of an amount representing 50% of the wages paid to its staff, the corporation is required to maintain a ratio of US $1.5 million of capital equipment to one worker.

This additional deduction is doubled if the activity is located in Less Developed Areas.

EXAMPLE: Same facts as above, but the project is located in Tawi-tawi province. In this situation, the project would qualify to receive an additional income tax deduction up to 100% of the wages paid (instead of only up to 50% as stated above).

c. Additional Incentives

BOI registered companies are likewise allowed to employ foreigners for supervisory, technical, and advisor positions for a period not exceeding five years from the time of the company's registration with the BOI. This employment period may be extended subject to the BOI's discretion. (For the normal rules applicable to employing foreigners see Chapter 28.)

Additional incentives available to BOI registered companies include

i.   simplified customs procedures for the importation of equipment, spare parts, raw materials and supplies, and exports of processed products by registered enterprises

ii.   access to the utilization of the bonded warehousing system in all areas required by the project (subject to such guidelines as may be issued by the BOI upon consultation with the Philippine Bureau of Customs)

2. Enterprises Registered with Special Economic Zone Authorities

Location-specific incentives are available to enterprises operating in the following areas (known as the Ecozones) and registered with the listed special economic zone authorities:

i.   Bases Conversion and Development Authority

ii.   Subic Bay Metropolitan Authority

iii. Clark Development Corporation

iv.   Philippine Economic Zone Authority

v.   Zamboanga City Special Economic Zone Authority

vi.   Aurora Special Economic Zone Authority

vii. Cagayan Economic Zone Authority

Some of the major incentives available to projects locating in Ecozones include the following:

i.   Net operating loss carry-over

ii.   Accelerated depreciation

iii. Exemption from export tax

iv.   Exemption from local taxes and licenses

Chapter 30

What Legal Issues Are Associated with Foreign Ownership of Land?

Foreigners are, as a general rule, prohibited from owning land in the Philippines, except as stated below.

1. Condominium Ownership

Philippine law allows foreign individuals and foreign-held companies to purchase and own condominium units, provided that title to the common areas is held by a corporation and foreign interest in the condominium corporation does not exceed 40% as further explained below.

a. Title to the Common Areas, Including the Land, Is Held by a Condominium Corporation, Not by the Condominium Owners Directly

EXAMPLE: A UK individual seeks to purchase a condominium unit in Manila in a building in which the land, the swimming area, lobby, and other common areas are all held proportionally by the unit owners. In this situation, the UK individual would not be allowed to purchase the unit.

If the common areas are held by a condominium corporation, Philippine law requires that owners of units in the condominium development automatically become shareholders of the condominium corporation in the same proportion to their ownership interests in the common areas.

EXAMPLE: A Singaporean holds 16% of the total sellable space in a condominium building, and therefore, has a corresponding 16% interest in the common areas. Under Philippine law, he would automatically be a 16% shareholder of the condominium corporation.

b. Foreign Interest in the Condominium Corporation Does Not Exceed 40%

EXAMPLE: A large condominium development is established with a condominium corporation as the owner of all of the development's common areas. The shareholding of the condominium corporation and ownership of the units in the development is as follows: US 15%, UK 10%, Japanese 15%, Philippine 60%. Later, a Philippine shareholder attempts to sell condominium units representing 5% of his shareholding in the condominium corporation to the US shareholder. Such transfer would not be permissible because the foreign interest would become more than 40%.

However, if the condominium project is located on leased land (not owned by the condominium corporation), the condominium corporation may be wholly owned by foreign investors.

EXAMPLE: Same facts as above, but the land upon which the condominium development is located is leased (not owned) by the condominium corporation. In this situation, the transfer by the Philippine shareholder to the US shareholder would be permissible.

2. Land Ownership by Foreign Companies

Under Philippine law, only corporations in which foreigners hold no more than 40% of the total corporation shares may own land.

EXAMPLE: A Philippine registered corporation in which Korean shareholders hold 41% percent of the shares seeks to purchase land. This would not be legally permitted (see Chapter 27).

Note that under Philippine law, foreigners and locals who enter into an arrangement to circumvent the above rule are subject to prosecution and criminal penalties.

EXAMPLE: A US citizen seeks to buy land in the Philippines and makes an arrangement with a Philippine citizen whereby the US citizen will pay for and make use of the land, but the land will be registered in the name of the Philippine citizen as the US citizen's nominee. This arrangement is considered unlawful and may subject both the US investor and the Filipino nominee to prosecution and criminal penalties.

3. Title Search

The legal status of land title is accessible to the general public and may be verified with the Register of Deeds where the land is located. Any interested individual may conduct a title search to determine the status of the land title, the land area, and whether or not there are registered liens, leases, and other encumbrances.

4. Lease of Private Lands

While foreigners are not allowed to own land, foreigners are allowed to lease private (not government owned) land.

a. Lease for Commercial Purpose

Under Philippine law, a foreigner who makes certain kinds of equity investments in the Philippines may enter into a long-term lease of private land for a commercial purpose for a period not exceeding fifty years, which may be renewed once for a period not exceeding twenty-five years.

The lease should be in connection with the establishment of industrial estates, factories, assembly or processing plants, agro-industrial enterprises, land development for tourism, industrial or commercial use, and/or other similar purposes.

Note here that "investment" means making an equity investment in the Philippines through actual remittance of foreign exchange or transfer of assets, whether in the form of capital goods, patents, formulae, or other technological rights or processes.

EXAMPLE: A Japanese individual forms a wholly owned subsidiary corporation in the Philippines to establish a semi-conductor manufacturing facility, and thereafter, leases private land in the Philippines for the manufacturing facility. Using these facts, the maximum period the Japanese individual would be allowed to lease the land would be fifty years, and at the end of such term, the lease would be renewable for an additional period of twenty-five years.

If, however, the foreigner does not invest in the Philippines, the foreigner may still lease private land for an initial term of twenty-five years and renew it for a term of twenty-five years. The lease may be for a commercial, residential (see below), or any other purpose.

EXAMPLE: Same facts as above, but the Japanese individual makes no equity investment in the Philippines. In this situation, the maximum lease period legally permissible would be twenty-five years, and it would be renewable for an additional twenty-five year period.

b. Lease for Residential Purpose

Foreigners are allowed to lease private land for a residential purpose for a total term of twenty-five years, which is renewable once for an additional twenty-five year period.

EXAMPLE: A Japanese man wishes to rent land with a house outside Manila from the owner. He would be legally allowed to rent the land for twenty-five years and renew the lease for another twenty-five years.

EXAMPLE: A Swiss national leases a condominium owned by a Philippine national in a condominium development which already has the legal limit of foreign ownership at 40% (see Section 1 above). This would be permissible because he is leasing, not seeking ownership.

Thailand

Capital City	Bangkok
Major Financial Center	Bangkok
Population (projected 2010)	65 million
Location	Southeastern Asia, bordering the Andaman Sea and the Gulf of Thailand, southeast of Burma
Major Languages	Thai
Legal System	Civil law
Square Miles	198,115 sq mi
Gross Domestic Product (projected 2010)	USD 280 billion
Major Exports	Food including rice, seafood and live animals, office equipment, textiles and clothing, rubber
Currency	Baht (THB)
U.S. Dollar Exchange Rate (as of November 2009)	USD 1 = THB 33.5699
Euro Exchange Rate (as of November 2009)	EUR 1 = THB 49.7483

Section Author
Michael Doyle
Partner
Seri Manop and Doyle Ltd.
Email: michael@serimanop.com
Website: http://www.serimanop.com

Chapter 31

Should Our Business Establish as a Company Limited, Branch, Representative Office, or Regional Office?

One of the first issues faced by prospective investors in Thailand is choosing the appropriate type of legal structure through which to operate their business. The most commonly used of the structures available are company limited, branch, representative office, and regional office.

When choosing the structure that is appropriate for your business you should consider a number of factors, including these issues:

i.   Capital requirements
ii. The intended business activities to be pursued
iii. Liability issues
iv. Tax treatment

The chart on the next page compares these, as well as other aspects of company limited, branch, representative office, and regional offices.

1. Company Limited

The private company structure (company) in Thailand is similar to a Limited Liability Company (LLC) structure in the US and is the most utilized type of legal entity in Thailand.

A company is owned by shareholders (minimum three) and managed by directors (minimum one). The liability of each of the shareholders is generally limited to the total par value of their shares. The shareholders' direct

Comparison Chart

	Company Limited	Branch	Representative Office	Regional Office
Minimum Investment Required	No minimum investment (unless foreign and engages in List 2 or List 3 activities)	At least 25% of the average estimated expenses for 1st 3 years but not less than 3 million baht	At least 25% of the average estimated expenses for 1st 3 years but not less than 3 million baht	At least 25% of the average estimated expenses for 1st 3 years but not less than 3 million baht
Shareholders	Yes, minimum 3	No	No	No
Activities	Generally any lawful activity (unless foreign)	Generally limited to activities stated in Foreign Business License	Limited to 5 specific activities specified by statute	Limited to 7 specific activities specified by statute
Income	Can receive	Can receive	Cannot receive	Cannot receive
Legal Liability	Separate liability	No separate liability	No separate liability	No separate liability
Tax Liability	Subject to normal tax rules	Subject to normal tax rules	Not subject to corporate income tax with exception of an interest accrued on funds received from head office	Not subject to corporate income tax with exception of an interest accrued on funds received from head office

participation in company affairs is normally quite limited. It is the directors who are responsible for managing company affairs and who owe various fiduciary duties to the shareholders and the company (duty of care, duty of loyalty, etc.).

Unlike a branch, representative office, and regional office, a company limited is treated under Thai law as a stand-alone legal entity.

EXAMPLE: If a multinational wishes to establish a subsidiary in Thailand it will likely do so as a privately held company. If individual investors wish to establish a stand-alone business to generate income in Thailand, they will most likely do so as a company.

EXAMPLE: Suppose a multinational establishes a wholly owned subsidiary in Thailand as a company limited. That new company limited then executes a contract with another Thailand company to supply auto parts, but then fails to supply those parts. In this situation, the Thailand purchaser would generally be limited to suing the Thailand subsidiary for the breach of contract, not its headquarters overseas.

2. Branch, Representative Office, and Regional Office

Many times, however, foreign investors will not want to operate as a company limited. This is most likely to be true when a multinational company seeks to establish a presence in Thailand, but does not wish to establish a separate legal entity. For accounting, tax, and other reasons, the multinational company may instead want the Thailand office to function as a part of the head office overseas. If that is the case, the multinational will normally choose to establish a representative office, branch office, or regional office, not a company limited.

Thai law treats each of these three entities as extensions of the head office overseas, not as separate legal entities. The employees are the employees of the overseas company.

Thai law requires that each of these three must employ an office manager who resides in Thailand. Such office managers may be either Thai or foreign.

a. Branch

In many ways the branch structure is very similar to that of the company limited. Both are allowed to earn income in Thailand, and similar tax rules apply to both. Also, the rules governing the activities of a branch are the same as the rules governing the activities of a foreign-held company limited.

It is with issues concerning liability where the branch and company limited structures fundamentally differ. For a company limited, liability arising from the actions of the business or its employees is generally limited to the Thailand company only. The same is not true for a branch. Thai law treats a branch as merely an extension of its head office overseas.

EXAMPLE: Suppose that the multinational establishes a branch (instead of a company limited), and the branch enters into the same contract to supply auto parts and fails to perform. The Thailand purchaser could then sue the head office of the multinational directly.

b. Representative Office and Regional Office

The representative office and regional office structures are very different from those of the branch office and company limited. Unlike a branch or company limited, representative offices and regional offices are not allowed to earn income. Just as with a branch, representative offices and regional offices merely serve as extensions of their head offices overseas. They are not stand-alone legal entities. They are also strictly regulated to performing specific functions designated by statute on behalf of their head offices overseas.

A representative office is limited to the following activities:

i.   Sourcing goods or services in Thailand for the head office

ii. Checking and controlling the quality and quantity of goods purchased or hired to be manufactured in Thailand by the head office

iii. Giving advice concerning goods of the head office sold to agents or consumers

iv. Propagation of information concerning new goods or services of the head office

v.   Reporting on business trends in Thailand to the head office

A regional office is limited to the following activities:

i.   Communicating, coordinating, and directing, on behalf of the head office, the operation of branches and affiliates that are located in the region

ii. Providing services in consulting and management

iii. Training and personnel development

iv. Financial management

v.   Marketing control and sales promotion planning

vi.   Product development

vii. Services in research and development

It is also required that the regional office's head office must have at least one other branch or affiliate in the Asia region.

These are some of the specific restrictions applicable to both representative offices and regional offices:

i.   Non revenue-generating activities only.

ii.   No authority to accept purchase orders, make offers to sell, or nego-tiate to carry out business with individuals or businesses in the coun-try where its head office is located.

iii. All expenditures incurred must be borne by the head office.

iv.   Not subject to corporate income tax with the exception of interest ac-crued from funds received from the head office.

To see a list of further activities both representative offices and regional of-fices are specifically prohibited from engaging in go to www.doylesguideasia.com/thailand/chapter31/appendixa.

3. Capital Required

The rules governing the amount of investment required for a company lim-ited are presented in Chapters 32 and 33.

The rules governing the amount of investment required for a branch, rep-resentative office, and a regional office are all the same. The investment by the head office for each of the three must be at least 25% of the average estimated operating expenses for the first three years, but in any event, not less than 3 mil-lion baht.

EXAMPLE: Suppose a Japanese company decides to establish a branch in Thai-land. The Japanese head office estimates that the operating expenses of the branch for the first three years will be as follows:

12 million baht (Year One)

13 million baht (Year Two)

14 million baht (Year Three)

39 million baht total estimated expenses during 1st three years

39 million / 3 years = 13 million baht average

13 million baht x 25% = 3.25 million baht minimum capital

Thai law also specifies a schedule as to when the capital must be remitted into Thailand by the head office. At least 25% of the total minimum capital must be remitted within the first three months of operation, and an additional 25% of the minimum capital must be remitted within its first year of operation. A minimum of 25% of the minimum capital must be remitted in Year Two, and the remaining 25% within Year Three.

EXAMPLE: Using the branch in the above example, its minimum capital of 3.25 million baht would be required to be remitted into Thailand according to the following schedule:

812,500 baht (25%) within first three months of operation
812,500 baht (25%) within Year One
812,500 baht (25%) within Year Two
812,500 baht (25%) within Year Three
3.25 million baht

The law also sets forth minimum requirements as to the capital required. As stated above, the minimum amount of investment capital required is calculated based on the average of the estimated operating expenses for the office for its first three years of operation. The law specifies, however, that this figure may *not* be less than 3 million baht.

EXAMPLE: Let's change the facts so that the head office in Japan estimates that the Thailand branch's operating expenses over the first three years are as follows:

1 million baht (Year One)
2 million baht (Year Two)
3 million baht (Year Three)
6 million baht total estimated expenses during 1st three years
6 million baht / 3 years = 2 million baht average

However, because the three-year average (2 million baht) is below the minimum capital required (3 million baht) such figure would be adjusted up to 3 million baht. The head office would be required to remit such amount into Thailand according to the following schedule:

750,000 baht (25%) within first three months of operation
750,000 baht (25%) within Year One
750,000 baht (25%) within Year Two
750,000 baht (25%) within Year Three
3 million baht total

For each of the three types of offices, the ratio of the business's investment capital to its total loans may not exceed seven to one.

EXAMPLE: If the business's capital is 10 million baht, the business's total loans may not exceed 70 million baht.

4. Registration and Official Fees

The procedure to register a company limited is presented in Chapter 32.

There is no registration procedure required for a branch, representative office, or regional office; however, each will be subject to the rules associated with operating as a foreign business (see Chapter 33).

The official fees payable to the Ministry of Commerce (MOC) for each of the three types of offices are calculated in the same way and are based upon the amount of the head office's registered capital. The official fee is 5 baht for every 1,000 baht of the head office's registered capital, with the minimum fee payable 20,000 baht and the maximum fee payable 250,000 baht (a fraction of capital of 1,000 baht is treated as 1,000 baht).

EXAMPLE: A German company seeks to establish a representative office in Thailand. The German company has a registered capital of the equivalent of 8 million baht. The official fee payable to the MOC upon registering the representative office would be 40,000 baht.

Each of the three types of offices will also be required to obtain a Tax ID Card, and a branch also may be required to obtain a VAT (Value Added Tax) Certificate, depending upon the activities it is to engage in.

Chapter 32

What Legal Issues Are Associated with the Start-Up of a Foreign-Held Company?

There are several legal and practical issues associated with the legal start-up of a private company limited (company). The start-up process involves registration with the Ministry of Commerce (MOC), obtaining the company's Tax ID card, and VAT Certificate, if required (from the Revenue Department), as well as obtaining other government licenses and approvals that may be required, depending upon the business activities the company seeks to engage in. Note that shelf companies are not readily available in Thailand, so this process must generally be followed each time a new company is formed.

To see the list of information required during the company registration process go to www.doylesguideasia.com/thailand/chapter32/appendixa.

To see the list of documents required to obtain the company's Tax ID Card go to www.doylesguideasia.com/thailand/chapter32/appendixb.

To see the list of documents required to obtain the company's VAT Certificate go to www.doylesguideasia.com/thailand/chapter32/appendixc.

1. Promoters

The parties responsible for registering the company with the MOC are referred to as the company's promoters. The promoters must be at least three individuals (not business entities), and they must be available to sign documentation, as required, during the registration process.

The promoters will be required to be among the company's initial shareholders immediately after the company's registration. Each of the promoters is required to hold a minimum of one share upon the company's registration; however, they are generally free to transfer those shares to existing shareholders or third parties, thereafter, if they wish to do so. It is not required for the individuals serving as promoters to reside in Thailand.

Promoters' potential legal liability is generally limited to the par value of the shares they will hold after registration is completed. The promoters are also responsible for paying expenses associated with the company's registration. After registration, however, the company may choose to reimburse the promoters for those expenses.

2. Timing

Registration of the company occurs at the MOC and can normally be accomplished between two weeks and six weeks, depending upon a number of factors. These factors include the types of business activities the company is to pursue, the speed with which the investor supplies required information and documents, and the availability of the parties who are required to sign various documents.

Note that if the company falls under the definition of "foreign" (as defined in the Foreign Business Act) it will normally be required to obtain Cabinet approval or a Foreign Business License prior to commencing operations (see Chapter 33).

Applying for and obtaining the company's Tax ID Card and VAT Certificate (if required) take place after registration with the MOC and can normally be accomplished within seven to ten days of the date of providing all required information and documents to the Revenue Department.

3. Filings

All documents associated with the company's registration must be submitted to the registrar of the Department of Business Development of the MOC, or if the company's office is to be located outside of Bangkok, at the filing office of the province where the office will be.

All documents associated with the registration of the company's Tax ID Card and VAT Certificate (if required) must be submitted to the District Revenue Office in Bangkok, or if the company office is to be located outside Bangkok, to the Revenue Office of the province where the office will be.

4. Company Name

The first step of the company registration process is the name reservation. In order to reserve the name, one of the promoters is required to submit a signed Name Reservation Form to the Department of Business Development of the MOC or apply via the Internet at www.dbd.go.th. To see this form together with an English translation go to www.doylesguideasia.com/thailand/chapter32/appendixd.

As you will see from Appendix D, a promoter is required to supply the requested company name together with two alternative names. The registrar will then examine the application in order to ensure that no similar company names have previously been reserved and that the names submitted do not violate any ministerial rules.

If the applicant's intended name is in conflict with either of the above, that name will be rejected, and the registrar will consider the alternative names submitted. This process can normally be completed within two to three days. If all three names submitted are rejected, the applicant will be required to resubmit the form with three new names.

The registrar has considerable discretion with regard to his consideration of the company names submitted. Many times, the first name or even the first two names are rejected for violating one of the two rules stated above.

The investors should, therefore, not invest in marketing materials containing the company's intended name until after the registrar's approval of a company name. This sounds like common sense, but many people make this mistake.

Note that the name may be reserved for only thirty days from the date of approval at a time. This means that if the applicant does not take the next step in the company application process (submitting a document called the Memorandum of Association) within thirty days of reserving the name, the applicant will be required to reserve the company name again.

5. Signatures

After the name is reserved, the company Memorandum of Association (MOA) must be submitted. To see the official MOA form together with an English translation go to www.doylesguideasia.com/thailand/chapter32/appendixe. You can see from the English translation that the MOA contains, among other things, the following information:

i.   The names and various personal information concerning the promoters (minimum seven individuals)

ii. Amount of the company's registered capital (see Section 7)

iii. Province in which the company will be located (see Section 6)

iv. The company's intended scope of business activities (these activities
     are not presented in Appendix E)

Each of the seven promoters is required to sign the MOA. This can cause
logistical problems if the promoters are scattered in different countries around
the world. This is because each of the seven or more individual promoters are
required to sign the same document.

6. Address

As stated above, the MOA must contain the physical address of the company
to be formed. A PO Box address will not be acceptable.

During the company registration process the sufficiency of the company
address is normally not an issue. The company's address, however, can become an issue if the company is later required to obtain a VAT Certificate.

As a part of the process to obtain a VAT Certificate, the company is required
to obtain the written permission of the owner of the premises where the company will be located (if the company is not the owner of the premises). To see
the permission form the owner or the owner's authorized representative is normally required to sign and an English translation go to www.doylesguideasia.com/
thailand/chapter2/appendixf.

If the company address is a residential (not commercial) space, the building
owner or landlord will often be reluctant to sign this permission. A common
reason for such refusal is that the owner does not want the business traffic in
the building that would be caused by allowing the company to be situated there.

Also, if the registered address is a condominium unit, be aware that some
condominium buildings include a specific provision, in their standard condominium sales agreements or the condominium juristic office's rules, prohibiting the condominium owner from using the condominium unit as a
business address.

7. Registered Capital

Registered capital refers to the total financial responsibility of the company's
shareholders with respect to the company. Each individual shareholder may
make this investment in the company by using either cash or non-cash assets.
If non-cash assets are to be contributed, the shareholder(s) contributing such
assets as capital should have the non-cash assets properly appraised during the

company registration process. Each shareholder is required to pay into the company a minimum of 25% of their shares' par value.

EXAMPLE: Suppose a company's registered capital is set at 10 million baht. If that is the case, 2.5 million baht would be required to be actually paid into the company by the shareholders upon final registration of the company. The amount of capital actually paid into the company by the shareholders is referred to as the company's "paid-up" or "paid-in" registered capital.

Each shareholder should note that although he is generally required to pay in only 25% of his shares' par value upon registration, that shareholder's potential liability associated with the company's activities is 100% of the shares' par value.

EXAMPLE: Suppose one of the shareholders of a company holds shares with a cumulative par value of one million baht. Upon registration, however, this shareholder elects to pay into the company the minimum of only 25% of the shares' par value or 250,000 baht. The company is later sued by a third party in Civil Court for 20 million baht, which exceeds the value of the company's total assets. The third party wins the lawsuit. As the shareholder has not paid in 100% of his shares' par value, the shareholder could potentially be required by the presiding court to pay into the company the remaining 750,000 baht in order to enable the company to pay the judgment.

Note that Thai law stipulates that the company's debt to equity ratio may not exceed seven to one, meaning that the company is not allowed to borrow more than seven times the amount of its equity.

EXAMPLE: Suppose a company is established and its registered capital is designated at 10 million baht. According to the above rule, this company may not borrow more than 70 million baht, unless the company's registered capital first increases accordingly.

8. Minimum Capital

The general rule is that there is only a very low minimum registered capital requirement for a company limited (registered par value of each share must not be less than five baht per share). An exception to this minimum registered capital requirement rule applies, however, if the company falls under the definition of a foreign company (see Chapter 33). If so, the following rules apply:

i.   If the foreign company engages in activities specified in the Foreign Business Act (see Chapter 33) its minimum registered capital would be the greater of 25% of the company's average per year expenses for its first three years of operation and 3 million baht (exceptions apply) fully (100%) paid up.

ii.   If the foreign company does not engage in specified activities its minimum registered capital would be 2 million baht fully (100%) paid up.

Also, note that if the company is to employ foreigners, other minimum registered capital requirements may also apply (see Chapter 34).

9. Articles of Association

Prior to final registration, the applicant will be required to submit the company's Articles of Association (Articles) to the MOC. The Articles state basic rules the company is required to follow after incorporation is successfully completed.

These rules generally include the frequency with which directors' and shareholders' meetings take place, what constitutes a quorum at meetings, notice requirements for meetings, the numbers required to pass a resolution at a meeting, etc.

A company is normally completely free (within legal limits and as long as proper regulatory procedures are followed) to submit its own unique Articles; however, many new companies will instead initially elect to adopt standard Articles upon incorporation.

Standard Articles represent very basic rules for the company's operation that are in compliance with Thai law. Normally, if standard Articles are presented to the presiding MOC official, they will be accepted without amendment. Therefore, in order to avoid potential delays, many promoters choose to register standard Articles at the time of registration and then adopt the company's own unique (non-standard Articles) at a later time. To see standard Articles, presented together with an English translation go to www.doylesguideasia.com/thailand/chapter32/appendixg.

10. Directors

After registration, the company's Affidavit remains on file with the MOC and states the names of the company's director(s) and their authority to sign on behalf of the company.

Directors are designated as authorized or unauthorized in the Affidavit. Authorized directors are allowed to sign on behalf of the company, unauthorized directors are not.

Many times, as a controlling mechanism, the company will designate that only a combination of two or more directors signing together are authorized to sign on behalf of the company. Also, many companies will designate that a director(s) may sign on behalf of the company only together with the company seal. This makes the physical presence of the company seal another kind of control mechanism.

To see the Affidavit form and an English translation go to www.doylesguide asia.com/thailand/chapter32/appendixh. The company is required to have a minimum of one director. Directors may be individuals only.

Note that, unlike shareholders, directors (both authorized and unauthorized) incur legal obligations and substantial liability associated with the actions of the company. A person should carefully consider this before agreeing to serve as a company director.

11. Auditor Information

During the company registration process, the promoters will be required to supply the name, license number, and remuneration of the auditor the company is planning to engage.

12. Official Fees

The amount of official fees payable to the MOC is calculated based upon the amount of the company's registered capital. There are two separate official fees payable at different stages of the incorporation process.

The first official fee is payable at the time of approval of the MOA. The fee is 50 baht for every 100,000 baht of the company's intended registered capital. The maximum fee payable is capped at 25,000 baht.

The second official fee is payable upon the company's final registration. This fee is 500 baht for every 100,000 baht of the company's registered capital. The maximum fee payable is capped at 250,000 baht.

EXAMPLE: If a company's registered capital is 10 million baht, the official fee payable to the MOC at the time of approval of the MOA would be as follows:

50 baht (statutory rate) x 100 = 5,000 baht payable.

The official fee payable at the time of the company's final registration would be calculated as follows:

500 baht (statutory rate) x 100 = 50,000 baht payable.

Accordingly, the total official fee payable in the above transaction would be 55,000 baht.

5,000 baht MOA fee + 50,000 baht incorporation fee = 55,000 baht total.

13. Bank Accounts

Immediately after registration is complete, most companies will want to open a corporate bank account. Requirements to open a corporate bank account vary from bank to bank, but generally, the company will be required by the bank to provide its Tax ID Card and VAT Certificate (if required), as well as other relevant documents. To see a sample list of the documents and information which may be requested by the bank go to www.doylesguideasia.com/thailand/chapter32/appendixi.

Note that if any of the signatories for the bank account are foreigners, many banks will require that each of the foreign signatories submit a valid work permit (see Chapter 34) prior to opening the account.

14. Public Access to Company Details

After the company is successfully registered, many details regarding the company's structure are easily available to the public at the MOC. These details include the company's list of shareholders and directors, registered capital, articles of incorporation, registered address, auditor's report, and balance sheet for the preceding year, etc.

Chapter 33

What Legal Issues Are Associated with Operating as a Foreign-Held Company?

Thai law regulates the activities in which companies designated as "foreign" may engage. Some activities are completely prohibited, some may be engaged in with prior approval from a designated government agency only, and some do not require any special approval at all. This chapter discusses the applicable rules associated with operating a business as a foreign company.

1. Definition of Foreign

According to Thai law, a company is foreign if it is registered under the laws of

i. another country (including all branches, representative offices, and regional offices of overseas companies operating in Thailand) or

ii. Thailand, and 50% or more of its shares are held by non-Thais (individuals or business entities).

EXAMPLE: Suppose a company has three shareholders and a total of 10,000 shares. One of the shareholders is German and the other two are Thai. If the German owns 5,000 shares, the company will be classified as foreign and therefore, subject to special regulations.

Conversely, if this company instead has two German shareholders and one Thai shareholder and the Thai holds 51% of the shares and the German shareholders hold 49%, the company would not be classified as foreign and therefore, not be subject to the special regulations.

2. Regulated Activities

Regulated activities are stated in the Foreign Business Act and are divided into three groups: List 1, List 2, and List 3.

Activities stated in List 1 are designated as "businesses not permitted for foreigners to operate due to special reasons." Foreign companies are completely restricted from engaging in the activities contained in List 1. To see the List 1 activities go to www.doylesguideasia.com/thailand/chapter33/appendixa.

Activities stated in List 2 are designated as "businesses related to national safety or security, or affecting arts and culture, traditional and folk handicraft, or natural resources and environment." Foreign companies may only engage in the activities stated in List 2 with prior Cabinet approval. To see the List 2 activities go to www.doylesguideasia.com/thailand/chapter33/appendixb.

Activities stated in List 3 are designated as "businesses in which Thai nationals are not yet ready to compete with foreigners." In order to engage in activities stated in List 3, the foreign company must apply for and obtain a Foreign Business License prior to commencing the activity. To see the List 3 activities go to www.doylesguideasia.com/thailand/chapter33/appendixc.

Note that there are two common exceptions to the above stated rules:

i.   If the foreign company obtains an exemption from the above stated rule from the Board of Investment or the Industrial Estates Authority of Thailand (see Chapter 35)

ii. If the foreign company is a US company which qualifies for Treaty of Amity protection

     (Treaty of Amity affords qualifying US investors in Thailand national treatment with only limited exceptions.)

Take special note of three things. One, manufacturing for export is not mentioned in any of the three lists. This means that a foreign company may engage in manufacturing for export without obtaining any special permission from the Ministry of Commerce (provided that the manufactured items themselves are not subject to restrictions, such as Thai handicrafts and firearms).

Two, note that "other service businesses" are shown in List 3. This effectively serves as a "catch-all" service category. That means that if the foreign company is to provide a service, not otherwise contained in List 3, the company must still apply for and obtain a Foreign Business License prior to commencing operation. This category includes the business activity of leasing both fixed and non-fixed assets. Also, the activities which representative offices and regional offices are allowed to engage in (see Chapter 31) are all services which fall under this category.

Three, note that special rules apply if the foreign company plans to engage in the activities of "retail sale of goods" or "wholesale sale of goods." Both of these activities are contained in List 3; therefore, in order for a foreign company to engage in either of these activities the company must first apply for and obtain a Foreign Business License.

This is a source of difficulty for many foreign investors because many times if the foreign investor(s) wants to engage in the general activity of "trading of goods" that will mean that the company will engage in retail selling, wholesale selling, or both. Thai law, however, grants narrow exceptions to the Foreign Business License requirement for those foreign companies seeking to engage in retail selling and/or wholesale selling. These exceptions are linked to the amount of the foreign company's registered capital.

For a foreign company to engage in the activity of retail selling, the exception is that if the company has a registered capital of 100 million baht (fully paid up) or more *or* capital for each retail store of 20 million baht or more, the company is exempt from the Foreign Business License requirement.

For a foreign company to engage in the activity of wholesale selling, the exception is that if the company has 100 million baht capital or more for *each* of its wholesale stores, the company is exempt from the Foreign Business License requirement.

3. Foreign Business License Application

As stated above, foreign companies seeking to engage in List 3 activities are required to apply for and obtain a Foreign Business License prior to commencing operations.

The Foreign Business Act sets forth the process by which the Foreign Business Committee (Committee) reviews the application. It states that the Committee is required to rule on the application within sixty days of submission. However, practically speaking, the application process has two distinct steps. The first is the process by which the presiding official at the MOC accepts the application for review by the Committee, and the second is the Committee's actual review of the application.

a. Acceptance by the MOC Official

An application for a Foreign Business License is submitted to the Ministry of Commerce (MOC) together with all required documents and information. To see the application form presented together with an English translation go to www.doylesguideasia.com/thailand/chapter33/appendixd. To see the initial list of supporting documents to be submitted with the application for a company limited go to www.doyleguideasia.com/thailand/chapter33/appendixe.

To see the list of supporting documents required to be submitted if the applicant is a foreign company seeking to operate as a branch, representative office, or regional office go to www.doylesguideasia.com/thailand/chater33/appendixf.

The presiding MOC official charged with accepting the application normally will not do so until he is satisfied that all documents are in order. Sometimes the official will perform the preliminary inspection upon presentation, but usually he will require the person submitting the application to leave it with him so that he can inspect the documents later. This can be frustrating, because unlike the Committee's review, the time frame for the official's review of the application is not specified by statute.

The process is further complicated by the fact that the applicant will normally be required to contact the same individual official each time he wants to follow up with the application until such time as it is officially accepted. This can easily cause delays if the official becomes sick, goes on vacation, etc.

In order to avoid these delays, make sure that the person designated to submit the application is familiar enough with the intended operations of the company to respond on the spot to the official's questions regarding the application.

Also, when the official requests additional documents and/or information, make sure that the designated person supplies those documents in a timely fashion.

b. Review by the Board

Once the official accepts the application and issues a receipt, the sixty-day consideration period begins. Factors considered by the Committee when reviewing applications include the following:

   i.   The advantages and disadvantages to the nation's safety and security

   ii.   Economic and social development

iii. Public order, good morals, art, culture and traditions of the country

iv. Natural resources, conservation, energy and environment, consumer protection, size of the enterprises, employment

v. Technology transfer and research and development

Technology transfer and research and development are probably the most important right now. In 2004, the Ministry issued a document advising foreign investors on how they should describe technology transfer in the license application. Technology here is not just limited to R&D and use of sophisticated equipment, but also specifically includes "administration, management and marketing." Also, any planned programs the company has with Thai universities are taken under consideration by the Committee.

In the event the Foreign Business License application is rejected, the law requires that the MOC inform the applicant within fifteen days of the decision. The notification of rejection must be in writing and expressly state the reasons why the application was rejected.

If the application is rejected, the applicant has the right to appeal the decision. The appeal must be submitted within thirty days of the date on which the applicant received the rejection notice. The MOC Minister is required to rule on the appeal within thirty days of receipt.

4. Nominee Shareholders

Generally, nominee shareholders are individuals or companies that agree to hold shares on behalf of the true owner(s) of the shares. Under this arrangement, typically the nominee shareholder and the true owner execute an agreement stating that the nominee shareholder agrees to hold the shares in name only. The true owner retains all rights of ownership and control (voting rights, rights to transfer, rights to receive dividends, etc.) of the shares.

This technique was commonly used in order for the company to avoid being legally classified as a "foreign company" and the associated restrictions.

In 1999, however, the Thai government introduced new and more severe penalties for Thais who act as nominees and foreigners who "cause" Thais to act as nominees. The penalties also extend to situations where Thai nationals aid foreigners in operating a business in contravention of the Foreign Business Act.

The new penalties prescribed under the Foreign Business Act range from fines of 100,000 baht to 1 million baht and terms of imprisonment of up to three years or both.

Chapter 34

What Is the Process to Obtain a Work Permit?

Obtaining a work permit for the first time in Thailand can be a lengthy, fairly involved process, and the applicant will be required to locate and prepare an extensive list of documents.

The application process is actually two applications being processed simultaneously:

i. An application to receive a work permit from the Ministry of Labor and Social Welfare

ii. An application for a One-Year Non-Immigrant Visa Extension (One-Year Visa Extension) from the Immigration Bureau

The work permit is the permission to work in Thailand. The visa is the permission to reside in Thailand. The applicant must obtain both. Foreigners normally focus on the importance of the work permit, but it is the One-Year Visa Extension that is normally the more difficult of the two to obtain.

The One-Year Visa Extension and work permit are normally valid for one year from the date the foreign applicant enters Thailand with a non-immigrant visa (see Section 1 below) as indicated by the immigration stamp in the applicant's passport. After one year, both the work permit and visa must be renewed (see Section 6 below).

There are two separate methods available to the applicant to obtain a work permit and One-Year Visa Extension. If the applicant already resides in Thailand there is one procedure, and if the applicant has yet to come to Thailand there is another procedure. However, because most applications are submitted by applicants already residing in Thailand, this chapter will focus on the procedures they must follow.

Keep in mind that if the employer company is promoted by the Board of Investment (BOI) or otherwise qualifies for BOI's One Stop Visa and Work Permit service the process is much simpler, and the normal rules stated below will not apply. To see the categories of foreign workers who qualify for One Stop Service go to www.doylesguideasia.com/thailand/chapter34/appendixa.

1. Non-Immigrant Visa

The first step in initiating the work permit process is to obtain a non-immigrant visa. There are many types of non-immigrant visas; however, in most cases the applicant will be required to obtain a Non-Immigrant Type "B" Visa before applying for the work permit. This visa is quite important because it allows the applicant to stay in Thailand for the initial ninety days, and it will serve as one of the supporting documents when the applicant's work permit application is later submitted.

There are two separate methods available to the applicant to obtain a non-immigrant visa. One method is an application process, recently introduced by the government, for applicants who have already entered Thailand on a tourist or transit visa. To see the list of documents required to apply to change from a tourist or transit visa to a non-immigrant visa go to www.doylesguideasia.com/thailand/chapter34/appendixb.

The other method is an application process for applicants who are outside of Thailand. This method is normally not so difficult for the applicant, although it may be inconvenient. The applicant submits the application to the Immigration Section of the Thai Embassy in any country. This process can usually be completed within one or two working days.

In addition to the application form for the non-immigrant visa, the embassy will require the applicant to submit a signed invitation letter from the Thailand employer (to see a sample invitation letter go to www.doylesguideasia.com/thailand/chapter34/appendixc) and supporting documentation. Each Thai embassy has it own requirements for supporting documentation to obtain the visa, and their requirements are not uniform.

EXAMPLE: The Thai Embassy in Hong Kong may require that the applicant provide a copy of the employer company's list of shareholders and its affidavit as a part of the visa application. However, the Thai Embassy in Vietnam may require only the application form and invitation letter, with no further supporting documentation.

Also, the time required to process the application varies from embassy to embassy. Some Thai embassies require as much as three days to process an application, some only one day. The amount of the application fee varies as well.

The applicant should, therefore, check in advance with the Thai Embassy to be visited to determine its particular requirements.

2. Required Documentation for Work Permit and Non-Immigrant One-Year Visa Extension

Once the applicant is in Thailand with a valid non-immigrant visa, he is ready to begin the work permit application process.

Along with the work permit application, the applicant must submit a list of supporting documents. To see the list of documents required go to www.doylesguideasia.com/thailand/chapter34/appendixd.

Note that the applicant will be required to later produce another list of documents associated with the One-Year Visa Extension. To see the list of documents required go to www.doylesguideasia.com/thailand/chapter34/appendixe.

The receiving government officials (both at the Ministry of Labor for the work permit application and the Immigration Bureau for the One-Year Visa Extension application) will normally take a quick look at the submitted documents to see if they appear to be in order. If so, they will then forward the individual applications for processing.

3. Deadlines

Once the process is under way, there is a thirty-day consideration period. That means that the applicant's passport is stamped at the Immigration Bureau stating that the applicant is allowed to reside in Thailand during the consideration period stated. At the end of the consideration period, the applicant or his representative will be required to go to the Immigration Bureau and then the Ministry of Labor.

Commonly, foreigners are surprised when they are informed that they should wait until two or three days before the expiration of the deadline before submitting the next set of required documents. This is true even when the documents are prepared well in advance. The reason for this lies in the working systems of the Ministry of Labor and Immigration Bureau.

The system used to process work permit and One-Year Visa Extension applications involves the rotating of applications "to the top of the pile" two or three days before the stated deadline. If the applicant comes to receive the official's ruling on his individual application within those two or three days of the stated deadline, it will be easy for the officials to locate the file. If the applicant instead, for example, comes two weeks before the deadline, the applicant's file will not be at the top of the pile, and it may be much more difficult for the official to find. This often results in delays in receiving final approval.

4. One-Year Visa Extension

The application for the One-Year Visa Extension may be processed and approved within one month of submitting the initial application.

Normally, the presiding official at the Immigration Bureau will accept the initial One-Year Visa Extension application. He will then take the application under consideration for a period of approximately thirty days. During this period the applicant is allowed to reside in the country.

At the end of the thirty-day period. the applicant (either in person or represented by a third party) will meet with the official. At that meeting the official will normally either grant the One-Year Visa Extension or reject the application and allow the applicant seven days to leave the country.

5. Leaving Thailand

During the time the applicant is applying for the One-Year Visa Extension and even after it is obtained, Thai law requires that the applicant obtain a valid Re-Entry Permit each time he leaves and returns again to Thailand.

If the applicant fails to secure this Re-Entry Permit before leaving, upon his return to Thailand the immigration official who checks his passport upon re-entry (at the airport, train station, etc.) will stamp his existing visa as cancelled, and the applicant will be required to re-initiate the entire One Year Visa Extension application process from the beginning. The good news is that the Re-Entry Permit is not difficult to obtain. In Bangkok, it can be accomplished at the Immigration Bureau on Chaeng Wattana Road.

The Re-Entry Permit can normally be obtained within one hour of submitting the application and paying the application fee. To see the form for the Re-Entry Permit application go to www.doylesguideasia.com/thailand/chapter 34/appendixf.

In the application you will see that the applicant can obtain either a Single Entry Permit or a Multiple Entry Permit. The Single Entry Permit may be used only one time and will be stamped "cancelled" by the Thai immigration official upon the traveling party's return to Thailand (applicant will not be able to use that Re-Entry Permit for future trips outside Thailand). The Multiple Entry Permit, by contrast, may be used as many times as desired up until the next deadline stated in the applicant's visa.

EXAMPLE: Suppose the One-Year Visa Extension applicant is required to re-submit documents for the immigration official's consideration on February 28th. The applicant intends to leave Thailand for a short trip on February 3rd and obtains a Multiple Re-Entry Permit. The applicant may use the Multiple Re-Entry Permit to leave and return to Thailand for as many trips as he likes before February 28th. After February 28th, however, the applicant will be required to obtain a new Re-Entry Permit before leaving Thailand again. Remember, if he does not secure a Re-Entry Permit before leaving, upon his return he will generally be required to start the One-Year Business Visa application process all over again.

An applicant would obtain a Single Entry Permit, rather than a Multiple Entry Permit, for only two reasons:

i. Cost considerations. The application fee for a Multiple Entry Permit is about four times that of a Single Entry Permit.

ii. The applicant is reasonably certain that he will leave Thailand only one time before his next appointment with the immigration official.

6. Subsequent Years

After the work permit and One-Year Visa Extension are secured, there will be a single deadline stated as to when the applicant must apply for renewals of the work permit and visa. Normally, renewals are much easier to obtain than the original work permit and visa. This is because the applicant has already compiled all or most of the required documentation to be submitted. If, however, the structure of the company has changed since the time the original applications were filed or the applicant's job description or title has changed during the period, additional documentation will be required.

7. Dependents

Throughout this process the applicant's spouse, children, and other dependents residing in Thailand are required to maintain a valid dependent's visa. Permission to stay in Thailand stated in the dependent's visa normally will mirror the period of stay stated in the applicant's visa.

Each time the applicant updates his visa the applicant's spouse, children, and other dependents must also update their visas. To see the list of documents submitted with the dependent visa application form go to www.doylesguideasia.com/thailand/chapter34/appendixg.

8. Employer Requirements

Thai law restricts the types of employers that may qualify to obtain work permits for their foreign staff. The applicable rules for private sector employers are presented below. The requirements vary depending upon whether the employer operates as a company limited, branch, representative office, or regional office.

a. Company Limited and Branch

The following are the applicable requirements for a company limited and a branch to obtain work permits for their foreign staff. Note the requirements for branches established in Thailand before October 30, 2002 and after October 30, 2002 differ.

	Company Limited:	Branch est. on or before Oct. 30, 02:	Branch est. after Oct. 30, 02:
Registered capital required	Paid up capital of 2 million baht with each additional 2 million baht allowing for an additional foreign employee	N/A	N/A
Amount remitted into Thailand	N/A	N/A	3 million baht with each additional 3 million baht allowing for an additional foreign employee
Amount in bank account over previous 6 months	N/A	3 million baht with each additional 3 million baht allowing for an additional foreign employee (requirement if no transfer information is available)	N/A

EXAMPLE: Suppose a German company decides to establish a branch in Thailand and remits 9 million baht for operation of the branch. That branch would qualify to employ three foreigners (subject to Section 9 below).

EXAMPLE: Suppose a new company limited wishes to employ two foreigners. Normally, in order to qualify for the employees to receive work permits, the company's paid-up registered capital would be required to be not less than 4 million baht.

Note, however, that if the employee is married to a Thai national and the couple lives together, the above described investment requirements for both a company limited and branch are reduced by 50%.

EXAMPLE: Same facts as above, but one of the two employees is legally married to a Thai national, and the two live together. In this situation, the company's investment requirement would be reduced from 4 million baht (normal requirement) to 3 million baht.

Under the above rules, the law normally limits company limiteds and branches to employing a maximum of ten foreigners.

However, in the event that a company limited or branch wishes to employ more than ten foreigners it shall be considered in the following situations:

i.   Employer paid tax in Thailand of not less than 3 million baht in the previous year

ii. Employer engages in the business of exporting products and brought into Thailand no less than 30 million baht during the previous year

iii. Employer engages in the business of tourism and brought into Thailand no less than five thousand tourists during the previous year

iv. Employer employs not less than one hundred Thai employees

Additionally, a company limited with paid-up registered capital of at least 2 million baht or a branch that has transferred into Thailand no less than 3 million baht shall be exempted from the normal employer's requirements if the foreigner is able to perform any one of these activities:

i.   Use technology that Thai people do not have or is in insufficient supply. In this situation, the foreigner is required to teach no fewer than two Thais the technology within a specific time frame.

ii. Use particular skills to complete a project with a specified time frame.

iii. Work in areas of entertainment, theater, or music that is not permanent employment (has a specified time frame).

Also, note that foundations, associations, and other organizations that have not for profit objectives or are useful to the public may also be exempted from the above requirements.

b. Representative Office

The number of foreigners a representative office in Thailand is allowed to employ depends upon the job description of the position to be filled by the foreigner. If a representative office employs foreigners in one of the following capacities it may qualify to employ up to two foreigners:

i.   Giving advice concerning the products of the head office in order to sell to agents or users

ii.   Publicizing information concerning new products or services from the head office and reporting business developments in Thailand to the head office

If the representative office employs foreigners in one of the following capacities it may qualify to employ up to five foreigners:

i.   Aiding in procuring goods or services in Thailand on behalf of the head office

ii.   Examining and controlling the quality and/or quantity of the goods that are purchased or produced in Thailand by the head office

There is an exception to the above rules, however, in the case where the representative office is procuring goods or services in Thailand, and the head office overseas purchases those goods or services for an amount not less than 100 million baht in the previous year. In such case the representative office would qualify to employ more foreigners than what would ordinarily be allowed.

EXAMPLE: A representative office in Thailand wishes to employ six foreigners to perform quality control on the goods its head office overseas purchases in Thailand. Last year the head office purchased 100 million baht worth of products from Thailand.

Normally, the representative office would qualify to employ only five foreigners. However, in this situation, because the head office purchased 100 million baht in goods from Thailand the year prior, the representative office would be able to employ all six foreigners instead of only five.

c. Regional Office

The number of foreigners a regional office in Thailand is allowed to employ depends upon the job description of the position to be filled by the foreigner. If the regional office employs foreigners in one of the following capacities it may qualify to employ up to five foreigners:

i.   Acting on behalf of the head office to coordinate and control the operation of a branch(es) or affiliate(s) outside of Thailand, but in the same region.

ii. Consulting and/or arranging for training and development for employees to prepare financial plans, monitor the market, plan for sales promotions and product development, and perform research and development without remuneration. However, these positions may have no authority to accept orders or make offers or to negotiate with an individual or company located in Thailand.

However, if the head office remits no less than 10 million baht into Thailand during the previous year, the regional office may qualify to employ more than five foreigners.

EXAMPLE: A regional office in Thailand wishes to employ six foreigners to coordinate activities between the head office and its affiliates outside Thailand. Last year the head office remitted 10 million baht to the regional office for its operation.

Normally, the regional office would be limited to employing five foreigners only; however, because the office remitted 10 million baht the previous year it would qualify to employ all six foreigners instead of only five.

9. Thai Staff Requirements

In addition to the above, Thai law requires employers (companies, branches, representative offices, and regional offices) to maintain a minimum number of Thai staff in order to qualify for its foreign staff to obtain business visas.

Type Entity	Minimum Number of Thai Employees
Company limited:	Four Thai employees for every foreigner
Branch, representative office, regional office:	One Thai employee for every foreigner

EXAMPLE: A Danish company establishes a company limited in Thailand and wishes to employ two foreigners. Among the requirements for the company to qualify to obtain the business visas for the two foreigners, the Thailand company would be required to employ a minimum of eight Thais.

10. Restricted Professions

In addition to the law regulating the types of companies that qualify to receive work permits for their foreign staff, Thai law also limits the professions in which foreigners may obtain work permits. To see the list of professions foreigners are normally prohibited from engaging in go to www.doylesguide asia.com/thailand/chapter34/appendixh. Note again, that if the employer is a BOI promoted company exceptions may apply.

11. Applicable Fees

The following are the normal government fees associated with obtaining a work permit and One-Year Non-Immigrant Visa Extension.

One-Year Non-Immigrant Visa Extension Fees:

Application fee for Non-immigrant "B" Visa extension	1,900 baht
Application fee for dependent	1,900 baht (per applicant)
Application fee for Re-entry Permit	
Single Re-entry Permit	1,000 baht
Multiple Re-entry Permit	3,800 baht

Work Permit Fees:

Application fee depends upon the length of the period for which the work permit is granted.

Application fee 100 baht

Approval fee:

If period is no longer than 3 months—750 baht

If period is no longer than 6 months—1,500 baht

If period is no longer than 12 months—3,000 baht

Chapter 35

What Investment Incentives Are Available to Foreign Investors?

Previous chapters discussed the generally applicable rules for foreign investors setting up business operations in Thailand. Different rules may apply, however, if the business activities qualify for Board of Investment (BOI) incentives, or the investors locate their factory in an industrial estate.

1. Board of Investment (BOI)

The Board of Investment (BOI) is the Thai government agency responsible for attracting investment to Thailand by offering a wide range of tax and non-tax incentives to investors to engage in specific kinds of projects.

The following are the most common incentives granted by BOI:

i.   Corporate income tax exemptions, reductions, and special carry forward loss provisions

ii. Customs duties reductions and exemptions for raw materials and machinery

iii. Permission for foreigners to own land in order to carry out promoted projects or to establish offices or residences

iv. Special rights with regard to the issuance of work permits and visas

v.   Special rights with regard to operating as a foreign-held company

Generally, when BOI awards one or more of these incentives to a given project these awards supersede the legal rules which would normally apply. Once the award expires or has otherwise been utilized, the normal legal rules would apply to the project.

EXAMPLE: Suppose a project is awarded an eight year exemption from corporate income tax (corporate income tax is normally 30% of annual net profits). During those eight years the normal corporate income tax rules would not apply as long as the project continues to comply with the terms and conditions issued by BOI (see Section 5 below). However, at the end of the promotion period the normal corporate income tax rules would then be applicable.

An exception to the above rule exists, however, for the incentives relating to the right of foreigners to own land and special rights concerning the issuance of work permits and visas for foreign employees. These incentives normally apply throughout the life of the project.

EXAMPLE: Same facts as above, but BOI also grants the project the right to own land and special rights concerning the issuance of work permits and visas. In this situation, even after the project's period of tax exemption expires, the project's special right to own land and its special rights with regard to work permits and visas for foreign staff continue on.

Also, note that the incentives awarded by BOI are applicable to the specific project promoted only and are not applicable to the business's other operations.

EXAMPLE: Suppose a company is granted BOI promotion for a project to produce electronic components for export. One of the BOI incentives granted is exemption from import duties for raw materials needed to produce the components. This company, however, also engages in the activity of producing car radios for sale in Thailand, and the same imported raw materials used to produce the electric components are also used to produce car radios. In this situation, the raw materials imported by the company to produce the components for export (promoted activity) would qualify for the exemption from import duty. However, the raw materials imported to produce car radios for sale in Thailand (non-promoted activity) would be subject to normal import duty.

a. BOI Benefits

The most common BOI investment incentives are discussed below. Note that which of these incentives (if any) would be awarded to a given project and the extent to which the incentives would be awarded depends upon many factors, including the project's intended activities, location, and amount of investment, as well as other factors.

i. Tax Incentives

The following are some of the normal tax rates applicable to businesses in Thailand:

	Normal Rate	BOI Rate
Corporate Income Tax	30%	*
Tax on Dividends	10%	*

BOI is authorized to grant qualifying projects tax reductions and exemptions from these rates during the period of promotion. Note that many times (but not always) BOI will limit the total corporate income exemption to an amount equal to the total capital investment in the project.

EXAMPLE: Suppose a company invests a total of 100 million baht in a project that is granted promotion by BOI. Among the incentives granted is an eight year corporate income tax exemption. There is a limitation placed on this exemption, however, that the total tax exemption applicable may not exceed the amount representing the total capital investment (100 million baht).

The project shows no profit in Year One or Year Two, but in Year Three, the project's total tax savings resulting from this exemption is 100 million baht. Because of this, the project's tax exemption stops at the end of Year Three, even though five more years remain in the exemption period.

Note, however, that the above described limitation normally excludes the amount representing the investment in land and working capital in the project.

EXAMPLE: Same facts as above, but the 100 million baht total investment includes 25 million baht to purchase land and 25 million baht as working capital. Using these facts, the total tax exemption available to the project would be limited to 50 million baht instead of 100 million baht as stated above.

An applicant can often obtain exemption from both the above described limitations by submitting a "Supplementary Application for Promotion Privileges in Accordance with BOI's Investment Promotion Policy to Develop Skill, Technology and Innovation (STI) for Groups of Enterprises which Reinforce STI." The application must be submitted with the standard BOI application. The cap is exempted in cases where the applicant meets at least one of the following criteria:

i.   Research and development expenses amount to at least 2% of annual sales not over 1,000 million baht and 1% over 1,000 million baht.

ii. Not less than 1–5% of the total workforce, depending on the industry, have a bachelor's degree or higher in the field of science or any field related to research and development or design technology for the first three years of operation.

iii. The proportion of Thai employee training costs of the monthly payroll is not less than 1% during the first three years of operation.

iv.   The average expenses for developing the capability of Thai subcon-
tractors or expenses for supporting related educational institutions is
not less than 1% of annual sales for the first three years.

If a company incurs a loss in any year during the exemption period, it is allowed
to carry forward the loss to deduct from its net profits (if any) within five years
of the expiration of the exemption period.

EXAMPLE: A project is awarded by BOI an eight year exemption from corporate income tax. In Year One the project incurs a loss of 8 million baht. Beginning from the time the exemption period ends after Year Eight the company
may still use the loss it incurred in Year One in any year until the end of Year
Thirteen.

ii. Reduction or Exemption of Customs Duties

Normally, when raw materials or machinery are imported into Thailand a
duty is levied by the Customs Department. This duty is calculated based upon
the imported items' value together with the duty rate applicable to the item.
BOI is authorized to award projects that qualify for reduction or exemption
of this duty.

Note that raw materials and machinery that can be produced or assembled in
Thailand which are of similar quality are normally excluded from this exemption. Additionally, used machinery and equipment considered obsolete (the
standard threshold is ten years' prior use) are also normally excluded.

iii. Foreign Ownership of Land

As discussed in Chapter 36, foreigners are normally prohibited from holding title to land in Thailand. However, BOI is authorized to grant qualifying
projects the right to own land. This right may extend to not only factories, but
for offices and residences purchased under the promoted company's name.

iv. Issuance of Work Permits and Visas

The normal rules and procedures associated with the issuance of work permits for foreign staff are discussed in Chapter 34. However, BOI is authorized
to grant qualifying projects these special rights concerning the issuance of work
permits and visas for the foreign employees working on those projects:

i.   An increase in the number of work permits and visas that the company
would normally qualify for, as well as an increase in the normal duration of those work permits and visas

ii.   Access to BOI's One Stop Visa and Work Permit Service Center (which processes work permits and long-term visas in three hours or less), instead of using the normal procedure discussed in Chapter 34

v. Operating as a Foreign Company

As stated in Chapter 33, companies legally classified as "foreign" that engage in List 3 activities (as stated in the Foreign Business Act) are required to obtain a Foreign Business License prior to commencing those activities.

The application process for this license normally takes a minimum of three months, and many times the outcome of the application is less than certain. BOI is, however, authorized to grant qualifying projects an exemption from this requirement.

b. Promoted Activities

In order for a project to qualify to receive the above incentives it must fall into one or more of the activities promoted by BOI at the time. To see the current list of activities promoted by BOI go to http://www.boi.go.th. Note that different activities are entitled to receive varying levels of incentives.

BOI also has a list of priority activities which may qualify for maximum incentives. To see the list of priority activities go to www.doylesguideasia.com/thailand/chapter35/appendixa.

c. Promotion Zones

One of the ways BOI determines the level of incentives to be granted to a particular project is through the use of promotion zones. BOI divides Thailand's seventy-six provinces into three zones. To see a list of the three zones stating where each province is located go to www.doylesguideasia.com/thailand/chapter35/appendixb.

Projects in Zone 1 (Bangkok and the five central provinces around Bangkok) and Zone 2 (the ten provinces that surround Zone 1 and the developed provinces of Phuket and Rayong) are eligible to receive reductions in import duties for machinery and exemptions from corporate income tax and import duties for raw materials of products for export.

Thailand's remaining fifty-eight provinces fall into Zone 3, which is designated as an Investment Promotion Zone. Projects located there are eligible to receive more extensive incentives than those located in Zone 1 or 2. Note that those projects located in the provinces designated by BOI as the twenty-two least developed in Zone 3 are eligible to receive maximum incentives.

d. Application Process

BOI has a well-defined criteria governing the evaluation of projects and the awarding of incentives. Basically, BOI evaluates the application from the perspective of "how the project would benefit Thailand." The primary factors considered when determining whether to grant awards are (1) the economic contribution of the project to the country and (2) compliance of the project with the government's investment promotion policies and strategies, as well as these other broad criteria:

i.   Project activity

ii. The amount of project investment

iii. Project location

iv. Technology and knowledge transfer

v.   Stature of the applicant internationally

vi. Number of Thai employees

Although producing goods for export is not formally considered in investment promotion awards, a project's ability to generate foreign exchange for the country is also generally considered by BOI to be important.

Applications for BOI promotion can normally be completed within two to four months of submission of all required information from the company. Note that the application may be submitted before the company's final registration with the Ministry of Commerce (MOC).

The following is BOI's normal procedure for processing promotion applications:

i.   A project officer is assigned by the BOI to each project.

ii. The project officer evaluates the application, writes up recommendations for approval or rejection, and presents the project to an investment subcommittee for approval.

iii. The evaluation is required to be completed in either sixty or ninety days depending on the circumstance.

It is not required, but is often a good idea for the applicant to meet with the director of the division handling the application and one or more senior BOI executives, to familiarize them with the benefits of the project to Thailand.

The application process normally involves a series of meetings between the applicant and BOI officials in order to discuss the details of the proposed project. The object of these meetings is to give the presiding BOI official a general understanding of the project's staffing requirements, logistic needs, production processes, etc.

Note that when explaining production procedures, often it is useful if the applicant prepares a simple flow chart with pictures describing the individual steps.

The following BOI divisions process applications:

1. Investment Promotion Bureau 1
    Agro-Industry and Light Industry
    Division Director Tel: 02-537-8163

2. Investment Promotion Bureau 2
    Metals, Metal Products, Machinery and Transport Equipment
    Division Director Tel: 02-537-8164

3. Investment Promotion Bureau 3
    Electronics and Electrical Industries
    Division Director Tel: 02-537-8165

4. Investment Promotion Bureau 4
    Chemical, Paper, Plastic, Services and Public Utilities
    Division Director Tel: 02-537-8166

The application form can be found on the BOI website at: http://www.boi.go.th/english/download/boi_forms/50/pp_01.pdf. Applicants may either submit the application at the appropriate division office (depending on the type activity) or submit it online.

Investors may also contact directly BOI divisions that process applications. BOI's Investment Services Center provides BOI publications and information and operates a "Help Desk" within its "One Stop Services Center" to assist investors with information, project development, government approvals, and trouble-shooting.

e. Terms and Conditions

If the application is approved, BOI will issue a list of terms and conditions. These are effectively the rules applicable to the project's promotion. The project's continued receipt of incentives will be contingent upon its ability to continue to comply with the terms and conditions during the promotion period.

EXAMPLE: Suppose a project is granted incentives for eight years. The terms and conditions, however, require that the shareholders of the company that own the project must not be less than 40% Thai. In that situation, if at any time during the eight-year promotion period, the Thai shareholders of the company fall below

40% (without first receiving permission from BOI to do so), the project will no longer qualify to receive the incentives granted and the normal rules would apply.

2. Industrial Estate Authority of Thailand (IEAT)

Industrial estates are developed and managed by the Industrial Estate Authority of Thailand (IEAT), which is a state enterprise attached to the Ministry of Industry. Industrial estates are equipped to provide infrastructure necessary for industrial operations (for example electricity, water supply, flood protection, waste treatment, solid waste disposal, etc.). To see a list of each of Thailand's thirty-eight industrial estates go to www.doylesguideasia.com/thailand/chapter35/appendixc.

IEAT is authorized to grant non-tax incentives to investors who choose to locate their factories on an industrial estate. The incentives include these special rights:

i.   Permission for foreigners to own land in order to carry out promoted projects or to establish offices or residences (see Chapter 36)

ii.   Special rights with regard to the issuance of work permits and visas

iii.   Special rights with regard to operating as a foreign-held company (see previous section)

Just as with BOI incentives, when IEAT awards one or more of these incentives to a project, the incentives supersede the normal legal rules which would apply.

Unlike most BOI incentives, however, the incentives granted by IEAT are normally applicable during the entire life of the project (as long as it remains on the industrial estate), instead of a specific period of time as with BOI.

For a description of the application process to obtain IEAT incentives see Chapter 36.

3. Export Processing Zone (EPZs)

Ten of the total thirty-eight industrial estates in Thailand operate Export Processing Zones (EPZs). An EPZ is a special area within an industrial estate designed to allow goods to enter Thailand for processing. As long as the goods remain in the EPZ no Thailand customs duty or VAT is applicable. For reference purposes, IEAT has recently changed the EPZ terminology to IEAT-Free

Zone or IEAT-FZ; however, the "EPZ" term will continue to be used for some time and thus, is the term used in this chapter.

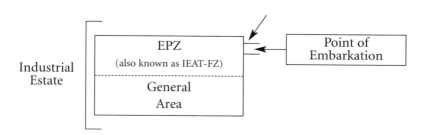

IEAT manages the EPZ; however, the Customs Department is in charge of the EPZ gate in order to monitor the goods entering and exiting the EPZ.

EXAMPLE: Suppose an international company decides to establish a factory in Thailand and then locates the factory on one of the ten industrial estates with an EPZ. All the goods produced in the factory are designated for export. The raw materials used to produce the product are sourced outside Thailand.

In this situation, as long as the imported raw materials are shipped, processed, and exported from the EPZ, no Thailand VAT or customs duties would be applicable, just as if the raw materials had never entered Thailand.

EXAMPLE: Same facts as above except the company decides to sell some of the finished products in Thailand as well. When the finished products designated for sale in Thailand exit the EPZ to be shipped to the place of sale (in Thailand) all of the duty and VAT which would have normally been applicable are applicable at that time.

Note, do not confuse EPZs with Customs Free Zones, which offer similar benefits to investors, but are managed by the Customs Department rather than IEAT.

Chapter 36

What Legal Issues Are Associated with Foreign Ownership of Land?

Contrary to popular belief, land ownership rules in Thailand as they apply to foreigners are quite straightforward. Foreign individuals and foreign companies are not allowed to own *any* direct interest in land unless an exception to the general rule applies.

This restriction is disappointing to many foreign investors who ideally would like to own the land occupied by their business premises or their individual home. The above stated general rule is, however, quite clear and allows for only limited exceptions, the most common of which are discussed below.

1. Condominium Ownership

Foreign individuals and foreign companies are allowed to hold title to condominium units in buildings that qualify. There are some conditions, however; the most potentially significant are listed below.

a. Financing

The foreign individual or foreign company purchasing the condominium unit is generally required to bring into Thailand 100% of the amount of the purchase price from a source offshore. This rule is quite significant because it precludes the foreign purchaser from obtaining local financing in Thailand for the purchase. (See next page.)

Normally what happens when a foreigner wishes to buy a condominium is that on the date scheduled for the transfer of title, the foreign purchaser and seller of the condominium unit meet at the Land Office in the district where

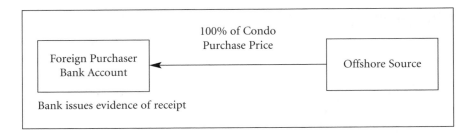

the condominium is located. The presiding official will require the parties to produce a number of documents, including evidence of receipt of the purchase price from a source offshore issued by the purchaser's bank. If the foreign purchaser does not present this document, the official will not approve the transfer of title.

There is an important exception to the above rule. Foreign individual condominium purchasers holding a Permanent Resident Certificate are exempt from the above foreign remittance requirement.

A Permanent Resident Certificate is issued to long-term foreign residents of Thailand who qualify. Note that in recent years, it has become more and more difficult to obtain a Permanent Resident Certificate.

b. Ratio of Foreign Ownership

The presiding official at the Land Office will also require the seller of the condominium unit to produce a letter from the condominium juristic person (the body that manages the condominium building) stating the ratio of foreign condominium owners to Thai condominium owners in the building.

The general rule is that foreigners may own no more than 49% of the total units in the building at any one time. If the proposed transfer would cause the building to exceed 49% foreign ownership it would violate the above rule, and the official would reject the transfer.

2. Land Ownership by Foreign Companies

Foreign businesses classified as "foreign" according to the Foreign Business Act (see Chapter 33) are generally not allowed to own any interest in land. You will recall one of the ways in which a company may be classified as "foreign" is if non-Thai parties hold 50% or more of its shares. Ownership of land is included under the category of "Land Trading" as specified in List 1 of the Foreign Business Act (To see List 1 activities go to www.doylesguideasia.com/thailand/chapter33/appendixa). This means foreign companies are completely prohibited from owning land unless the government grants a special exemption from this restriction (see Section 3 and 4).

If, on the other hand, Thai parties hold more than 50% of the company's shares and more than half of the company's shareholders are Thai nationals, the company technically should have the legal right to hold title to land according to the law. In this situation, the company would not technically fall under the definition of "foreign"; therefore, the restriction would not apply. In practice, however, it is not quite that simple. When a Thai party wishes to sell land, the parties must go to the Land Office of the district in which the land is located to transfer the title. At the Land Office, the presiding official will request the purchasing company's list of shareholders. In practice, if the company's foreign shareholders hold more than 39% of the shares of the purchasing company the official will not approve the transfer.

EXAMPLE: Suppose a Thai majority-held company with inactive foreign shareholders holding 45% of the total shares, wishes to purchase land. Even though this company technically qualifies as a Thai company (non-foreign) according to applicable law, when the parties attempt to transfer the title at the local Land Office the presiding official may withhold approval. This is because the foreign shareholders hold 45% of the shares of the purchasing company. 45% is more than 39%; therefore, the proposed transfer is unlikely to be approved.

If the foreign shareholders instead would have held only 39% of the total shares and the transaction otherwise qualifies, the presiding official would likely have approved the transfer of title.

3. Industrial Estate Authority of Thailand— IEAT

As discussed in Chapter 35, Industrial Estates are developed and managed by the Industrial Estate Authority of Thailand (IEAT), which is a state enterprise attached to the Ministry of Industry. IEAT is authorized to grant foreigners rights to own land within these estates. Industrial Estates are equipped to provide infrastructure necessary for industrial operations (such as ample electricity, water supply, flood protection, waste water treatment, solid waste disposal, etc).

In order to purchase land in an industrial estate the foreign applicant must receive a series of approvals from the IEAT in Bangkok. This is normally not so difficult as long as the foreign applicant's primary activity on the property to be purchased will be manufacturing. Purchasing land for speculation purposes is not allowed.

The first approval the applicant must receive from IEAT is a Land Utilization License. In order to receive this license the applicant must already be established as a company with the Ministry of Commerce. An applicant may not generally purchase such land as a branch, representative office, or regional office. The applicant must then complete necessary forms and submit them together with the application fee (10,000 baht) to the IEAT office in Prathunam in Bangkok.

This license is usually issued within one to two weeks of the submission of the application. After the license is issued, it must be renewed every four years.

After the Land Utilization License is acquired, the next step is for the applicant to apply for the Land Ownership License. The Land Ownership License serves as the notification to the Land Department in the district where the land is located that the applicant has been granted permission by IEAT to own the land. Once the applicant obtains this Land Owner License the purchaser and the seller may go to the Land Office in the district where the land is located and effect transfer of title.

If the applicant intends to construct a factory on the land purchased he will also be required to obtain a Construction License from the IEAT. The final step is for the purchaser to submit a Notice to Start Industrial Operation with IEAT. Note that other licenses and/or approvals may also be required depending upon the company's intended operations.

4. Board of Investment — BOI

As discussed in Chapter 35, the BOI is the branch of the Thai government set up to encourage specific types of business projects in Thailand. Foreign companies that engage in these special types of projects, and otherwise qualify, may receive special privileges, including the right to own land. Unlike the land right granted by IEAT, the BOI is authorized to grant the right to own land outside of Industrial Estates. This can be quite significant from a pricing standpoint because the purchase price of land outside an Industrial Estate is generally much less than inside. There may be other indirect advantages in obtaining the right to own land outside industrial estates as well, such as less likelihood of staff turn over and logistic advantages.

5. Title Search

A very simple step that many foreign purchasers of property in Thailand overlook is performing a title search. This seems like common sense, but many foreigners make mistakes by not doing this. You will almost always learn something new about the property by performing a title search.

The legal status of the title is accessible to the general public at the local Land Office where the land is located. By conducting a title search one can determine the land's legal boundaries, whether the land has registered liens, mortgages, leases, etc.

6. Long Term Leases

Many foreigners avoid the above restrictions associated with owning land by instead leasing the designated land over the long term. This option is generally completely acceptable, and the foreigner may be afforded very broad rights to the land during the term of the lease. There are, however, some legal and practical limitations associated with this option.

Foreigners are generally allowed to lease land (outside an industrial estate) for up to thirty years. Foreigners may (depending on the terms of the lease) also own improvements erected on the leased property. However, no matter how broad the rights the foreign tenant has to the land during the lease period, the foreigner does not own any interest in the land. This is a very important distinction.

If the foreign tenant wishes to divest his rights to the land, he will be limited to assigning those rights to the land to a third party assignee (if the terms of the lease permit such assignment) or waiting until the conclusion of the lease term. Because of this, the foreign tenant's interest in the land is generally regarded as much less marketable than if he owned the land outright.

Also, in order to be enforceable after the initial three-year lease period, all leases of land for a period of longer than three years must be registered with the local Land Office where the land is located. After registration, the lease appears on the land title. If the lease is not registered, the terms of the lease are enforceable for the initial three-year period only.

EXAMPLE: Suppose a foreigner enters into a thirty-year lease of a plot of land, but does not register the lease with the local Land Office. The lease would be enforceable by the foreign tenant for the initial three-year period of the lease only.

Registering the lease with the Land Department effectively places prospective third party purchasers of the land on notice of the tenant's rights to the land during the period of the lease.

EXAMPLE: Suppose a foreign individual leases land for a period of thirty years and registers the lease with the local Land Office. The owner of the land then sells the land to a third party without mentioning the lease to the purchaser. That purchaser would acquire the land subject to the foreign tenant's rights for the remainder of the term of the lease. That is because by registering the lease the foreign tenant placed all future purchasers of the land on notice that any purchase of the land during the lease period would be subject to the current tenant's rights.

Vietnam

Capital City	Hanoi
Major Financial Center	Ho Chi Minh City
Population (projected 2010)	89 million
Location	Bordered with China in the north, Laos and Cambodia in the west, and South China Sea in the east
Major Languages	Vietnamese
Legal System	Civil law
Square Miles	127,123 sq mi
Gross Domestic Product (projected 2010)	USD 94 billion
Major Exports	Petroleum, rice, coffee, clothing, fish
Currency	Dong (VND)
U.S. Dollar Exchange Rate (as of November 2009)	USD 1 = VND 17,872
Euro Exchange Rate (as of November 2009)	EUR 1 = VND 27,958.26

Section Authors
Benjamin Yap and Nguyen Hoang Long
Kelvin Chia Partnership
Email: benjamin.yap@kcpartnership.com
Website: http://www.kcpartnership.com

Chapter 37

Should Our Business Establish as a Shareholding Company, Limited Liability Company, Branch, or Representative Office?

One of the first issues faced by prospective investors in Vietnam is choosing the appropriate type of legal entity through which to operate their business. The most commonly used of the entities available are shareholding company, limited liability company, branch, and representative office. When choosing the structure that is appropriate for your business you should consider a number of factors, including

i.   capital requirements

ii. the intended business activities to be pursued

iii. liability issues

iv. tax treatment

1. Shareholding Company and Limited Liability Company

A shareholding company and a limited liability company are similar in that the investors' potential legal liability in both is generally limited to the capital contributed and that management and ownership are separated in each. Also, unlike a branch and representative office (see below), both the shareholder company and limited liability company are treated under Vietnam law as stand-alone legal entities.

EXAMPLE: If a multinational company wishes to establish a subsidiary in Vietnam to operate as a stand-alone business to generate income it will likely do so either as a privately held shareholding company or a limited liability company, depending on the circumstances.

a. Shareholding Company

The private shareholding company (also know as joint-stock company) is owned by shareholders (minimum three) and managed by directors (minimum one). The liability of each of the shareholders is generally limited to the total par value of their shares. The shareholders' direct participation in company affairs is normally quite limited. It is the directors who are responsible for managing company affairs and who owe various fiduciary duties to the shareholders and the company (duty of care, duty of loyalty, etc.).

EXAMPLE: A French electronics company seeks to establish a presence in Vietnam and to eventually do a listing on the Vietnam stock exchange. Under these circumstances, the French company would likely establish in Vietnam as a shareholding company.

EXAMPLE: A Korean company and a local Vietnamese company wish to establish a joint venture in Vietnam to produce water heaters, and they wish to issue shares and be managed by a board of directors. In this situation, the joint venture would likely be established as a shareholding company.

b. Limited Liability Company

In Vietnam, a limited liability company's (LLC) paid-up capital is referred to as the charter. It does not issue shares, but is rather formed by the contributions of its members. Each member holds a percentage of equity proportionate to his/her contribution. Thus, voting power in an LLC is dependent on the amount of capital contribution. An LLC may not have more than fifty members.

An LLC may consist of only one member (single member LLC) or two or more members. Since the LLC is not permitted to issue shares, it may be suitable for investment where there are only one or two investors and/or if the company does not intend to list on a stock exchange.

EXAMPLE: A Singapore company wishes to establish a wholly owned subsidiary in Vietnam with no other investors/owners. In this situation, the Singapore company would likely do so as an LLC.

In an LLC the highest authority is the members' council, which consists of members or representatives authorized by members. Presiding over the members' council is the chairman of the council. A single-member LLC may, if the sole member so chooses, appoint only one authorized representative. In this case, the single authorized representative is the president of the company. The members' council or the president appoints or recruits the general director of the company.

Shareholding Company and LLC Comparison

	LLC	Shareholding company
Membership	Minimum 1 Maximum 50	Minimum 3 No maximum limitation
Highest authority	Members' Council	Shareholders' Meeting
Issuing shares	No	Yes
Listing	No	Yes
Liability	Limited liability	Limited liability

2. Representative Office and Branch

Many times, however, foreign investors will not want to operate as a shareholding company or as an LLC. This is most likely to be true when a multinational company seeks to establish a presence in Vietnam, but does not wish to establish a separate legal entity. For accounting, tax, and other reasons, the multinational company may instead want the Vietnam office to function as a part of the head office overseas. If that is the case, the multinational will normally choose to establish a representative office or branch office, instead of a shareholding company or LLC.

Vietnam law treats both a representative office and a branch as extensions of the head office overseas, not as separate legal entities. The employees are the employees of the overseas company.

a. Representative Office

Vietnam law requires that a foreign registered company must be incorporated or be in operation for not less than one year in order to qualify to establish a representative office in Vietnam.

EXAMPLE: A Japanese registered company seeks to establish a representative office in Vietnam. In order to qualify to establish the representative office, the Japanese head office must be able to show that it has been registered or has otherwise been in operation for not less than one year.

A representative office is restricted to conducting liaison and promotional (non-income generating) activities on behalf of the head office only, principally

i.   functioning as a liaison office

ii.   facilitating the formation of cooperative projects of the foreign company in Vietnam

iii. conducting market research to promote opportunities for purchase and sale of goods and for the provision and sale of commercial services of the foreign company that it represents

iv.   monitoring and facilitating the execution of contracts entered into by the foreign company that it represents

Vietnam law requires that the head office overseas appoint a chief representative of the representative office who may be either a Vietnamese national or a foreigner. The law does not require the chief representative to reside in Vietnam; however, his income from working as the chief representative is subject to Vietnamese personal income tax.

EXAMPLE: A Taiwan registered company establishes a representative office in Vietnam and appoints a Taiwanese national to be the representative office's chief representative. It is not necessary that the Taiwanese national reside in Vietnam; however, it is required that the Taiwanese national pay Vietnam income tax on the compensation he receives from working as the chief representative.

Furthermore, if the chief representative is a foreigner (i.e. a person holding citizenship of any country other than Vietnam), he must apply for a work permit, irrespective of whether or not he actually works and/ or resides in Vietnam during his term of employment.

EXAMPLE: A Canadian company establishes a representative office in Vietnam and appoints a Canadian national as the representative office's chief representative. The Canadian national will be required to obtain a Vietnamese work permit, irrespective of whether or not he actually works and resides in Vietnam.

The chief representative may be authorized to enter into contracts on behalf of the head office overseas; however, authorization for this must be made on a case-by-case basis, normally through a power of attorney. A general authorization for the chief representative to execute any contract is not valid under the laws of Vietnam.

EXAMPLE: A Singapore company with a representative office in Vietnam wishes to enter into a contract with a local Vietnamese company to purchase floor tiles from Vietnam and wants the chief representative of its Vietnam branch to sign the contract on behalf of the Singapore company. In order for this to happen, the Singapore company would be required to first execute a power of attorney or other such authorization. A general power of attorney or other such authorization would not be accepted.

Note that special rules apply to overseas companies seeking to establish a representative office if they engage in certain activities such as banking, finance, legal services, culture, education, tourism, and advertising.

b. Branch

A foreign company must be incorporated or in operation for no less than five years to be eligible to establish a branch in Vietnam.

EXAMPLE: A German registered company seeks to establish a representative office in Vietnam. In order to qualify to establish the representative office, the German head office must be able to show that it has been registered or has otherwise been in operation for not less than five years.

Unlike a representative office, a branch is permitted to enter into contracts and to engage in the sale and purchase of goods. Also, a branch is allowed to engage in profit generating activities.

3. Capital Required

The rules governing the amount of investment required to establish a shareholding company and an LLC are presented in chapters 38 and 39.

Note that there is no minimum capital requirement to establish a representative office.

Generally, there are no minimum capital requirements to establish a branch office; however, certain minimum requirements may apply if the branch is to engage in certain special industries such as banking, finance, legal services, culture, education, tourism, and advertising. To see a complete list go to www.doylesguideasia.com/vietnam/chapter37/appendixa.

4. Registration and Official Fees

The process to register a shareholding company and a limited liability company is described in Chapter 38.

Foreign companies seeking to establish a representative office in Vietnam must submit the designated application form, together with required supporting documents.

Foreign companies seeking to establish a branch office in Vietnam must submit the designated application form, together with required supporting documents.

In order to establish either a representative office or a branch, the applicant will be required to obtain an Establishment License prior to commencing operations in Vietnam. The government authority is required by statute to issue this license within fifteen working days of receipt of a "complete and valid" file of application documents.

Note that because government authority has a wide discretionary power on what is a "complete and valid" file and due to the lack of implementing regulations, this process may take longer.

Applicants seeking to establish either a representative office or a branch also must publish a notice of its establishment in a local newspaper for three consecutive issues, officially commence its operations, and notify the licensing authority within forty-five days from the date of issuance of the Establishment License.

Note that, to date, the Ministry of Industry and Trade has not provided any guidelines with regard to establishing a branch for the purpose of selling goods.

Therefore, even though it is theoretically possible for a foreign company to establish a branch in Vietnam for the purpose of selling goods, in practice, it may not be possible due to the absence of government issued guidelines.

In other special commercial sectors, such as banking, finance, legal services, culture, education, tourism, and advertisement, foreign companies are generally permitted to set up branches to carry on business in Vietnam.

Chapter 38

What Legal Issues Are Associated with the Start-Up of a Foreign-Held Company?

There are many legal and practical issues associated with the start-up of a company in Vietnam.

Some requirements are generally applicable to all companies in Vietnam, and other requirements are specifically applicable to foreign-held companies. Note that shelf companies are not available in Vietnam.

1. General Start-Up Requirements

A company name, legal representative, company seal, and charter are required to establish a company in Vietnam.

a. Company Name

Company names are registered and managed by the provincial or municipal Department of Planning and Investment; however, there is no formal system of name reservation.

A company name in Vietnam consists of two elements—a specification of the type of legal entity and the company's proper name.

For a limited liability company (LLC) (see Chapter 37), the name is required to be presented as

CONG TY TRACH NHIEM HUU HAN or CONG TY TNHH (Vietnamese language for LLC) + Proper Name (may be presented in foreign or Vietnamese language).

EXAMPLE: CONG TY TRACH NHIEM HUU HAN Glisten Shoe Polish
EXAMPLE: CONG TY TNHH Ever Star Batteries

For a shareholding company (see Chapter 37), the name is required to be presented as

CONG TY CO PHAN or CONG TY CP (Vietnamese language for shareholding company) + Proper Name (may be presented in foreign or Vietnamese language).

EXAMPLE: CONG TY CO PHAN Sparks Electronics

EXAMPLE: CONG TY CP Low Fat Doughnuts

The proper name of a company must consist of letters, numbers, or a combination of the two and must be pronounceable.

EXAMPLE: A Dutch consulting company seeks to establish a company in Vietnam with VPJL as the company's proper name. As VPJL is not pronounceable, the presiding official at the Department of Planning and Investment would likely withhold approval for that name.

Vietnamese law technically prohibits names which are identical to or names which cause confusion with names of other companies already registered within the same province or city; however, practically speaking, as there is no centralized system of company name registration, there could be a case where one party registers a name in one province, and then another party registers the same name in another province.

EXAMPLE: In a northern province, a name is reserved and the company is registered with the name CONG TY TNHH Stardust Apparel, and then later in a southern province a third party registers the exact same name.

In order to avoid this situation, where possible, the party who has reserved the company name should also register that name as a trade name with the intellectual property authority of Vietnam. If this is done, that company name should not be registerable by a third party unless the previous party registering the name consents.

EXAMPLE: Same facts as above, except the first company registered the name Stardust Apparel Inc. with the intellectual property authority in Vietnam shortly after registering the company name. In this situation, when a third party later attempts to register the same company name, it should not be allowed, unless the trade name owner first consents.

In practice, the licensing authorities usually wield a wide discretion as to whether to permit the registration of a proper name. It is, therefore, always prudent to prepare more than one name for the company.

b. Legal Representative

Every company in Vietnam is required to have an individual serve as the company's legal representative.

The role of a legal representative of a company is to act on the company's behalf signing documents and in representing the company when dealing with third parties.

The legal representative must reside in Vietnam; therefore, if the legal representative is not a Vietnamese national, he must apply for a temporary residence. If the legal representative is absent from Vietnam for thirty days or more, he must authorize another person to act as a legal representative in his absence.

EXAMPLE: A Vietnamese company seeks to have a Dutch national serve as its legal representative. In order to qualify, the Dutch national must first apply for temporary residence with the proper authority in Vietnam (see Chapter 40).

EXAMPLE: The Dutch national is named as the legal representative. Any time the Dutch national is to be outside of Vietnam for a period of thirty days or more he is required to authorize another qualified party to act as the company's legal representative in his absence.

As stated in Chapter 37, the most common types of companies in Vietnam are a shareholding company and a limited liability company, with each having their own distinctive requirements of a legal representative.

In a shareholding company, either the chairman of the board of management or the director/general director may be appointed the legal representative.

In a limited liability company, only the president, the chairman of the members' council, or the director/general director may be appointed as the legal representative.

Note that in some cases, the legal representative can be held personally liable for certain omissions or failures on the part of the company, such as failure of the company to pay taxes, failure to make required corporate filings, and in certain litigation situations. Therefore, an individual should consider these liability issues carefully before agreeing to be a company's legal representative.

c. Company Seal

Under the laws of Vietnam, a company is required to possess a single company seal, which must be officially registered and kept at the company's head office. The seal must be affixed to all documents to be executed, together with the signature of the legal representative (see above section). The absence of either the seal or the signature will render the documents unenforceable.

d. Charter

The charter of a company sets forth the company's scope of activities, the company regulations and authorizations of various parties, and the company's organizational structure. A copy of the draft charter must be submitted together with other application documents for the establishment of the company.

To see the information that must be stated in the charter go to www.doylesguideasia.com/vietnam/chapter38/appendixa.

2. Foreign Company Start-Up Requirements

In addition to the above requirements, Vietnamese law requires that foreign companies (companies in which non-Vietnamese parties hold any ownership interest) comply with investment project law and minimum capital requirements. They must also state their investment capital, enter into a lease agreement, register to pay taxes, and open a bank account.

a. Investment Project and Investment Certificate

A foreigner investing in Vietnam for the first time must apply for and obtain an investment project certificate (investment certificate) for each project the company is to engage in from the Department of Planning and Investment in the province that is the site of the project.

To see the application go to www.doylesguideasia.com/vietnam/chapter 38/appendixb, and to see a list of industries requiring the certificate, go to www.doylesguideasia.com/vietnam/chapter38/appendixc.

The law specifies that the evaluation period for the application shall not exceed forty-five days.

The term of operation of an investment project is normally fifty years. In some exceptional cases the term may extend to seventy years.

Note that a company may implement more than one investment project, and the term of operation of its project(s) does not affect the lifetime of the company.

The application for the investment certificate is required to contain the following information:

i.   Name of the investment project (could be different from the name of the company to be established)

ii. Objective and scale

iii. Location

iv. Total investment capital and charter (i.e. paid-up) capital

v.   Term of operation

vi. Schedule for implementation

vii. Investment incentives (if any)

b. Legal Capital

Vietnamese law sets forth minimum capital requirements for foreign companies engaging in certain business activities. This requirement (when applicable) is known as the company's legal capital. The business activities in which the minimum legal capital requirements apply are listed below.

Securities Trading

i.   Finance and securities/stock investment advice: VND 10 billion

ii. Securities/stock brokerage: VND 25 billion

iii. Securities/stock trading: VND 100 billion

iv. Securities/stock underwriting: VND 165 billion

Finance and Banking

i.   Joint-venture bank or wholly-owned foreign bank: VND 1,000 billion (2008) and VND 3,000 billion (2010)

ii. Branch of foreign bank: US $15 million

iii. Financial company: VND 300 billion (2008) and VND 500 billion (2010)

iv. Finance-leasing company: VND 100 billion (2008) and VND 150 billion (2010)

Travel Agency

i.   Domestic travel agency: VND 50 million

ii. International travel agency: VND 250 million

Employment Agency: VND 300 million

Real Estate Business: VND 6 billion

The government authorities will many times request evidence of the availability of capital in the form of a deposit into a Vietnam bank account prior to granting the investment certificate. This may cause inconvenience for some foreign investors, as not everyone is prepared to deposit funds without any certainty as to whether a certificate will be issued in the first place.

EXAMPLE: A Belgian company seeking to engage in the employment agency business establishes a company and applies for an investment certificate to do that business. Before the certificate is granted, the presiding government official may require that the Belgian company deposit an amount representing the minimum legal capital (VND 300 million) in a bank in Vietnam.

c. Investment Capital

Investment capital is separate from legal capital and represents the total amount of capital that an investor agrees to contribute throughout the life of the project. It consists of paid-up capital (also referred to as charter capital) and unpaid capital (also referred to as loan capital).

The investment capital is stated in the application for the investment certificate, and later, if the certificate is granted, it will be stated in the certificate itself.

EXAMPLE: A Swiss company establishes a shareholding company in Vietnam for the purpose of establishing a factory to produce hard drives. In its investment certificate application the company states that its total paid-in (or charter) capital is set at VND 100 billion and the unpaid (or loan) capital is an additional VND 100 billion.

Note that after the certificate is issued, whenever the investor intends to increase its investment capital, it must apply for an amendment of the investment certificate, which may take several weeks.

It is therefore recommended that investors consider the total amount of investment required for the project from the beginning and set the investment capital accordingly, in order to avoid the inconvenience and added costs of amending their investment certificate.

There are no specific minimum investment capital requirements; however, the amount of investment capital as set forth in the application for the investment certificate may impact on whether or not the application is approved.

d. Land/Office Lease Agreement

In the application for the issuance of an investment certificate, the investor must state the location of the head office (i.e. registered office) of the company in Vietnam and the location where the investment project is to be implemented (if it is a different place from the head office). As a matter of principle, a lease is a pre-requisite condition for the authorities to issue the investment certificate.

e. Tax Registration

Within ten days from the date of issuance of the investment certificate, the company must register with the tax authorities. In practice, the tax authorities of the provincial/municipal Tax Department normally accept application documents even after the deadline; however, the company may be subject to a fine for late submission.

f. Bank Accounts

A newly established company must open a bank account to carry out business in Vietnam. The bank account opening procedures will vary from bank to bank, and it is prudent to consult with the bank in advance.

The following documents are generally required to open a bank account:

i.   Investment certificate

ii. A copy of the charter

iii. Minutes/resolution of the members' council (in the case of an LLC) or the board management (in the case of a shareholding company) appointing the signatories of the company

iv. A copy of the identification paper (e.g. passport or identity card) of the signatories

v.   Seal registration certificate

Chapter 39

What Legal Issues Are Associated with Operating as a Foreign-Held Company?

Vietnam law broadly regulates the activities of companies which are legally classified as foreign invested, as set forth below.

1. Definition of Foreign

There is no clear definition of what constitutes a foreign invested company under Vietnamese laws; however, the commonly held view is that a company registered in Vietnam with any foreign shareholders will be legally classified as foreign-invested, and therefore, subject to regulation.

EXAMPLE: A company registered in Vietnam with one foreign individual shareholder holding one share may be legally classified as a foreign-invested company and therefore, subject to regulation.

2. Regulated Activities

Both foreign and local companies are not allowed to engage in activities which are legally prohibited. Accordingly, any activities are prohibited which are

i.   detrimental to national defense and security and public interests

ii. harmful to historical and cultural relics, morality, and Vietnamese fine customs

iii. harmful to the people's health or destroy natural resources and the environment

iv. related to the treatment of hazardous waste brought from overseas into Vietnam or to the manufacture of toxic chemicals or the use of toxic agents prohibited under treaties

To see a complete list of the activities prohibited for investment go to www.doylesguideasia.com/vietnam/chapter39/appendixa.

Foreign-invested companies seeking to engage in activities which are legally classified as "conditional to foreign investors" must comply with sector specific requirements as set by Vietnamese law and international treaties. Examples of these activities include radio and television broadcasting, publishing and distribution of cultural products, mining, and processing of minerals, as well as many other activities.

In addition, note that recently certain foreign investment restrictions are being liberalized by the government, per Vietnam's World Trade Organization Commitments.

EXAMPLE: Previously foreign-invested companies were generally prohibited from engaging in courier services. However, now foreign investors seeking to engage in courier services may generally do so, as long as the foreign equity participation does not exceed 51%.

3. Business License Application

In addition to complying with normal company registration procedures to obtain an investment certificate(s) as set forth in Chapter 38, foreign invested companies seeking to engage in distribution services are also required to apply for and obtain a business license prior to beginning operations.

Distribution services have a specific definition under Vietnamese law, which include the retail and wholesale sale of goods, operating a commercial agency, and operating as a commercial franchise.

A commercial agency is defined as commercial activity in which the principal and the agent agree that the agent conduct in its own name the sale or purchase of goods for the principal or provide the services of the principal to customers in order to receive remuneration.

A commercial franchise is defined as commercial activity in which a franchisor authorizes and requires a franchisee to conduct on its own behalf the purchase and sale of goods or provision of services that is in line with the method of business organization specified by the franchisor. It must be associated with the trademark, trade name, business know-how, business mission statements, business logo, and advertising of the franchisor. The franchisor has the right to control and offer assistance to the franchisee in the conduct of the business.

EXAMPLE: German investors seek to establish a company in Vietnam to sell hot water heaters produced outside of Vietnam. In this situation, in addition to complying with the normal company registration procedures and obtaining an investment certificate(s) necessary to engage in the activity, the investors would also be required to obtain a business license.

EXAMPLE: Italian investors seek to establish a coffee house chain in Vietnam. In this situation, in addition to complying with the normal company registration procedures and obtaining an investment certificate(s) necessary to engage in the activity, the investors would also be required to obtain a business license.

Foreign investors seeking to engage in distribution services are required to submit for approval an application with the provincial People's Committee in the district where the company is located.

The procedure to obtain a business certificate involves three steps:

i.   Submission of application documents to the provincial People's Committee: To see the list of supporting documents required to be submitted together with the application go to www.doylesguideasia.com/vietnam/chapter39/appendixb. The relevant provincial People's Committee will review the application, and when it is satisfied that the application documents are "valid and complete," it will forward the application to the Ministry of Industry and Trade for its consideration.

ii.   Processing by the Ministry of Industry and Trade: The Ministry of Industry and Trade is required to rule on the application within fifteen days upon its receipt from the provincial People's Committee.

iii. Issuance of the Business License: If the Ministry of Industry and Trade approves the application, the provincial People's Committee will issue the Business License within fifteen days.

Foreign investors and their companies must meet the following criteria in order to receive a business license:

i.   The foreign investor is from a country which is a member of the WTO or is a signatory of the international treaties to which Vietnam is also a signatory.

ii.   The form and structure of the investment is consistent with the schedule undertaken in the international treaties to which Vietnam is a signatory, as well as the laws of Vietnam.

iii. The goods and services traded and the scope of operation is consistent with Vietnam's commitments to open its market to increased foreign participation, as well as consistent with the laws of Vietnam.

Note that where a foreign invested company merely intends to carry out import services (without the right to distribute, but only to sell to local licensed distributors), the foreign invested company will be exempt from having to apply for the Business License.

EXAMPLE: A Japanese auto parts company seeks to establish a company in Vietnam for the purpose of selling its auto parts produced in Japan to licensed distributors in Vietnam. In this situation, although the company would be required to follow the normal company registration procedures and obtain an investment certificate to establish a company in Vietnam to engage in this activity, it would not be required to obtain a business license.

To see a list of goods not allowed to be imported go to www.doylesguideasia.com/vietnam/chapter39/appendixc.

4. Nominee Shareholders

Generally, nominee shareholders are individuals or companies that agree to hold shares on behalf of the true owner(s) of the shares. Under this arrangement, typically the nominee shareholder and the true owner execute an agreement stating that the nominee shareholder agrees to hold the shares in name only. The true owner retains all rights of ownership and control (voting rights, rights to transfer, rights to receive dividends, etc.) of the shares.

The laws of Vietnam do not recognize the separation of legal and beneficial ownership of shares and, therefore, the use of nominee shareholders to establish a company in order to avoid legal restrictions is illegal. Further, any arrangements entered into to try to protect the foreign investor in this situation would also be unenforceable.

EXAMPLE: A French company seeks to establish a book distribution company in Vietnam. The French company enters into an agreement with a Vietnamese company, where the French company pays the Vietnamese company an amount of money equal to the total registered capital of the book distribution company, which the Vietnamese company uses to form a 100% domestically-owned company using its own name. The book distribution company makes a profit and declares dividends, but the Vietnamese company does not pass on the profits to the French company as agreed. The French company sues the Vietnamese company for breach of their agreement. In this situation, the Vietnam court would likely rule that the nominee arrangement was meant to circumvent the rules prohibiting foreign investment, so it is unenforceable. Also, both the French company and the Vietnam company may be subject to civil and criminal penalties.

Chapter 40

What Is the Process to Obtain a Work Permit?

The Vietnam government limits the issuance of work permits to foreigners who hold management positions in a foreign company and foreign experts.

A management position is defined as a job in which the person is directly in charge of the management of a foreign parent company that has set up a subsidiary or commercial presence in Vietnam and reports to the board or to the shareholders' meetings of that foreign company.

An expert is defined as a person who possesses specialist and highly technical qualifications concerning services, and technical and research skills, as well as considerable experience concerning production, business coordination, and/or management.

EXAMPLE: A locally owned Vietnamese company seeks to employ a foreigner. In order for that foreigner to qualify to receive a work permit one of the things that will have to be established is that the foreigner is an expert according to the above criteria.

1. Exceptions to the Work Permit Requirement

All foreigners working in Vietnam must obtain a work permit, subject to the following exceptions:

i.   A foreigner enters Vietnam to work for no longer than three months within the same calendar year.

EXAMPLE: A UK national is a director of a UK company which has registered a subsidiary in Vietnam. He is in charge of the supervision of subsidiary operations and must often travel to Vietnam to fulfill his duties. In (calendar) Year One he resides and works in Vietnam for seventy-eight days and in (calendar) Year Two, one-hundred-twelve days. In this situation, the UK national would not be required to obtain a work permit in Year One, but would be required to in Year Two.

    ii.   A foreigner enters Vietnam to represent a foreign service provider negotiating a service and does not receive remuneration from any source in Vietnam, offer any service to the public in general, or directly engage in providing the service being negotiated.

EXAMPLE: A representative of a US software company goes to Vietnam to negotiate with the primary contractor of a banking services project at a Vietnam bank to supply certain technical services. The representative does not enter into any other business activities while in Vietnam and is not paid from any source in Vietnam. In this situation, the representative would not need a work permit to enter Vietnam.

    iii.   A foreigner enters Vietnam to resolve a technical emergency and/or complicated issue beyond the capability of local technicians. If the foreigner fails to resolve the issue within three months, he must apply for a work permit.

EXAMPLE: A telecommunication company in Vietnam experiences a serious problem with its service network, and there is no local technician available who can assist. The company then locates a German expert with special skills to resolve the problem. In this situation, the German could come to Vietnam to solve the problem without obtaining a work permit. If, however, he is required to work in Vietnam for a period exceeding three months, he would be required to obtain a work permit.

    iv.   A foreigner is a member of a limited liability company with two or more members or is the owner of a single-member limited liability company (see Chapter 37).

    v.   A foreigner is a member of the board of management of a shareholding company (see Chapter 37).

    vi.   A foreigner is a foreign licensed lawyer holding a certificate to practice issued by the Ministry of Justice.

In a case where the foreign employee is exempted from applying for a work permit, the employer must send a notice in the required form to the Department of Labor, Invalids and Social Affairs (DOLISA) in the province/city where the foreign employee is to work. The notice must be submitted within seven working days prior to the date when the foreign employee is to start working.

2. Visa

A visa (for a duration of one year or less) or a temporary residence card (a type of longer term visa for a duration of up to three years) is the foreign employee's permission to reside in Vietnam. The work permit is the foreign employee's permission to work in Vietnam. The foreign employee is required to obtain both. The application for a visa and the application for a work permit are two different forms, processed by two different authorities. The visa application is processed by the Immigration Department of the Ministry of Public Security, while the work permit application is processed by the DOLISA.

The employer must submit the application for the visa to the Immigration Department on the foreign employee's behalf prior to the foreign employee entering Vietnam. Shortly after receipt of an in-principle approval of the application from the Immigration Department, the foreign employee may collect the visa at the Vietnamese embassy or consulate in the foreign country where he is then residing.

To see a list of the supporting documents required to be submitted together with the application go to www.doylesguideasia.com/vietnam/chapter40/appendixa.

3. Work Permit

A work permit is the authorization granted to a foreigner to work for a specific employer in Vietnam and within a specific scope of work. Work permit applications are processed by the DOLISA. Upon issuance, the work permit remains valid so long as the foreigner is working for the same employer within the period stated in the work permit, which may not exceed thirty-six months.

EXAMPLE: A Canadian national is employed by a Vietnam registered company as the quality control director for its factory and receives a work permit for this position. If, in the future, the Canadian employee's job within the company changes or he accepts employment with another company, he would be required to obtain a new work permit for that position.

The work permit application must be submitted to the DOLISA in the province/city where the head office of the employer is located or where the employee is to work, at least twenty working days prior to the date when the employee is scheduled to start working.

The DOLISA is then required to issue the work permit within fifteen days of receiving the application or, in the event the application is rejected, the

DOLISA is required to provide a written explanation as to the grounds for the rejection.

Foreign employees may qualify to receive a work permit in the following situations:

i.   Recruitment by way of an Employment Contract: The foreigner works under an employment contract with a Vietnamese employer (such as a company established in Vietnam, including a foreign-invested company under the Law of Investment, or the commercial presence of a foreign company in Vietnam).

ii. Internal Transfer: The foreigner is transferred to work in Vietnam at a subsidiary or a commercial presence of a foreign company.

iii. Contract of Employment Service: The foreigner works under a contract entered into between a Vietnamese partner and a foreign party in which it was agreed that the foreigner will be sent to work in Vietnam.

a. Recruitment by Way of an Employment Contract

Under this option, an employer in Vietnam may only recruit a foreign employee for a management position or as a foreign expert when the employer is unable to hire a suitable Vietnamese person. There is, therefore, a requirement for the employer to first attempt to recruit a local for the position before hiring a foreigner. To do this, the employer may either engage a recruitment service provider or do the recruitment himself.

In the event that the employer chooses to recruit the person(s) himself, he is required to place a newspaper ad announcing the vacancy and giving Vietnamese applicants thirty days to apply prior to recruiting a foreigner.

If a foreigner then applies for the position, he will be required to submit two sets of applications: one application to the prospective employer and a second application to be used by the employer to apply for the foreign employee's work permit (if he is hired) with the DOLISA. This second application must contain the following documents:

i.   Judicial record (or certificate of no criminal conviction) issued by the authorized body of the country where the foreigner lived prior to coming to Vietnam. If the foreigner has currently resided in Vietnam for six months or more, then there need only be a legal record issued by the Vietnamese Department of Justice of the address where the foreigner is residing.

ii. Curriculum vitae of the foreigner on the standard form prescribed by the Ministry of Labor, Invalids and Social Affairs.

iii. Health certificate issued overseas or health certificate issued in Vietnam in accordance with the regulations of the Ministry of Health.

iv. Copies of certificates of specialist or highly technical qualifications of the foreigner.

v. Three color photos (3cm by 4cm in size, bareheaded, frontal view, showing the face and ears clearly, without glasses, and on a white background) taken within six months of the date on which the foreigner submits the application file.

Upon obtaining the work permit, the employer and the foreign employee are required to enter into an employment contract and then submit a copy of the executed contract to the DOLISA within five days from the date of execution. The terms and conditions of the employment contract must not be contradictory to the provisions of the work permit.

EXAMPLE: A German owned company registered in Vietnam recruits a US engineer to work in its factory and submits an application for a work permit, which is eventually granted. The company and employee also enter into an employee contract; however, the job description as stated in the employment contract is different from the job description stated in the work permit. This would be in violation of Vietnam law.

b. Internal Transfer

Under Vietnam law, a foreign employee who works for a foreign company which has established a commercial presence in Vietnam, holds a management position or is an expert in the company, and has worked for the company for at least twelve months, may temporarily work (maximum thirty-six months, renewable) for the foreign company in Vietnam by way of internal transfer and qualify to receive a work permit.

In addition, a minimum of 20% of the total management personnel and experts of such company must be Vietnamese. However, the employer company is allowed to have a minimum of three foreigners (total) who hold positions as managers or experts, irrespective of the foreign local percentage.

EXAMPLE: A Korean national who has worked for a Singaporean company as the CFO of its India office for the past five years learns that he will be transferred to work in the Singapore company's office in Ho Chi Minh City. Currently, ten of the Vietnam offices' twenty-five managers are Vietnamese nationals. In this situation, the Korean would qualify to receive a work permit as an internal transfer.

The person being transferred to Vietnam must receive an appointment letter from the foreign company, and the employer must apply for a work permit on his behalf before he enters Vietnam.

EXAMPLE: Same facts as above: In order for the Korean employee to obtain a work permit as an internal transfer, the Vietnam office is required to issue a letter appointing the Korean to the position in Vietnam, and the Singaporean company must apply for a work permit on the Korean employee's behalf before he enters Vietnam to work.

c. Contract of Employment Service

A Vietnamese company entering into a service contract with a foreign party in which the foreign party will be required to send a person(s) to Vietnam in order to perform the contract is responsible for applying for the work permit for that foreign person(s).

EXAMPLE: A German company and a Vietnamese company establish a joint venture in Vietnam. One provision of the joint venture agreement states that the German company will send one person to Vietnam to assist with the installation of equipment in the joint venture company's factory. Using these facts, the joint venture company would be required to apply for the work permit for the individual the German company is to send.

4. Required Documents

The work permit application is submitted to the relevant official within the DOLISA together with supporting documents.

To see a complete list of the supporting documents required go to www.doylesguideasia.com/vietnam/chapter40/appendixb.

The foreign employee must also submit the document that indicates how he was hired:

i.   His employment application if he was Recruited by Way of an Employment Contract (see above)

ii. The letter of appointment from the foreign company if he is an Internal Transfer (see above)

iii. A copy of the service contract if he is a Contract of Employment Service hire (see above)

Note that any document submitted by the foreign employee which is issued by a foreign government authority must be notarized and legalized at the Vietnam embassy in the country where the document was issued and translated into Vietnamese before being submitted to the DOLISA.

5. Single Entry/Re-Entry Permit

A foreigner intending to make multiple trips to Vietnam should apply for a multiple entry visa. Otherwise, the visa that is issued will be only for a single entry.

6. Dependents

A foreign employee who is permitted to reside in Vietnam for six months or more may apply for a visa(s) for his dependents to live with him in Vietnam. The dependent visa application is submitted to the Immigration Department in Vietnam, and the visa should be issued within five working days of submission if all documents are in order. The time period of the dependent visa is subject to the discretion of the official; however, it may be granted for a period up to the expiration of the foreign employee's business visa.

7. Work Permit Extension

A work permit will only be extended if the nature of the work to be performed by the foreign employee requires more than thirty-six months or if a Vietnamese employee who was trained to replace the foreign employee fails to satisfy the job requirement.

To see a list of the required supporting documents go to www.doylesguideasia. com/vietnam/chapter40/appendixc.

The extension request application and all supporting documents must be submitted to the DOLISA at least thirty days prior to the date of expiration of the current work permit. The DOLISA then has fifteen days to either issue the Work Permit with the requested extended term or provide a written explanation as to why the application is rejected.

The extension term may not exceed an additional thirty-six months.

8. Official Fees

The official fee payable to the DOLISA at the time the work permit application is submitted is VND 400,000.

Chapter 41

What Investment Incentives Are Available to Foreign Investors?

The Ministry of Planning and Investment (MPI) is the Vietnam government agency responsible for attracting certain types of investment projects to Vietnam. The government incentives available to investors in Vietnam by MPI and the requirements and application procedures are discussed below.

1. Investment Incentives Available

The following are investment incentives normally available to qualifying foreign investment projects in Vietnam:

i.   A special corporate income tax rate

ii.   Corporate income tax exemptions and reductions

iii. Customs duties exemptions for raw materials and machinery

iv.   Land rental exemption

Investment incentives are granted for a fixed period of time. After the expiration of that period of time, the incentives no longer apply, and the project is subject to the ordinary rules and regulations.

EXAMPLE: A project is granted a corporate income tax exemption for a period of five years, starting from the date of commencement of operations. Upon the expiration of that five-year period, the project would be subject to normal corporate income tax rules going forward.

Also, note that the incentives awarded by MPI are applicable in a general manner to all the company's promoted activities but not to the business's other operations (if any).

EXAMPLE: Suppose a company is granted MPI promotion for a project to produce electronic components for export. One of the MPI incentives granted is exemption from import duties for raw materials needed to produce the components. This company, however, also produces stereos for sale in Vietnam, and the same imported raw materials used to produce the electric components are also used to produce stereos. In this situation, the raw materials imported by the company to produce the components for export (promoted activity) would qualify for the exemption from import duty. However, the raw materials imported to produce stereos for sale in Vietnam (non-promoted activity) would be subject to normal import duty.

Tax incentives are applicable only to newly established companies. The laws define a newly established company as a company to which an investment certificate (see Chapter 38) has been issued for the first time.

EXAMPLE: A German investor registers a company in Vietnam and is issued an investment certificate and then five years later seeks to start a new project which qualifies for tax incentives according to the MPI. In this situation, it would appear to be more favorable if the German investor registers a new company and applies for a new investment certificate, as his existing company would not qualify for such incentives.

When a project qualifies to receive more than one tax incentive the investor may choose the more favorable incentive.

EXAMPLE: A Danish company invests to engage in education services (which qualifies for the special tax rate of 10%) and is also located in a geographical area with socio-economic difficulties (which qualifies for the special tax rate of 20%). In this situation, the investor may choose the more favorable 10% rate.

a. Tax Incentives

The MPI has broad authority to grant qualifying projects one or more tax incentives. For example, a company which engages in any of the following activities qualifies for a special tax rate of 10% for a period up to 15 years:

i.   The company invests in a geographical area with special socio-economic difficulties. To see a list of these areas go to www.doylesguideasia.com/vietnam/chapter41/appendixa.

ii. The company invests in an economic zone or a high-tech zone established by way of a decision of the Prime Minister.

iii. The company invests in the high-tech sector (including software development), research and development, or key infrastructure such as water plants, electric plants, roads, bridges, airports, marine ports, etc.

In addition to a preferential tax rate, companies investing in the aforementioned areas or in the high tech sector (referred to as Group A Companies) are also granted a tax exemption for the initial four years of the project, as well as a tax reduction of 50% for the subsequent nine years.

EXAMPLE: A Singapore investor establishes a microchip plant which qualifies as being in the high-tech sector, and therefore, the investor qualifies for Group A Company incentives. In this situation, the Singapore investor would qualify to receive the following tax rates:

i.   A tax exemption for the first four years.

ii. Starting in year 5, the project would qualify for the special tax rate of 10%.

iii. In years 5 to 13 the project would receive an additional 50% tax reduction (to be applied on top of the special tax rate).

iv. In years 14 and 15 the project would be granted the special tax rate of 10% (without the benefit of the 50% reduction).

The special tax rate of 10% also may apply during the entire lifetime of a company in respect to income derived from its business operations in the following areas: education, training, healthcare, culture, sports, and environment (referred to as Group B Companies).

Group B Companies operating in geographical areas with socio-economic difficulties are also entitled to a tax exemption for four years, as well as a tax reduction of 50% for nine subsequent years.

EXAMPLE: A US held company in Vietnam establishes a hospital in Gia Lai (an area with special socio-economic difficulties), which qualifies the Vietnam registered company as a Group B Company. In this situation, this project would qualify for the following tax rates:

i.   Four years of tax exemption.

ii. Starting in year 5 the project would qualify for the special tax rate of 10%.

iii. In years 5 thru 13 an additional 50% tax reduction would be applied on top of the special tax rate.

iv. After year 13 the 10% tax rate (without the 50% additional reduction) would be applicable each year thereafter.

Group B Companies operating in other areas (outside of areas with socio-economic difficulties) are entitled to a tax exemption for the initial four years, as well as a tax reduction of 50% for the subsequent five years.

b. Exemption from Import Duties

MPI may also grant promoted projects an exemption on import duties for equipment, machine and machinery spare parts, special-purpose transportation vehicles and their spare parts, and materials which may not be domestically produced in Vietnam. To see a list of the types of projects which may qualify to receive an exemption from import duties go to www.doylesguide asia.com/vietnam/chapter41/appendixb.

Investment in sectors such as hotels, offices, residential apartments, commercial complexes, supermarkets, golf courses, tourist, sportive or recreational areas, or other industries such as healthcare, education, training, culture, finance, banking, insurance, auditing and consulting services are entitled to exemption from import duties for the following goods (imported for the first-time only):

i.   Hotel room furniture and interior decoration (beds, cupboards, tables, chairs, telephones)

ii.   Sanitary ware (bathtubs, toilets, wash basins, supplies for installing sanitary ware, mirrors)

iii.   Living-room sets (tables, chairs)

iv.   Equipment and facilities for kitchens, dining-rooms, restaurants, and bars (assorted cookers and cooking devices)

v.   Paintings, statues, carpets, and other decorative articles

vi.   Refrigerators, televisions, microwave ovens, smoke absorbers, vacuum cleaners, and machines for deodorizing cups, plates and bowls

vii.   Audio and video equipment

viii. Golfing gear

c. Land Rental Exemption or Reduction

Normally, manufacturing and other types of projects in Vietnam are required to lease their production facilities from the Vietnam government. Projects promoted by MPI, however, may be granted either an exemption from land rental payments entirely or a reduction in the rental. This incentive may be granted for the entire life of the project or for a fixed term.

The following investment projects are entitled to an exemption from land rental payments for the entire life of the project:

i.   Investment projects in investment sectors entitled to special investment incentives and carried out in geographical areas with special socio-economic difficulties.

       To see the list of these sectors go to www.doylesguideasia.com/vietnam/chapter41/appendixc.

To see the list of these areas go to www.doylesguideasia.com/vietnam/chapter41/appendixd.

ii. Investment projects for the development of residential apartments for workers working in industrial zones; student hostels; or public construction works (for profit) in education, healthcare, culture, sports, science, and technology.

Fixed term exemptions apply to eligible investment projects upon the completion of construction work according to project type:

Project Type	Exemption Period
Investment projects in investment sectors entitled to investment incentives	3 years
Investment projects in geographical areas with socio-economic difficulties	7 years
Investment projects in investment sectors entitled to (special) investment incentives	7 years
Investment projects in geographical areas with (special) socio-economic difficulties	11 years
Investment projects in investment sectors entitled to investment incentives in geographical areas with socio-economic difficulties	11 years
Investment projects in investment sectors entitled to investment incentives in geographical areas with (special) socio-economic difficulties	15 years

Land rental reduction is not a common investment incentive as it only applies to investors suffering from difficulties caused by a major force, such as natural disaster or fire.

2. Application Process

The application for MPI investment incentives is required to be submitted, together with the application for the issuance of the investment certificate (see Chapter 38) with the provincial MPI office where the project will be located.

Note that it is the duty of the applicant to set forth all the incentives that the project qualifies for in the application.

The application process normally takes between three and six months.

If approved, the investment incentives granted will be stated in the investment certificate issued by MPI.

Chapter 42

What Legal Issues Are Associated with Foreign Ownership of Land?

Vietnam law does not recognize the private ownership of land by individuals or companies, (either local or foreign), as ownership of all land in Vietnam resides with the government. Instead, the law allows for degrees of (non-ownership) rights associated with use of the land (land use rights) to be transferred to individuals and companies (both foreign and local), as explained below.

Note, however, that Vietnam law does allow for the ownership of immovable property erected on land that has been leased.

EXAMPLE: A Hong Kong company acquires land use rights to a piece of land and constructs a factory. In this situation, although the Hong Kong company is not legally allowed to own the land, it is allowed to own the factory.

1. Land Use Rights

As mentioned above, instead of allowing for land ownership, Vietnam law allows for varying degrees of land use rights, which are less than ownership rights. These rights are referred to as land grants and land leases.

Land grants (which transfer comparatively greater rights) are only available to Vietnamese parties from the government by way of an administrative decision. A land grant is given either on a "stable long term basis" or for a fixed duration and may be made either with or without the payment of land fees, depending on the situation.

For the purpose of this chapter, any reference to a land grant means land in which the payment of land fees is applicable.

Land leases (transferring comparatively fewer rights) may be transferred to Vietnamese parties and foreign invested companies. A land lease is a contract between the government and the lessee where the land use rights will be leased for a fixed duration (see rules concerning period of lease below), and the lessee pays rent to the government (see conditions below).

Note that one of the major differences between a land grant and a land lease is that a land grant may be granted on a "stable long term basis," which means for an indefinite amount of time, and a land lease will always be for a specified amount of time.

EXAMPLE: Swedish investors seek to establish a company in Vietnam in order to acquire rights to a particular piece of land and build a factory. Normally, the Swedish investors would be limited to leasing land for a period of fifty years (see below).

EXAMPLE: Same facts as above, but the company is Vietnamese owned. In this situation, the Vietnamese company may potentially be able to secure a land grant on a "stable long term basis" for an indefinite period.

An exception to this rule applies in the situation where a joint venture company has been established between a foreign investor and a locally owned Vietnamese company, and the Vietnamese company's contribution to the joint venture company is land (it has received by way of a land grant), instead of cash.

EXAMPLE: A local Vietnamese company and Canadian investors enter into a joint venture to establish a new company in Vietnam. The Canadian company seeks to contribute cash and technology to the new joint venture company, and the Vietnamese company seeks to contribute land it has received by way of a land grant from the government. In certain situations, it would be permissible for the Vietnamese company to contribute its land grant to the joint venture company, despite the fact that the company has foreign shareholders.

2. Land Use Period

Foreign invested companies (not foreign individuals) are allowed to lease land for the purpose of carrying out an approved investment project for a period up to fifty years or, in exceptional cases, up to seventy years.

The lease period is determined by the authorized land officials, based upon the merits of the investment project as stated in the lease application.

EXAMPLE: A German company establishes a shareholding company (see Chapter 37) in Vietnam for the purpose of operating a jewelry factory and finds an appropriate site for the factory. After the company has applied for and obtained its investment project certificate from the Department of Planning and

Investment (see Chapter 37), it would be allowed to apply for a land use rights certificate (see below) in order to lease the land.

EXAMPLE: A US global hotel chain constructs a multimillion US Dollar mega resort in Halong Bay, Vietnam. The normal maximum period of land lease for the property would be fifty years; however, if the US investor can establish that due to the size of the project, the investor's return on investment will likely be slow, the project may be granted a seventy-year lease.

3. Application for Lease

Foreign companies carrying out investment projects in Vietnam seeking to lease land must first apply for and receive a LUR Certificate from the provincial People's Committee. Below is a summary of the application procedure for the issuance of the LUR Certificate:

i. Submit application for LUR certificate.

ii. Receive ruling on application. The approximate time required is either ten working days or thirty working days, depending upon whether or not the land has already been vacated.

iii. Pay financial obligations.

iv. Execute land lease contract.

v. Transfer possession of the land.

vi. Receive the LUR Certificate.

The statutory timeline for the execution of the land lease contract, transfer of possession of the land, and receipt of the LUR Certificate is ten days from the foreign tenant's rental payment. However, the statutory timeline is not always strictly observed by the authorities, causing delays to occur.

If the land is still occupied, the government land management authorities will carry out site clearance procedures and settle all land compensation issues so that the land in question may be vacated for the purpose of the investment project.

Note that site clearance procedures (which include dealing with land compensation issues) may take a long time. Further, the amount of land compensation payable may be an important factor in the government's determinate of rental price.

The lease will normally be renewable subject to the tenant submitting an application to the provincial People's Committee at the end of the lease term and receiving the government's approval.

4. Assigning Leasehold

A foreign tenant is generally allowed to assign his rights to the land to a third party as long as he has already paid the rent for the entire period of the lease term, and the party receiving the land rights applies for and receives a new LUR Certificate.

EXAMPLE: A Singaporean company secures a lease of fifty years and pays rent for the entire period of the lease in advance. Five years later the Singaporean company wants to transfer its rights to the land to a German company. Normally it would be allowed to do so, subject to the German company's application for and receipt of a LUV Certificate.

5. Title Search

Note that although the law does provide a mechanism to carry out title searches, in practice, many provincial land authorities will only provide land title information to the land owner.

6. Ownership of Residential Apartments

The following types of foreign individuals and companies are allowed to purchase units in apartment buildings that are not located in an area where such purchase and ownership is prohibited:

i.   Individuals entering Vietnam to pursue an approved direct investment or individuals hired in a managerial capacity

EXAMPLE: An Italian individual who is the director of a Vietnam registered company with a project in Vietnam finds an apartment and seeks to purchase a term of ownership for the apartment. This should be permissible under the law.

ii. Individuals working in a socio-economic sector with a university or higher degree and possessing special knowledge and skills which Vietnam requires, such as lawyers, accountants, and other professionals

iii. An individual married to a Vietnamese citizen

iv. Foreign-held companies that purchase residential housing for their employees

Foreign individuals in any of the above categories are required to be currently living in Vietnam and have permission to reside in Vietnam for one year or more at the time of purchase.

EXAMPLE: A retired Dutch national marries a Vietnamese national, and the two live in Amsterdam. The Dutch national seeks to purchase an apartment for a period of twenty-five years. In this situation, the Dutch national would not qualify to purchase the apartment as he is not living in Vietnam.

EXAMPLE: Same facts above, but instead the Dutch national is residing with his wife in Ho Chi Minh City and has a valid visa/temporary residence card which is valid for one year. In this situation, he would qualify to purchase the apartment.

The law expressly limits foreign individuals to purchasing one apartment only (purchase of a house and townhouses is not allowed). Also, the apartment may not be located in an area that is prohibited to foreigners.

EXAMPLE: Same facts as above, but the Dutch national also seeks to purchase a second apartment in Danang. The purchase of the second apartment would not be legally permissible.

EXAMPLE: A French company with a subsidiary in Vietnam purchases a term of ownership to three apartments to be used by members of the subsidiary's board of directors. This should be permissible.

Index

Acknowledgments

I just want to mention a few people who have assisted in the production of this book. Without their help, this book would not have been possible. First, I would like to thank my production dynamic duo of (Ms.) Sunan Tanurak-pairoj and (Mr.) Anucha Phrakarul. They kept me organized and on time, and I really appreciate their efforts. Millie Lindsay, my editor, did a great job (as always), and there is no way I could have finished without her. I also want to thank my co-authors and their staffs who worked tirelessly to make deadlines and answer all of my questions. Also, special thanks to Kyung Jin Lee (KJ), my law clerk from the University of Wisconsin School of Law for all of her efforts, to Joe Lindsay who gave me the idea for the name, and to Rob Glasco for all his technical expertise. Finally, I would like to thank my wife Koy, who has always been very supportive, even when writing this book took away a lot of nights and weekends together.

About the Author

Michael Doyle is a U.S. attorney who has practiced in Asia since 1996 in the areas of foreign direct investment, mergers and acquisitions, cross border transactions, and corporate law. He resides with his family in Bangkok, Thailand where he is a partner with the law firm of Seri Manop and Doyle. If you have any questions or comments, feel free to contact him at michael@serimanop.com.